ALSO BY ORLANDO FIGES

Peasant Russia, Civil War:
The Volga Countryside in Revolution, 1917–1921

A People's Tragedy: The Russian Revolution, 1891–1924

Interpreting the Russian Revolution:
The Language and Symbols of 1917 (with Boris Kolonitskii)

Natasha's Dance: A Cultural History of Russia

The Whisperers: Private Life in Stalin's Russia

The Crimean War: A History

Just Send Me Word: A True Story of Love and Survival in the Gulag

REVOLUTIONARY RUSSIA

1891–1991

REVOLUTIONARY RUSSIA

1891–1991

A HISTORY

ORLANDO FIGES

METROPOLITAN BOOKS

HENRY HOLT AND COMPANY   NEW YORK

Metropolitan Books
Henry Holt and Company, LLC
Publishers since 1866
175 Fifth Avenue
New York, New York 10010
www.henryholt.com

Metropolitan Books® and m® are registered trademarks of
Henry Holt and Company, LLC.

Library of Congress Cataloging-in-Publication Data
Figes, Orlando, author.
Revolutionary Russia, 1891–1991 : a history / Orlando Figes.
      pages ; cm
Includes bibliographical references and index.
ISBN 978-0-8050-9131-1 (hardcover) — ISBN 978-0-8050-9598-2 (electronic copy)
  1. Insurgency—Russia—History—19th century.   2. Revolutions—Russia—History—
20th century.   3. Revolutions—Soviet Union—History.   4. Russia—History—19th century.
5. Russia—History—20th century.   6. Soviet Union—History.   I. Title.
  DK43.F54 2014
  947.084—dc23   2013042580

Henry Holt books are available for special promotions and
premiums. For details contact: Director, Special Markets.

First U.S. Edition 2014

Designed by Kelly S. Too

Printed in the United States of America
1   3   5   7   9   10   8   6   4   2

CONTENTS

REVOLUTIONARY RUSSIA

1891–1991

INTRODUCTION

My aim is to provide a brief account of the Russian Revolution in the *longue durée*, to chart one hundred years of history as a single revolutionary cycle. In this telling the Revolution starts in the nineteenth century (and more specifically in 1891, when the public's reaction to the famine crisis set it for the first time on a collision course with the autocracy) and ends with the collapse of the Soviet regime in 1991.

It might seem odd to plot the Revolution in one hundred years of history. Most short books on the subject focus on the years immediately before and after 1917. But to understand the Revolution's origins, its violent character and tragic course from freedom to dictatorship, one must look more closely at the tsarist past; and to perceive its lasting outcomes, one must see it in the broader context of Soviet history. Many of the themes of the first chapters on the tsarist period—the absence of a political counter-balance to the power of the state; the isolation of the educated classes from the common people; the rural backwardness and poverty that drove so many peasants to seek a better life in the industrial towns; the coercive basis of authority in Russia; and the extremism of the socialist intelligentsia—will reappear in the later chapters on 1917 and the Soviet regime.

When did the Russian Revolution end? Historians have chosen various dates, depending on the stories which they wish to tell, and these of course can all be justified. Some have ended their accounts in 1921 with the ending of the Civil War, when armed opposition to the Bolsheviks was finally defeated, and the consolidation of the Soviet dictatorship. Others have concluded with the death of Lenin in 1924, as I did in *A People's Tragedy*, a work on which I draw in these pages, on the grounds that by this time the basic institutions, if not the practices, of the Stalinist regime were in place. One or two have ended in 1927, with the defeat of Trotsky and the Left Opposition; or in 1929, with the onset of a new revolutionary upheaval, the forced industrialization and collectiviza-tion of the first Five Year Plan, implying that the Stalinist economy was the significant outcome of 1917.

One of the most influential historians of the Soviet period, Sheila Fitzpatrick, concluded her short history of the Revolution in the mid-1930s, a period of 'retreat' from its utopian objectives when the struc-tural economic changes of Stalin's Revolution were consolidated as a permanent system. By her own later admission, this was to suggest that the Great Terror of 1937-8 was a 'monstrous postscript' to the Revolu-tion, an aberration explained by the regime's fear of war, when in fact it was a part of it—the biggest in a series of waves of terror whose origins can only be explained by the insecurities of the Soviet regime going back to 1917. To omit the Great Terror from a history of the Russian Revolution, Fitzpatrick acknowledged, would be the equivalent of writ-ing an account of the French Revolution of 1789 without the Reign of Terror (1793-4) for which it was chiefly known.[1]

The Great Terror was not the final wave of violence by the Soviet state. The population of the Gulag labour camps, which Solzhenitsyn placed at the very core of the Bolshevik experiment, reached its peak, not in 1938, but in 1952. So it does not make much sense to end a his-tory of the Revolution with the halting of the Great Terror. But then it doesn't make much sense either to break it off in 1939 or 1941. The Sec-ond World War did not interrupt the Revolution. It intensified and broad-ened it. Bolshevism came into its own during the war—with its military discipline and cult of sacrifice, its willingness to expend human life to meet its goals, and its capacity to militarize the masses through its planned economy, it was made to fight. The Revolution was reforged and toughened by the war. Through the Red Army and its NKVD units, the Soviet empire tightened its control of its borderlands in West Ukraine and the Baltic, purging towns and villages and sending to the Gulag, in their hundreds of thousands, nationalist insurgents, repatriated Soviet servicemen and 'collaborators' with the Germans. By force of arms, the Bolsheviks exported the Russian Revolution into Eastern Europe—first in 1939–40 and again in 1945.

The Cold War, in this sense, has to be seen as a continuation of the international civil war started by the Bolsheviks in 1917. The global ambitions of the Revolution's leaders remained essentially unchanged, from their first attempts to extend Soviet power into Europe through the invasion of Poland in 1920 to their final foreign adventure in Afghanistan after 1979. Lenin's power seizure had been based on the idea that the Revolution could not survive on its own in a backward peasant country such as Russia, that it needed the support of revolutions in the more advanced industrial states or in countries that could give it the resources it needed to industrialize: a life-or-death conflict between socialism and the capitalist powers was unavoidable as long as capitalism existed. Stalin, Khrushchev, Brezhnev and Andropov, if not Gorbachev, were all Leninists in this belief.

Until the end of their regime, the Soviet leaders all believed they were continuing the Revolution Lenin had begun. Their means of rule altered over time, of course, particularly after Stalin's death, when they gave up on the use of mass terror, but they always saw themselves as Lenin's heirs, working to achieve the same utopian goals envisaged by the founders of the Soviet state: a Communist society of material abundance for the proletariat and a new collective type of human being. That is why I think a good case can be made for the Revolution being treated as a single cycle of one hundred years, ending with the collapse of the Soviet system in 1991.

Within this longer cycle I aim to explain the Revolution's rise and fall in three generational phases. The first corresponds to the lifetime of the

Old Bolsheviks, mostly born in the 1870s or 1880s and, if not already dead, eliminated in the Great Terror. Their utopian ideals and austere party culture of military unity and discipline had been shaped by years of struggle in the conspiratorial underground. But they obtained their revolutionary power from the cataclysm of the First World War—which seemed at once to undermine the value of a human life and to open up the possibility of altering the nature of humanity out of the destruction it had caused—and reached the height of their destructive fury in the Civil War, from which the Bolsheviks emerged victorious and strengthened in their conviction that any fortress could be stormed. From these killing fields they set about the building of a new society. But they could not overcome the problem of the peasantry—the small-holding family farmers who made up three quarters of the country's population and dominated its economy—with their individualistic attitudes, patriarchal customs and attachment to the old Russian world of the village and the church. To so many of the Party's new supporters— peasant sons and daughters who had fled the 'backward' village for a better life—the Revolution could not banish peasant Russia fast enough.

Here were the roots of Stalin's 'revolution from above', the second phase of the cycle charted here, beginning with the Five Year Plan of 1928–32. Stalinism's vision of modernity gave fresh energy to the utopian hopes of the Bolsheviks. It mobilized a whole new generation of enthusiasts—young ambitious workers, officials and technicians born around the turn of the century and schooled in Soviet values—who forced through Stalin's policies of crash collectivization and industrialization and who, through the purges of the 1930s, took the places of the old élites. Collectivization was the real revolution of Soviet history—the complete overturning of a peasant way of life that had developed over many centuries—and a catastrophe from which the country never recovered. It was a social holocaust—a war against the peasants—uprooting millions of hardworking families from their homes and dispersing them across the Soviet Union. This nomadic population became the labour force of the Soviet industrial revolution, filling the great cities, the building-sites and labour camps of the Gulag.

The industrial infrastructure built by Stalin in the 1930s remained in place until the end of the Soviet system. His Five Year Plans became the model for Communist development throughout the world. They were said to be the cause of the Soviet military victory in 1945—the justifying rationale for everything accomplished by the October Revolution according to Soviet propaganda. But these achievements came at an enormous human cost—far bigger than we had imagined before the archives opened after 1991—so big that they challenge us to think about the moral nature of the Stalinist regime in ways reserved previously for historians of Nazism.

Khrushchev's speech denouncing Stalin's crimes marks the start of the Revolution's third and final phase. The Soviet system never recovered from the crisis of belief caused by Khrushchev's revelations at the Twentieth Party Congress in 1956. For the next thirty years the leadership was split about how far they could build on Stalin's legacies, or even recognize his influence, except as a war leader. The country was divided between Stalin's victims and those who revered his memory or took pride in Soviet achievements under Stalin's leadership. But the speech was the defining moment for a younger generation that identified itself by the years of Khrushchev's 'thaw' (the *shestidesiatniki* or 'people of the sixties'), among them a 1955 law graduate from Moscow University called Mikhail Gorbachev, whose ideas of socialist renewal were first sown by Khrushchev's programme of de-Stalinization.

The challenge facing all the later Soviet leaders was to sustain popular belief in the Revolution as it became a remote historical event. The problem was particularly acute for the generation born since 1945: they were too young even to relate to the 'Great Patriotic War', the other main legitimizing Soviet myth after the 'Great October Socialist Revolution'. Better educated and more sophisticated than the Stalin-era generation, the post-war Soviet baby boomers were less engaged in the Revolution's history or ideas than in Western music, films and clothes. Did this make the demise of the Soviet system unavoidable? Is any revolution destined to run out of energy, to die from old age, if it lives as long as the Soviet Union did? The Chinese endgame (liberalizing the economy within the one-party state) could briefly have been an alternative for the Soviet leadership under Andropov and Gorbachev, although it is doubtful whether economic modernization could have saved the system in the longer term (the Soviet population had forgotten how to work). But in the end it was Gorbachev's commitment to political reform—a belief rooted in his Leninist ideals—that brought the system down.

In 2017 the world's media will reflect on the Revolution during its centenary. It is a good time to look back at 1917. A generation after the collapse of the Soviet regime, we can see it more clearly, not as part of Cold War politics or Sovietology, but as history, a series of events with a beginning, a middle, and an end.

Retrospective distance enables us to see the Revolution from a fresh perspective and to ask again the big questions: why Russia? why Lenin? why Stalin? why did it fail? and what did it all mean? Questions as worth engaging with at the start of the next hundred years as they were during the last.

Seen from today's perspective the Revolution appears very differently from the way it looked in 1991. Communism now seems, more than ever, like something from a stage of history that has been passed. Capitalism may have its crises, but outside North Korea no one sees the Soviet model of the planned economy as a viable alternative, not even China or Cuba any more. Russia has become very much weaker as a power in the world. Its loss of empire and foreign influence has been so dramatic that it makes one wonder how it held the Soviet Union and Eastern Europe for so long. Russia is no longer an aggressive state. It does not start foreign wars. Economically it is a pale shadow of the powerhouse it was on the eve of the First World War. Seventy years of Communism ruined it. Yet the authoritarian state tradition has revived in Russia in a manner unexpected twenty years ago. This resurgence, based on Putin's reclamation of the Soviet past, demands that we look again at Bolshevism—its antecedents and its legacies—in the long arc of history.

1

THE START

After a year of meteorological catastrophes the peasants of south-east Russia faced starvation in the summer of 1891. The seeds planted the previous autumn had barely time to germinate before the frosts arrived. There had been little snow to protect the young plants during the severe winter. Spring brought with it dusty winds that blew away the topsoil and then, as early as April, the long dry summer began. There was no rain for one hundred days. Wells and ponds dried up, the scorched earth cracked, forests turned brown, and cattle died by the roadsides.

By the autumn the famine area spread from the Ural mountains to Ukraine, an area double the size of France with a population of 36 million people. The peasants weakened and took to their huts. They lived on 'hunger bread' made from rye husks mixed with goosefoot, moss and tree bark, which made the loaves turn yellow and bitter. Those who had the strength packed up their meagre belongings and fled wherever they could, jamming the roads with their carts. And then cholera and typhus struck, killing half a million people by the end of 1892.

The government reacted to the crisis clumsily. At first it buried its head in the sand, speaking euphemistically of a 'poor harvest', and warned newspapers not to print reports on the 'famine', although many did in all but name. This was enough to convince the public, shocked and concerned by the rumours of starvation, that there was a government conspiracy to conceal the truth. There were stories of the obstinate bureaucracy withholding food relief until it had 'statistical proof' that the population for which it was intended had no other means of feeding itself. But the greatest public outrage was caused by the government's postpone-ment of a ban on cereal exports until the middle of August, several weeks into the crisis, so that merchants rushed to fulfil their foreign contracts, and foodstuffs which could have been used for the starving peasants van-ished abroad. Even then the ban had been opposed by the Ministry of Finance, whose economic policies (raising taxes on consumer goods so that the peasants would be forced to sell more grain) were seen by the public as the main cause of the famine. As the unfortunately worded offi-cial slogan went: 'We may not eat enough, but we will export.'[1]

Unable to cope with the situation, the government called on the pub-lic to help. It was to prove a historic moment, for it opened the door to a powerful new wave of public activity and debate which the government could not control and which quickly turned from the philanthropic to the political.

The public response was tremendous. Hundreds of committees were formed by 'public men' to raise money for the starving peasants. Thou-sands of well-meaning citizens joined the relief teams organized by the zemstvos—district councils dominated by the liberal gentry which had done 'good works' for the rural population (building schools and hospi-tals, providing agronomic help and credit, gathering statistics about peas-ant life) since their establishment in 1864. Famous writers such as Tolstoy and Chekhov (who was also a doctor) put aside their writing to join the relief campaign. Tolstoy blamed the famine on the social order, the Ortho-dox Church and the government: 'Everything has happened because of our own sin. We have cut ourselves off from our own brothers, and there is only one remedy—to repent, change our lives, and destroy the walls between us and the people.'[2] His message struck a deep chord in the moral conscience of the liberal public, plagued as it was both by feelings of alienation from the peasantry and by guilt on account of its privileges.

Russian society was politicized by the famine, and from 1891 it became more organized in opposition to the government. The zemstvos expanded their activities to revive the rural economy. Doctors, teachers and engineers formed professional bodies and began to demand more influence over public policy. In the press and periodicals, in universities and learned societies, there were heated debates on the causes of the crisis in which Marx's ideas of capitalist development were generally accepted as the most convincing explanation of the peasantry's impoverishment. The global market system was dividing peasants into rich and poor; manufacturing was undermining rural crafts, and a landless proletariat was being formed. The socialist movement, which had been largely dormant in the 1880s, sprang back into life as a result of these debates. In the words of Lydia Dan, a teenager in 1891 but later to become one of the founders of the main Russian Marxist party, the Social Democrats (SDs), the famine was to prove a vital landmark in the history of the Revolution because it had shown to the youth of her generation 'that the Russian system was completely bankrupt. It felt as though Russia was on the brink of something.'[3]

When does a 'revolutionary crisis' start? Trotsky answered this by distinguishing between the objective factors (human misery) that make a revolution possible and the subjective factors (human agency) that bring one about. In the Russian case the famine by itself was not enough. There were no peasant uprisings as a consequence of it, and even if there had been, by themselves they would not have been a major threat to the tsarist state. It was the expectations of the upper classes—and the Tsar's refusal to compromise with them—that made the famine crisis revolutionary.

In 1894, the country's most progressive zemstvo leaders presented a list of political demands to Nicholas II on his accession to the throne, following the premature death of his father, Alexander III. They wanted to convene a national assembly to involve the zemstvos in the work of government. In a speech that infuriated public opinion Nicholas denounced such 'senseless dreams' and emphasized his 'firm and unflinching' adherence to the 'principle of autocracy' which he had sworn to uphold in his coronation oath. The Tsar's sovereignty was absolute, unlimited by laws or parliaments, by bureaucrats or public opinion, and his personal rule was guided only by his conscience before God.

Nicholas believed it was his sacred mission to emulate his father's autocratic rule, but he lacked his domineering personality and the where-withal to provide effective government. He was only twenty-six when he came to the throne. 'What is going to happen to me and to all of Russia?' he had wept on his father's death. 'I am not prepared to be a Tsar. I never wanted to become one. I know nothing of the business of ruling. I have no idea of even how to talk to the ministers.'[4]

Had circumstances and his own inclinations been different, Nicholas might have saved the monarchy by moving it towards a constitutional order during the first decade of his reign, when there was still hope of sat-isfying liberal hopes and isolating the revolutionaries. In England, where being a 'good man' was the sole requirement of a good king, he would have made an admirable sovereign. He was certainly not inferior to his look-alike cousin, George V, who was a model of the constitutional king. He was mild-mannered and had an excellent memory and a perfect sense of decorum, which made him ideal for the ceremonial tasks of a consti-tutional monarch. But Nicholas had not been born into that world: he was the Emperor and Autocrat of All the Russias; Tsar of Moscow, Kiev, Vladimir, Novgorod, Kazan, Astrakhan, Poland, Siberia, the Tauric Cher-sonese and Georgia, et cetera, et cetera. Family tradition and pressure from the crown's conservative allies obliged him to rule with force and resolution and, in the face of opposition, to assert his 'divine authority'.

Here, then, were the roots of the monarchy's collapse, not in peasant discontent or the labour movement, so long the preoccupation of Marx-ist and social historians, nor in the breakaway of nationalist move-ments on the empire's periphery, but in the growing conflict between a dynamic public culture and a fossilized autocracy that would not con-cede or even understand its political demands.

Russia had been a relatively stable society until the final decades of the nineteenth century. It was untroubled by the revolutions that shook

Europe's other monarchies in 1848–9, when Marx called it 'the last hope of the despots'. Its huge army crushed the Polish uprisings of 1830 and 1863, the main nationalist challenge to the Tsar's Imperial rule, while its police hampered the activities of the tiny close-knit circles of radicals and revolutionaries, who were mostly driven underground.

The power of the Tsar was only weakly counter-balanced by a landed aristocracy. The Russian nobility was heavily dependent on military and civil service to the state for its landed wealth and position in society. Nor were there real public bodies to challenge the autocracy: most institutions (organs of self-government, professional, scientific and artistic societies) were in fact creations of the state. Even the senior leaders of the Orthodox Church were appointed by the Tsar.

The Church retained a powerful hold over rural Russia, in particular. In many villages the priest was one of the few people who could read and write. Through parish schools the Orthodox clergy taught children to show loyalty, deference and obedience, not just to their elders and betters but also to the Tsar and his officials.

For all its pretensions to autocracy, however, the tsarist state was hardly present in the countryside and could not get a grip on many basic aspects of peasant life, as the famine had underlined. Contrary to the revolutionaries' mythic image of an all-powerful tsarist regime, the *under-government* of the localities was in fact the system's main weakness. For every 1,000 inhabitants of the Russian Empire there were only four state officials at the end of the nineteenth century, compared with 7.3 in England and Wales, 12.6 in Germany and 17.6 in France. The regular police, as opposed to the political branch, was extremely small by European standards. For a rural population of 100 million people, Russia in 1900 had no more than 1,852 police sergeants and 6,874 police constables. For most intents and purposes, once the peasants had been liberated from the direct rule of their landowners, with the abolition of serfdom in 1861, they were left to look after themselves.

Despite the abolition of serfdom, its legacies continued to oppress the peasants in the following decades. Most of the arable land remained the private property of the gentry landowners, who rented it out to the land-hungry peasants at rates that increased steeply in the later nineteenth century as the population rose. Legally the peasants remained excluded from the sphere of written law. Their affairs were regulated by the customary law of the village commune (*mir* or *obshchina*), which in most of Russia upheld the old peasant moral concept that the land belonged to nobody but God and that every family had the right to feed itself by cultivating it with its own labour. On this principle—that the land should be in the hands of those who tilled it—the squires did not hold their land rightfully and the hungry peasants were justified in their struggle to take it from them. A constant battle was fought between the state's written law, framed to defend the property rights of the landowners, and the customary law of the peasants, used by them to defend their own transgressions of those rights—poaching and grazing cattle on the squire's land, taking wood from his forest, fishing in his ponds, and so on.

Gentry magistrates were responsible for the judicial administration of the countryside. As late as 1904, they retained the power to have peasants flogged for rowdy drunkenness or trespassing on the landowner's land. It is difficult to overestimate the psychological impact of this corporal punishment—forty-three years after the serfs had been 'freed'. One peasant, who had been flogged for failing to remove his hat and bow before the magistrate, was later heard to ask: 'What's a poor peasant to a gentleman? Why he's worse than a dog. At least a dog can bite, but the peasant is meek and humble and tolerates everything.'[5]

The coercive basis of authority was replicated everywhere—in relations between officers and men in the armed services, between employers and workers, between peasant elders and wives and children. According to Russian proverbs, a woman was improved by regular beatings, while: 'For a man that has been beaten you have to offer two unbeaten ones.' At Christmas, Epiphany and Shrovetide there were huge and often fatal fights between different sections of the village, sometimes even between villages, accompanied by heavy bouts of drinking. However one explains this violence—by the culture of the peasants, the harsh environment in which they lived, or the weakness of the legal order—it was to play a major part in the overturning of authority during 1917.

The tsarist system could not cope with the challenges of urbanization and the development of a modern market-based economy which brought so many democratic changes in the final decades of the nineteenth century. The 1890s were a watershed in this respect. From this decade we can date the emergence of a civil society, a public sphere and ethic, all in opposition to the state.

Profound social changes were taking place. The old hierarchy of estates (*sosloviia*), which the autocracy had created to organize society around its needs, was breaking down as a new and more dynamic system—too complicated to be described in terms of 'class'—began to take shape. Men born as peasants, even serfs, rose to establish themselves as merchants, engineers and landowners (like the character Lopakhin who buys the cherry orchard in Chekhov's play). Merchants became noblemen. The sons and daughters of noblemen entered the liberal professions. Social mobility was accelerated by the spread of higher education. Between 1860 and 1914 the number of university students in Russia grew from 5,000 to 69,000 (45 per cent of them women). Public opinion and activity found a widening range of outlets in these years: the number of daily newspapers rose from thirteen to 856; and the number of public institutions from 250 to over 16,000.

These changes also helped the rise of nationalist movements on the periphery of the empire. Until the development of rural schools and networks of communication, nationalism remained an élite urban movement for native language rights in schools and universities, literary publications and official life. Outside the towns its influence was limited. The peasants were barely conscious of their nationality. 'I myself did not know that I was a Pole till I began to read books and papers,' recalled a farmer after 1917.[6] In many areas, such as Ukraine, Belorussia and the Caucasus, there was so much ethnic intermingling that it was difficult for anything more than a localized form of identity to take root in the popular consciousness. 'Were one to ask the average peasant in the Ukraine his nationality,' observed a British diplomat, 'he would answer that he is Greek Orthodox; if pressed to say whether he is a Great Russian, a Pole or an Ukrainian, he would probably reply that he is a peasant; and if one insisted on knowing what language he spoke, he would say that he talked "the local tongue".[7]

The growth of mass-based nationalist movements was contingent on the spread of rural schools and institutions, such as peasant unions and cooperatives, as well as on the opening up of remote country areas by roads and railways, postal services and telegraphs—all of which was happening very rapidly in the decades before 1917. The most successful movements combined the peasants' struggle for the land (where it was owned by foreign landlords, officials and merchants) with the demand for native language rights, enabling the peasants to gain full access to schools, the courts and government.

This combination was the key to the success of the Ukrainian nationalist movement. In the Constituent Assembly elections of November 1917, the first democratic elections in the country's history, 71 per cent of the Ukrainian peasants would vote for the nationalists—an astonishing shift in political awareness in only a generation. The movement organized the peasants in their struggle against foreign (mainly Russian and Polish) landowners and against the 'foreign influence' of the towns (dominated by the Russians, Jews and Poles). It is no coincidence that peasant uprisings erupted first, in 1902, in those regions around Poltava province where the Ukrainian nationalist movement was also most advanced.

Throughout Russia the impact of modernization—of towns and mass communications, the money economy and above all rural schools—gave rise to a generation of younger and more literate peasants who sought to overturn the patriarchal village world. Literacy rose from 21 per cent of the empire's population in 1897 to 40 per cent on the eve of the First World War. The highest rural rates were among young men in those regions closest to the towns (nine out of ten peasant recruits into the Imperial army from the two provinces of Petersburg and Moscow were considered literate even by 1904). The link between literacy and revolution is a well-known historical phenomenon. The three great revolutions of modern European history—the English, the French and the Russian—all took place in societies where the rate of literacy was approaching 50 per cent. Literacy promotes the spread of new ideas and enables the peasant to master new technologies and bureaucratic skills. The local activists of the Russian Revolution were drawn mainly from this newly literate generation—the beneficiaries of the boom in rural schooling during the last decades of the old regime, now in large enough numbers to pass on the new ideas to those still illiterate. In its belated efforts to educate the common people, the tsarist regime was helping to dig its own grave.

A study of rural schoolchildren in the 1900s found that almost half of them wanted to pursue an 'educated profession' in the city, whereas less than 2 per cent wanted to follow in the footsteps of their peasant parents. 'I want to be a shop assistant,' said one schoolboy, 'because I do not like to walk in the mud. I want to be like those people who are cleanly dressed and work as shop assistants.'[8] For these youths the desire for social better-ment was often synonymous with employment in the town. Virtually any urban job seemed desirable compared with the hardships and dull rou-tines of peasant life. They saw the village as a 'dark' and 'backward' place of superstition and crippling poverty—a world Trotsky would describe as the Russia of 'icons and cockroaches'—and looked towards the city and its modern values as a route to independence and self-worth. Here was the basis of the cultural revolution on which Bolshevism would be based. The Party rank and file was recruited in the main from peasant boys like these; its modernizing ideology was based on their rejection of the peas-ant world. The Revolution would sweep that village world all away.

Forced off the land by poverty, over-population and the growing cost of renting land, millions of peasants came into the towns, or worked in rural factories and mines. In the last half-century of the old regime the empire's urban population grew from 7 million to 28 million people. The 1890s saw the sharpest growth as the effects of the famine crisis coincided with the accelerated programme of industrialization and railway construction pushed through by Count Witte, the Minister of Finance from 1892.

There was a pattern in the peasant in-migration to the towns: first came the young men, then the married men, then unmarried girls, then married women and children. It suggests that the peasants tried to keep their failing farms alive for as long as possible. Young peasant men were sending money earned in mines and factories to their villages, where they themselves returned at harvest time ('raiding the cash economy' as is common in developing societies). There was a constant to-and-fro between the city and the countryside. We can talk as much about the 'peasantization' of Russia's towns as we can about the disappearance of the farming peasantry.

Factory conditions were terrible. According to Witte, the worker 'raised on the frugal habits of rural life' was 'much more easily satisfied' than his counterpart in Europe or North America, so that 'low wages appeared as a fortunate gift to Russian enterprise'.[9] There was little factory legislation to protect labour. The gains made by British workers in the 1840s, and by the Germans in the 1880s, remained out of reach of Russian workers at the turn of the century. The two most important factory laws—one in 1885 prohibiting the night-time employment of women and children, and the other in 1897 restricting the working day to eleven and a half hours—had to be wrenched from the government. Small workshops were excluded from the legislation, although they probably employed the majority of the country's workforce, and certainly most of its female contingent. By 1914, women represented 33 per cent of the industrial labour force, and in sectors like textiles and food processing they were a clear majority. The inspectorates, charged with ensuring that the factories complied with the regulations, lacked effective powers, so employers ignored them. Unventilated working areas were filled with noxious fumes. Shopfloors were crammed with dangerous machinery: there were frequent accidents. Yet most workers were denied a legal right to insurance and, if they lost an eye or a limb, could expect no more than a few roubles' compensation. Workers' strikes were illegal. There were no legal trade unions until 1905.

Many factory owners treated workers like serfs. They had them searched for stolen goods when they left the factory gates, and fined or even flogged for minor breaches of the rules. This degrading 'serf regime' was bitterly resented by workers as an affront to their dignity, and 'respectful treatment' was a prominent demand in strikes and labour protests that broke out after 1905.

Russian workers were the most strike-prone in Europe. Three quarters of the factory workforce went on strike during 1905. Historians have spent a lot of time trying to explain the origins of this labour militancy. Factory size, levels of skill and literacy, the number of years spent living in the city, and the influence of the revolutionary intelligentsia—all these factors have been scrutinized in microscopic detail in countless monographs, each hoping to discover the crucial mix that explained the rise of the 'workers' revolution' in Russia. The main disagreement concerns the effects of urbanization.

Some have argued that it was the most urbanized workers, those with the highest levels of skill and literacy, who became the foot soldiers of the Revolution. But others have maintained that the recent immigrants—those who had been 'snatched from the plough and hurled straight into the factory furnace', as Trotsky once put it[10]—tended to be the most volatile and violent, often adapting the spontaneous forms of rebellion associated with the countryside to the new and hostile industrial environment in which they found themselves.

There is no doubt that the peasant immigrants added a combustible element to the urban working class. Labour unrest often took the form of riots, pogroms, looting and machine-breaking, or the 'carting out' of bosses from the factory and dumping them in a cesspool or canal—all actions one might associate with an uprooted but disorganized peasant mass struggling to adapt to the new world of the city and the discipline of the factory. Nevertheless, it is going too far to suggest that such 'primitive' actions, or the raw recruits behind them, were the crucial factor in the rise of labour militancy. During the 1890s strikes became the main form of industrial protest and they required the sort of disciplined organization that only the most skilled and literate workers could provide.

Here Russia stood in stark contrast to Europe, where these worker types tended to be the least revolutionary and labour parties representing them were entering parliaments. There were few signs of such a 'labour aristocracy' emerging in Russia and certainly no parliament to which it could aspire. The print workers were the most likely candidates for such a role. Yet even they stood firmly behind the Marxist and other revolutionary socialist parties. Had they been able to develop their own legal trade unions, the workers might have gone down the path of moderate reform taken by the European labour movements. But the Russian political situation pushed them to extremes. They were forced to rely upon the leadership of the revolutionary underground. To a large extent, then, the workers' revolutionary movement was created by the tsarist government.

The famine crisis gave new life to the revolutionary parties, bringing them supporters, not just from the working class, but from a widening range of liberal professionals, students, writers and other members of the intelligentsia—a caste defined by its sense of debt to and commitment to 'the people'. The key to that commitment was moral: a stance of uncompromising opposition to the autocracy and a willingness to take part in the democratic struggle against it.

There was a revival of the Populist movement, culminating in 1901 with the establishment of the Socialist Revolutionary Party (SR). Populism had its roots in the intelligentsia's mission to improve the peasants' lot and to involve them in a democratic movement against the autocracy following the serf emancipation in 1861. The Populists idealized the peasant way of life. From the 1870s, they had gone into the countryside to educate and organize the peasantry, some of them (they called themselves the People's Will) increasingly resorting to violence and terror as they became frustrated by the failure of the peasants to respond to their revolutionary call. The Populists believed that the village commune could become the basis of a socialist society, thus enabling Russia to take a separate path to socialism from that of the West, where capitalist development was destroying the peasantry and Marxist hopes of revolution rested on the industrial working class. In contrast to the Marxists, the Populists believed that peasant Russia could advance directly to a socialist society without passing first through the capitalist stage of history.

The famine crisis undermined that view. Partly caused by the tax squeeze on the peasants to pay for industrialization, the crisis suggested that the peasantry was literally dying out, both as a class and a way of life, under the pressures of capitalist development. Marxism alone seemed able to explain the causes of the famine by showing how a capitalist economy created rural poverty. In the 1890s it fast became a national intelligentsia creed. Socialists who had previously wavered in their Marxism were converted to it by the crisis, as they realized that there was no more hope in the Populist faith in the peasantry. Even liberal thinkers such as Petr Struve found their Marxist passions stirred by the famine: it 'made much more of a Marxist out of me than the reading of Marx's *Capital*'.[11]

The SRs were swept along by this intellectual drift. Led by Viktor Chernov, a law graduate from Moscow University, the Party accepted the Marxist view of capitalist development in sociological terms whilst still adhering politically to the Populist belief that workers and peasants alike—what it called the 'labouring people'—were united by their poverty and their opposition to the government.

Marx's *Capital* had been published in Russia as early as 1872. It was the book's first foreign publication, just five years after the original German edition and fifteen years before its appearance in English. The tsarist censors had passed it by mistake, assuming that 'very few people in Russia' would read the heavy tome of political economy, and 'even fewer understand it'.[12] Contrary to expectations, Marx's critique of the capitalist system would lead to revolution earlier in Russia than in any of the Western societies to which it had been addressed.

The intelligentsia were drawn to Marxism by its 'scientific' nature—it was seen as a 'path of reason', in the words of Lydia Dan, offering 'objective solutions' to the misery of poverty and backwardness—and by its promise that Russia would become more like the capitalist West. 'We were attracted by its *European* nature,' recalled a veteran of the movement in Russia. 'Marxism came from Europe. It did not smell and taste of home-grown mould and provincialism, but was new, fresh, and exciting. Marxism held out a promise that we would not stay a semi-Asiatic country, but would become part of the West with its culture, institutions and attributes of a free political system. The West was our guiding light.'[13]

Here perhaps was the root of Marxism's attraction to the Jews, who played such a conspicuous role in the Social Democratic movement, providing many of its leaders (Trotsky, Martov, Axelrod, Kamenev and Zinoviev, to name just a few). Where Populism had proposed to build on peasant Russia—a land of pogroms and discrimination against the Jews—Marxism offered a modern Western vision of Russia. It promised to assimilate the Jews into a movement of universal human liberation—not just the liberation of the peasantry—based on principles of internationalism.

Even the young Lenin only became fully converted to the Marxist mainstream in the wake of the famine crisis. Contrary to the Soviet myth, in which Lenin appeared as a fully fledged Marxist theorist in his infancy, the leader of the Bolshevik Revolution came late to politics. In his last school year he was commended by his headmaster (by an irony of fate the father of Kerensky, his arch-rival in 1917) as a model student, 'moral and religious in his upbringing', and never giving 'cause for dissatisfaction, by word or deed, to the school authorities'.[14]

Lenin's father was a typical gentleman-liberal of the type his son would come to despise. His noble background was a source of embarrassment to Lenin's Soviet hagiographers. But it was a key to his domineering personality. It can be seen in his intolerance of criticism from subordinates, and his tendency to look upon the masses as no more than human material needed for his revolutionary plans (during the famine he argued that the peasants should be denied aid because it would make a revolution more likely). As Maxim Gorky wrote in 1917, 'Lenin is a "leader" *and* a Russian nobleman, not without certain psychological traits of this extinct class, and therefore he considers himself justified in performing with the Russian people a cruel experiment which is doomed to failure beforehand.'[15]

Lenin came to Marx already armed with the ideas of the People's Will, the terrorist wing of the Populist movement which had carried out the assassination of Alexander II in 1881. Lenin's elder brother, who had belonged to the People's Will, was executed for his participation in the abortive plot to kill Alexander III in 1887. There is a Soviet legend that on hearing of his brother's death Lenin said to his sister Maria: 'No, we shall not take that road, our road must be different.' The implication is that Lenin was already committed to the Marxist cause—the 'we' of the quotation—with its theoretical rejection of terror in favour of the organization of the working class. But this is nonsensical (Maria at the time was only nine). And while it may be true that his brother's execution was a catalyst to Lenin's involvement in the revolutionary movement, his first inclination was, like his brother's, towards the People's Will. Lenin's Marxism, which developed slowly after 1889, remained infused with the Jacobin spirit of the terrorists and their belief in the overwhelming importance of the seizure of power.

Lenin was particularly influenced by the 'Jacobinism' of the revolutionary theorist Petr Tkachev (1844–86), who in the 1870s had argued for a seizure of power and the establishment of a dictatorship by a disciplined and highly centralized vanguard on the grounds that a social revolution was impossible to achieve by democratic means: the laws of capitalist development meant that the richer peasants would support the status quo. Tkachev insisted that a coup d'état should be carried out as soon as possible, because as yet there was no real social force prepared to side with the government, and to wait would only let one develop.

All the main components of Lenin's ideology—his stress on the need for a disciplined 'vanguard'; his belief that action (the 'subjective factor') could alter the objective course of history (and in particular that the seizure of the state apparatus could bring about a social revolution); his defence of terror and dictatorship; his contempt for liberals and democrats (and indeed for socialists who compromised with them)— stemmed not just from Marx but from Tkachev and the People's Will. He injected a distinctly Russian dose of conspiratorial politics into a Marxist dialectic that would otherwise have remained passive—tied down by a willingness to wait for the revolution to mature through the development of objective conditions rather than bringing it about through political action. It was not Marxism that made Lenin a revolutionary but Lenin who made Marxism revolutionary.

Lenin was made for a fight. He gave himself entirely to the revolutionary struggle. 'That is my life!' he confessed to the French socialist (and his lover) Inessa Armand in 1916. 'One fighting campaign after another.'[16] There was no 'private Lenin' behind the professional revolutionary. The odd affair apart, he lived like a middle-aged provincial clerk, with precisely fixed hours for meals, sleep and work. There was a strong puritanical streak in Lenin's character which later manifested itself in the political culture of his dictatorship. He suppressed his emotions to strengthen his resolve and cultivate the 'hardness' he believed was required by the successful revolutionary: the capacity to spill blood for the revolution's ends. There was no place for sentiment in Lenin's life. 'I can't listen to music too often,' he once admitted after a performance of Beethoven's Appassionata Sonata. 'It makes me want to say kind, stupid things, and pat the heads of people. But now you have to beat them on the head, beat them without mercy.'[17]

After his arrival in the capital, St Petersburg, in 1893, Lenin moved much closer to the standard Marxist view—that Russia was only at the start of its capitalist stage and that a democratic movement by the workers in alliance with the bourgeoisie was needed to defeat autocracy before a socialist revolution could commence. No more talk of a coup d'état or terror. It was only after the establishment of a 'bourgeois democracy', granting freedoms of speech and association to the workers, that the second and socialist phase of the revolution could begin.

The influence of the exiled Marxist theorist Georgi Plekhanov was vital here. It was he who first mapped out the two-stage revolutionary strategy. With it the Russian Marxists at last had an answer to the problem of how to bring about a post-capitalist society in one only now entering the capitalist phase. It gave them grounds for their belief that in forsaking the seizure of power—which, as Plekhanov put it, could only lead to a 'despotism in Communist form'—they could still advance towards socialism.

Marxist groups set about the education of the workers for the coming revolution through propaganda. Some of the skilled and educated workers were more inclined to improve their lot within the capitalist system than to overthrow it. They were supported by a group of Marxists, the Economists, who sought to channel the workers' movement away from revolutionary goals. Lenin led the attack on Economism with the sort of violence that would become the trademark of his rhetoric. Its tactics, he argued, would destroy socialism and the revolution, which could only succeed under the centralized political leadership of a disciplined vanguard party in the mould of the People's Will. If the police regime was to be defeated, the Party had to be equally centralized and disciplined. It had to match the tsarist state.

In his polemics against the Economists Lenin came out with a pamphlet that would become the primer for the Bolsheviks through the revolution of 1917 and the founding text of international Communism. The implications of *What Is to Be Done?*—that the Party's rank and file should be forced to obey, in military fashion, the leadership's commands—were not fully realized when it first appeared in 1902. 'None of us could imagine,' recalled one of the SDs, 'that there could be a party that might arrest its own members.'[18]

That only began to emerge at the Second Party Congress, which met in London (at the Communist Club at 107 Charlotte Street)* from August 1903. The result was a split in the Party and the formation of two distinct SD factions. The cause of the split was seemingly trivial: the definition of Party membership. Lenin wanted all members to be activists in the Party's organization, whereas Martov thought that anyone who agreed with the Party's manifesto should be admitted as a member. Beneath the surface of this dispute lay two opposing views of what the Party ought to be: a military-revolutionary vanguard (tightly controlled by a leader such as Lenin) or a broad-based party in the Western parliamentary style (with a looser style of leadership). Lenin won a slender majority in the vote on this issue, enabling his faction to call themselves the 'Bolsheviks' ('Majoritarians') and their opponents the 'Mensheviks' ('Minoritarians'). With hindsight it was foolish of the Mensheviks to allow the adoption of these names. It saddled them with the permanent image of a minority party, which was to be an important disadvantage in their rivalry with the Bolsheviks.

---

* Today, ironically, the headquarters of the global advertising agency Saatchi and Saatchi.

2

THE 'DRESS REHEARSAL'

On a sunny Sunday morning the long columns of protestors marched across the ice towards the centre of St Petersburg. Church bells rang and their golden domes sparkled in the sun. In the front ranks were the women and children, dressed in their Sunday best, who had been placed there to deter the soldiers from shooting. At the head of the largest column was the bearded figure of Father Gapon in a long white cassock carrying a crucifix. Gapon had made a name for himself as a preacher in the workers' districts of the capital. He told his followers in simple terms, with arguments drawn from the Bible, that the Tsar was obliged before God to satisfy their demands if 'the people' went to him in supplication. The petition he had drawn up for the marchers to present to the Tsar began:

> Sire—We, the workers and inhabitants of St Petersburg, of various estates, our wives, our children, and our aged, come to THEE, O SIRE to seek justice and protection. We are impoverished; we are oppressed, overburdened with excessive toil, contemptuously treated . . . We are suffocating in despotism and lawlessness.[1]

Behind Gapon was a portrait of the Tsar and a large white banner with the words: 'Soldiers do not shoot at the people!' Red flags, the banner of the revolutionaries, had been banned by the organizers of the march.

As the column neared the Narva Gates it was charged by a squadron of cavalry. Some of the marchers ran away but most continued to advance towards the lines of infantry, whose rifles were pointing directly at them. Two warning salvoes were fired into the air, and then at close range a third volley was aimed at the unarmed crowd. People screamed and fell to the ground but the soldiers, now panicking themselves, continued to fire steadily into the mass of people. Forty people were killed and hundreds wounded as they tried to flee. Gapon was knocked down in the rush. But he got up and, staring in disbelief at the carnage around him, was heard to say: 'There is no God any longer. There is no Tsar!'[2]

There were bloody incidents in other parts of the city. On Palace Square a huge body of cavalry and several cannons had been posted in front of the Winter Palace to stop another group of 60,000 protestors. The guards tried to clear the crowds using whips and the flats of their sabres. But when this proved unsuccessful they took up firing positions. Seeing the rifles pointed at them, the demonstrators fell to their knees, took off their caps and crossed themselves. A bugle sounded and the firing began. When it was all over and the survivors looked around at the dead and wounded bodies on the ground there was one vital moment, the turning-point of the whole revolution, when their mood changed from disbelief to anger. 'I observed the faces around me,' recalled a Bolshevik in the crowd, 'and I detected neither fear nor panic. No, the reverend and almost prayerful expressions were replaced by hostility and even hatred. I saw these looks of hatred and vengeance on literally every face.'

In a few seconds the popular myth of a Good Tsar—which had sustained the regime through the centuries—was suddenly destroyed. Only moments after the shooting had ceased an old man turned to a boy of fourteen and said to him, with his voice full of anger: 'Remember, son, remember and swear to repay the Tsar. You saw how much blood he spilled, did you see? Then swear, son, swear!'[3]

There was a wave of strikes and demonstrations against the massacres of 'Bloody Sunday', as the events of 9 January 1905 became known.* In that month alone, more than 400,000 workers downed tools across the country. It was the largest ever labour protest in Russian history. But the strikes were not really organized; their demands were formulated as they went along; and the socialist parties were still much too weak, too closely watched by the police, their main leaders in exile in Europe, to play a leading role. The workers could not bring about a revolution on their own.

It was the response of the liberal middle classes and nobility that turned the events of Bloody Sunday into a revolutionary crisis of authority for the tsarist government. Since 1903 liberal professionals and zemstvo activists had been campaigning for political reforms, including a demand for a national assembly. Together they had formed a Union of Liberation, whose petitions to the Tsar had influenced Gapon.

Bloody Sunday was not the first blow to the Tsar's authority. Russia's military humiliation in a war against Japan had turned a broad section of the public against him and added strength to the Union's campaign. It is hard to overestimate the shock caused in Russia as the news of reported defeats by the Japanese came in—the first time a modern European power had been beaten by an Asian people. In January 1904, the war had begun when the tsarist fleet in Manchuria was ravaged by a Japanese surprise attack. The Japanese had been angered by Russia's aggressive economic expansion in the Far East and by the implications of the Trans-Siberian Railway as it approached completion. Despite this initial setback the Russians were confident of an easy victory. Government posters portrayed the Japanese as puny little monkeys, slit-eyed and yellow-skinned, running in panic from the giant white fist of a robust Russian soldier. Swept along by the patriotic mood, liberals contended that Russia was defending European civilization against the 'yellow danger, the new hordes of Mongols armed by modern technology'.

---

* Until February 1918 Russia adhered to the Julian (Old Style) calendar, which ran thirteen days behind the Gregorian (New Style) calendar in use in Western Europe. Dates relating to domestic events are given in the Old Style up until 31 January 1918, and in the New Style after that. Dates relating to international events are given in the New Style throughout the book.

The zemstvos sprang back into action and sent medical brigades to the Manchurian Front.

Had the war been won, the regime might have been able to make political capital from this patriotic upsurge. But it was hard for the Russian military to fight a war 6,000 miles away. The biggest problem was the sheer incompetence of the High Command, which stuck rigidly to the military doctrines of the nineteenth century and wasted thousands of Russian lives by ordering hopeless bayonet charges against well-entrenched artillery positions (a mistake it would repeat in 1914–17).

As the war went from bad to worse, the liberals turned against the government, using its bungled military campaign as a patriotic argument for political reform. Even the country's main industrialists, who had in the past relied on the state for protection, joined the chorus of criticism as they suffered from the economic dislocations of the war. So unpopular had the government become that in July 1904, when Viacheslav von Plehve, its reactionary Minister of the Interior, was blown to pieces by a terrorist bomber, there was hardly a word of public regret. In Warsaw, Plehve's murder was celebrated by crowds in the street.

Shocked by Plehve's murder, the Tsar had intended to replace him with another hardliner, but bad news from the Front and the strength of the opposition at home finally persuaded him to appoint a liberal, Prince Mirsky, who called himself a 'zemstvo man'. Encouraged by Mirsky's appointment, 103 zemstvo representatives met at a congress in St Petersburg and passed a ten-point resolution for political reform, including a legislative parliament. Convened illegally in various palaces, the congress was, in effect, the first national assembly in Russian history. People at the time compared it to the French Estates-General of 1789. Civic bodies and associations held meetings to support its resolutions. The Union of Liberation organized a series of banquets (like those in France in 1847–8) attended by the zemstvos' supporters where toasts were drunk to freedom and a constitution.

Mirsky presented the Tsar with a carefully worded digest of the zemstvo assembly's resolution in the hope of winning him over to a programme of moderate reform. It asked only for a consultative parliament (rather than a legislative one) and for zemstvo delegates to sit in the State Council, an advisory legislative body appointed by the Tsar. But even this was too much for Nicholas, who ruled out any talk of political reform as 'harmful to the people whom God has entrusted to me'. On 12 December, the Tsar issued an Imperial Manifesto promising to strengthen the rule of law, to ease restrictions on the press, and to expand the authority of the zemstvos. But it said nothing on the controversial subject of a parliamentary body. Hearing of its contents, Mirsky fell into despair. 'Everything has failed,' he said to his colleagues. 'Let us build jails.'[4]

If there is a single, repetitive theme in the history of Russia during the last decades of the old regime, it is that of the need for reform and the failure of successive governments to achieve it in the face of the Tsar's opposition. Mirsky's initiative was probably the main chance the government would have to avert a revolution. In a crisis of authority a regime's best hope of survival is to make concessions soon enough to satisfy and split off the opposition's moderate wing.

Bloody Sunday ended the Tsar's chance of keeping the political initiative. It drove the liberals to the left, creating a more radical, united opposition to the government. Educated society was outraged by the massacre. Students went on strike and turned their campuses into centres of political agitation. By the end of February, the government had been forced to close down virtually all institutions of higher learning until the end of the academic year. Professional unions organized themselves at a national level into a Union of Unions, later joined by a Women's Union for Equality and similar unions for semi-professional groups (e.g. railway workers and employees), which gave the intelligentsia a direct link to the masses.

The protest movement quickly spread to the non-Russian borderlands. It was particularly strong in Poland, Finland, the Baltic provinces and the Caucasus, where social and political tensions were reinforced by a widespread hatred of Russian rule. In the ten Polish provinces there were more strikes in the spring and summer of 1905 than in the rest of the empire combined. In Warsaw and Łodz strikers put up barricades and clashed with the police. News of Russia's humiliating defeat by Japan was celebrated in Poland, Finland and the Baltic lands in the belief that it would bring down the government and pave the way for their own autonomy.

The mood of rebellion spread to the countryside as well. Seeing the government's weakness, the peasants took their chance and organized rent strikes against the landowners. They trespassed on the gentry's land, felled their trees and cut their hay. From the early summer, they began to launch full-scale attacks on their estates, seizing property and setting fire to the manors, forcing the landowners to flee. Witnesses spoke of the night sky lit up by the blaze of burning manors and the lines of horse-drawn carts moving along the roads, loaded with plundered property. Nearly 3,000 manors were destroyed (15 per cent of the total) during the jacquerie of 1905–6. Most of the violence was concentrated in the central agricultural zone south of Moscow, where the largest estates were located and peasant poverty was most acute.

The local gentry appealed for help against the peasants, and the government sent in the troops. From January to October 1905 the army was deployed no fewer than 2,700 times to put down peasant uprisings, accelerating the breakdown of army discipline which had begun with the despatch of the troops to Manchuria. It was the growing threat of a mutinous revolution at home combined with the prospect of defeat abroad which forced the Tsar to sue for peace with Japan. It proved impossible—as it would again in 1917—to conduct a foreign war in the midst of a domestic social revolution. The vast majority of the infantry were peasants, and resented being used to suppress agrarian discontent. Whole units refused to carry out orders and mutinies spread through the ranks. Even the Cossack cavalry—known to be among the Tsar's most loyal soldiers—succumbed to the mood of rebellion. And then, on 14 June, the unrest spread to the Black Sea Fleet.

The mutiny began with a piece of maggoty meat. The ship's doctor on the battleship *Potemkin* declared it was fit to eat. When the sailors complained to the captain he had their spokesman, Vakulenchuk, shot. The crew rebelled, killed seven officers and raised the red flag on the

ship. The mutineers took the *Potemkin* to Odessa, where striking workers had been in a state of virtual war with the city government for the
past two weeks. Surrounded by a guard of honour, Vakulenchuk's body
was placed at the foot of a set of marble steps (later immortalized by
Eisenstein's film) leading from the harbour to the city. Huge crowds gathered on the harbour front, placing wreaths around the bier of the mar-
tyred revolutionary. Troops were sent in to disperse the crowd. Moving
down the steps, they fired indiscriminately into the hemmed-in civilians below: 2,000 people were killed and 3,000 wounded before the firing stopped. The mutineers sailed to Constanza in Romania, where they
gave up the *Potemkin* for safe refuge. In itself the mutiny had been a
minor threat. But it was a major embarrassment to the government, for
it showed the world that the revolution had spread to the heart of its own
military machine.

With the Russian Empire on the verge of collapse, the regime responded
to the crisis with its usual incompetence and obstinacy. Nicholas seemed
oblivious to the dangers of the situation: while the country sank into
chaos he filled his diary with trivial notes on the weather and the company at tea. His advisers told him that foreign agents had been responsible for the demonstration on Bloody Sunday. A carefully selected
delegation of 'reliable' workers was summoned to his palace and lined
up like children to hear a lecture from the Tsar in which he blamed the
workers for allowing themselves to be deceived by 'foreign revolutionaries' but promised to 'forgive them their sins' because he believed in
their 'unshakeable devotion'. When advised by his new Minister of the
Interior, A. G. Bulygin, that political concessions might be needed to
calm the country, Nicholas was astounded. He told the Minister: 'One
would think that you are afraid a revolution will break out.' 'Your Maj-
esty,' Bulygin replied, 'the revolution has already begun.'[5]

On 18 February 1905, Nicholas issued an Imperial Manifesto calling
on the people to unite behind the throne and send in ideas for 'improvements in the government'. Bulygin was instructed to draw up proposals

for a national assembly. For the next four months tens of thousands of reform petitions were sent in to the Tsar from village assemblies, army regiments, towns and factories. Like the *cahiers*, the letters of grievance during the French Revolution of 1789, they gave expression to the evolving language of democracy. But their demands were much too radical for Nicholas. Most called for a national parliament with sovereign rights of legislation, effectively establishing a constitutional monarchy, whereas the only sort of assembly which the Tsar was prepared to concede (the Bulygin Duma, presented for his signature on 6 August) was a purely consultative one (what Mirsky had proposed) elected on a limited franchise to ensure the domination of the aristocracy.

The Bulygin Duma (parliament) was too little too late: six months earlier it would have been welcomed, and might have enabled the government to regain the political initiative. But now all but the most moderate reformers found it unsatisfactory. Less than 1 per cent of St Petersburg's adult residents would qualify for the vote, while in many provincial cities the number would be even tinier. The socialist parties chose to boycott the elections and support the already growing movement of mass civil disobedience to pressure the government into making further concessions.

During 1905 the workers' strikes and protests had become increasingly organized and militant. This was partly the result of the socialist parties' growing influence, but mainly of the workers themselves becoming more class-conscious and violent as their conflicts with employers and police became more bitter and intense.

The general strike was a classic example of a spontaneous yet disciplined uprising by the working class. It began on 20 September with a walk-out by the Moscow printers—the most educated workers—for better pay and conditions. The strikers made contact with the students (the printing works were near the university) and held a demonstration, which came under attack by the police. The workers threw stones at the police and erected barricades to defend 'their' streets. By the start of

October the printers of St Petersburg and several other cities had come out in solidarity with their comrades.

Next the railway workers joined the strike. The Union of Railway Employees and Workers was affiliated to the Union of Unions, which had been discussing the idea of a general strike to further its campaign for political reform since the summer. By 10 October virtually the entire railway network had come to a halt. Millions of workers—factory, shop and transport workers, bank and office employees, hospital staff, teachers, lecturers, even the actors of the Imperial Theatre of St Petersburg— came out in support of what became a national strike against the government.

The organization of the general strike owed much to the Soviet of Workers' Deputies established in St Petersburg on 17 October. The word 'soviet' means 'council' in Russian (there was nothing particularly Communist about it until after 1917). The Petersburg Soviet was really no more than an ad hoc council of workers to direct the general strike. It published its own newspaper, *Izvestiia*, to keep strikers informed of developments, organized a militia, distributed food supplies, and by its example inspired workers in fifty other cities to set up Soviets of their own.

The Mensheviks dominated the Petersburg Soviet. They saw it as the embodiment of their social democratic ideology to build a political movement in which the working masses would play a leading role. Trotsky (then a Menshevik) was the real force behind the Soviet. He framed its resolutions and wrote the editorials for *Izvestiia*. The Bolsheviks, by contrast, were mistrustful of working-class initiatives that were not led by their own vanguard of professional revolutionaries, and they did not play much part in the Soviet's activities. Not even Lenin, who returned from his Geneva exile in November, got to speak in the Technological Institute, where the Soviet was housed, although after 1917 a plaque was put up in the building claiming that he had. It was important for the Bolsheviks to date their foundation myth from the 'first revolution' of 1905.

The government had lost control of the capital. It could not count on the support of enough loyal troops to end the general strike and restore order in the country as a whole. Under pressure from his advisers, who feared he would lose his throne, Nicholas reluctantly agreed to sign a Manifesto, drawn up by Count Witte, granting civil liberties, cabinet government and a legislative Duma elected on a wide franchise. It was in effect the political programme of the Union of Liberation. Witte's aim was to isolate the Left by pacifying the liberals.

The Manifesto's proclamation was met with jubilation in the streets. There was a euphoric sense of national unity, a feeling that all classes might at last be brought together by this 'people's victory'—a sentiment expressed by Ilia Repin's painting *Manifesto of 17 October*. Despite the rainy weather, huge crowds assembled in front of the Winter Palace with a red banner bearing the inscription 'Freedom of Assembly'—a symbolic victory on the site of the Bloody Sunday massacre. Officers and society ladies wore red armbands and sang the 'Marseillaise' in solidarity with the workers and students. The general strike was called off.

The unity of 'the people' was illusory. For the liberal upper classes, whose interests were political, the October Manifesto was the victorious end to their struggle. It seemed to them that Russia was becoming part of the family of European nations based on constitutional liberties. Newspapers were filled with daring editorials, as the old censorship laws ceased to function. Socialist leaders returned from exile. Political parties were organized to compete in the Duma elections. Streets, squares and parks became debating grounds, as people became conscious of themselves as citizens. There was talk of a new Russia being born.

But for the workers and peasants the political concessions of the Manifesto offered no solutions to their social grievances, the eight-hour working day, respectful treatment by the employers, better pay and conditions. For them the revolution had only just begun. After October, there were renewed strikes and agrarian disturbances, which continued during 1906. Many peasants thought mistakenly that the Manifesto had given them licence to overturn the rules they did not like. There was also a new wave of mutinies—much bigger than before—in the armed services, with 211 separate mutinies recorded in the army between late October and December.

Encouraged by these revolutionary signs, the SDs resolved to stage an armed uprising in Moscow. Lenin was keen on an action. Under Trotsky's leadership, the Petersburg Soviet was also preparing for a showdown with the government. It supported a series of militant strikes and talked about the idea of an armed revolt to assert the 'hegemony of the working class'. On 3 December its leaders were arrested on charges of preparing an armed rebellion. The Moscow SDs announced a general strike and distributed arms to the workers. Barricades went up and the streets of Moscow were turned into a battlefield between the workers and police. The Presnia district, the centre of the textile industry, became a rebel stronghold with its own revolutionary council and militia. Tsarist reinforcements were brought in. The Presnia district was bombarded. More than a thousand unarmed civilians were killed in the suppression of the uprising. During the weeks that followed the authorities launched a brutal crackdown with mass arrests and summary executions. Workers' children were rounded up in barracks and beaten by police to 'teach them a lesson'. The prisons filled up, militant workers lost their jobs, and the socialist parties were forced underground. Slowly, through terror, order in the country was restored.

The Moscow uprising was to occupy a prominent position in the Soviet cult of 1905. Its 'fallen heroes' were commemorated with a morbid veneration in 1917 and during the Civil War, when the Bolsheviks required martyrs for their cause. The uprising had had no real chance of victory, and it failed disastrously, but that was not the point. It stood as an example of the principle that one should *act* whenever it was possible to seize power—however unlikely that possibility—because only action could change things. 'On s'engage et puis on voit!' Napoleon once said. That would be Lenin's principle in October 1917.

———

What were the lessons of 1905? Although the tsarist regime had been shaken, it was not brought down. The reasons are clear enough. First, the various opposition movements—the liberal urban classes and the workers, the peasants, the mutineers in the armed services, and the nationalists—had all followed their own separate rhythms and failed to combine politically. This would be different in February 1917, when the Duma and the Soviet performed a co-ordinating role for the revolution as a whole. Second, the armed forces remained loyal, despite the rash of mutinies, and helped the regime to stabilize itself. This too would be different in February 1917, when the traditional military had been ruined by the First World War and the crucial units of the army and the navy went over quickly to the people's side. The relatively quick cessation of hostilities against Japan was also an important factor behind the government's recovery in 1905. Things might well have turned out differently. With a longer war (or a less favourable peace than the one secured by Russia at the Treaty of Portsmouth in September) the Tsar might have lost the support of the military and patriotic classes in society. Finally, there was a fatal split within the revolutionary camp between the political interests of the liberals and the Left's demands for radical social reforms. By issuing the October Manifesto the tsarist regime succeeded in driving a wedge between the liberals and the socialists. Never again would the Russian masses support the constitutional democratic movement as they had done between January and October 1905.

But if the tsarist regime had managed to survive the revolutionary crisis through repression and reform, its authority was undermined. People could no longer trust the Tsar. They had tasted freedom. They could not go back to the situation before 1905. And they were ready to rise up again if the regime gave up on reform.

The 'first revolution' was a formative experience for all those who lived through it. Many of the younger comrades of 1905 were the elders of 1917. They were inspired by its memory. Boris Pasternak, who was fifteen at the time, summed up its significance in his 1927 poem '1905':

This night of guns,
Put asleep
By a strike.
This night—
Was our childhood
And the youth of our teachers.[6]

In the countryside 1905 was a watershed, though nothing had strictly changed. The peasants were frustrated but not defeated in their struggle for the gentry's land. When the squires returned to their estates, they noticed a change in the younger peasants' mood. Their old deference was gone, replaced by a sullenness in their behaviour towards their old masters. Many nobles complained of a rise in peasant crime, vandalism and 'hooliganism'. This new surliness towards the gentry was reflected in village songs, like this one from 1912:

At night I strut around,
And rich men don't get in my way.
Just let some rich guy try,
And I'll screw his head on upside-down.[7]

The peasants resented having to relinquish control of the land they had briefly taken in the 'days of freedom'. Through hostile looks and petty acts of vandalism they were letting it be known that the land was 'theirs' and that as soon as the tsarist regime was weakened once more they would again reclaim it.

The squires were not the only gentlemen who feared the lower classes more and more. The urban élites had been forced to confront the frightening reality of a violent revolution; the prospect of it erupting again—with still more violence—filled them with horror. The next revolution, it seemed clear, would not be a celebration of Liberty, Equality and Fraternity. It would come as a terrible storm, a violent explosion of suppressed anger and hatred from the dispossessed which would sweep away the old Imperial civilization. Here was the terrifying vision of poets such as Blok and Belyi, who portrayed Russia after 1905 as an active and unstable volcano.

In the long run the Bolsheviks were the real victors of 1905. They only emerged as a distinct movement afterwards, as Lenin, back in exile in Europe, digested the practical lessons of the failed revolution, and the ideological and tactical divisions between Bolsheviks and Mensheviks became clear. Until 1905 the differences between the Social Democratic factions had been largely personal—Bolshevism having been defined by a personal pledge of loyalty to Lenin, and Menshevism by the rejection of any dominant leader.

In Lenin's view, three things had been made clear by 1905: the bankruptcy of the 'bourgeoisie' and its liberal parties as a political force against the power of autocracy; the immense revolutionary potential of the peasantry; and the capacity of the nationalist movements in the borderlands to undermine the empire fatally.

It was these conclusions that led him to advance the essential Bolshevik idea (a heresy for orthodox Marxists) that a 'vanguard' of the working class could seize power and carry out a socialist revolution without first having to go through a 'bourgeois-democratic revolution', so long as it formed an alliance with the peasantry and the nationalities to destroy the old regime.

Trotsky advanced a similar idea in his theory of the 'permanent revolution' which emerged from his analysis of 1905. The Russian bourgeoisie, Trotsky argued, had shown itself incapable of leading a genuinely democratic revolution. Yet its weakness made it possible for the working class to carry out a socialist revolution in backward Russia earlier than in the more advanced societies of the capitalist West, where Marxist theory had supposed that socialism would develop from the revolution's 'bourgeois democratic' phase. Trotsky thought that a workers' state in Russia would not be able to survive the organized resistance of the capitalist states. Its survival would depend on its international development—the ability of the revolution to spread to other countries through an alliance of the proletariat and the peasantry—a permanent imperative in view of the global nature of the capitalist system. Although

Trotsky was still a Menshevik, his theory already fitted better with the Bolshevism which he would espouse in 1917 than with the Marxist orthodoxy of Menshevism, which insisted that undeveloped countries such as Russia had to pass through a bourgeois-democratic phase (when political and civil rights allowed the growth of labour parties and trade unions) before it could begin a socialist revolution.

Lenin and Trotsky drew their revolutionary tactics of 1917 from the lessons they had learned from 1905. That is why, in 1920, Lenin would famously describe the 1905 revolution as the 'dress rehearsal' without which 'the revolutions of 1917 . . . would have been impossible'.[8]

3

LAST HOPES

Russia's parliamentary era started with a ceremonial opening of the Duma in the Coronation Hall of the Winter Palace in St Petersburg on 27 April 1906. On one side of the hall stood the great and good of autocratic Russia: ministers, senators, admirals, generals and members of the court, all in their dress uniforms dripping with medals and golden braid. Opposing them were the parliamentary deputies of the new democratic Russia, a motley collection of peasants dressed in cotton shirts and tunics, professional men in lounge suits, monks and priests in black, Ukrainians, Poles, Armenians and Tatars in colourful national costumes, a few noblemen in evening dress, but almost no workers. 'The two hostile sides stood confronting each other,' recalled a Crimean delegate. 'The old and grey court dignitaries, keepers of etiquette and tradition, looked across in a haughty manner, though not without fear and confusion, at the "people of the street", whom the revolution had swept into the palace, and quietly whispered to one another. The other side looked across at them with no less disdain or contempt.'[1]

The ceremonial confrontation was only a foretaste of the war to come. The whole period of Russian political history between the two revolutions of 1905 and February 1917 could be characterized as a battle between the royalist and parliamentary forces. To begin with, when the country was still emerging from the revolutionary crisis, the court was forced to concede ground to the Duma. But as the memory of 1905 passed, it tried to roll back its powers and restore the old autocracy.

The constitutional reforms of 1905–6 were ambivalent enough to give both sides hope. Nicholas had never accepted the October Manifesto as a limitation on his sovereignty. He had granted the Manifesto as a concession to save his throne but at no time had he sworn to act upon it as a 'constitution' (the word had nowhere been mentioned) so his coronation oath to uphold the principles of autocracy remained in fact, at least in his own mind. There was nothing in the Fundamental Laws (passed in April 1906) to suggest that from now on the Tsar's authority should be deemed to derive from the people, as in Western constitutional states. The Tsar retained the title 'Autocrat', albeit only with the prefix 'Supreme' in place of 'Unlimited'. Nicholas took this to mean business as usual.

The court remained the centre of political power. The Tsar appointed the Prime Minister (Ivan Goremykin) and the government (the Council of Ministers). He could dissolve the Duma and (under Article 87 of the Fundamental Laws) rule by emergency decree when it was not in session—a loophole used to bypass parliament when it opposed the government's bills. The Duma was elected by an indirect system of voting heavily weighted in favour of the court's traditional allies, the nobility and the peasantry (mistakenly assumed to be monarchists). Although it was a legislative parliament, it could not pass its own laws without the endorsement of the Tsar and the upper chamber (the State Council), dominated by the aristocracy.

The make-up of the Duma turned out to be far more radical than the government had bargained for when it drew up the Electoral Law. From its opening session in the Tauride Palace, it was turned into a revolutionary tribune, a rhetorical battering ram against the fortress of autocracy. The SRs and SDs had boycotted the Duma elections, which they denounced as a sham democracy, but the largest party, the Constitutional Democrats (Kadets), with 153 of the 448 seats, was radically inclined and set about demanding far-reaching political reforms, including the appointment of a government responsible to the Duma, the abolition of the State Council, and universal adult male suffrage. The second-largest party were the 107 Trudoviks (Labourites), a peasant-based party, whose deputies smoked cheap tobacco and spat sunflower seeds on to the floor of the elegant palace. Their main goal was a radical solution of the land question through the compulsory expropriation of the gentry's property. With the Kadets (who wanted compensation to the landowners) they introduced a bill for land reform in the Duma.

There had been a time, in 1905, when many landowners would have been prepared to accept some form of expropriation in order to save their class. Even the reactionary D. F. Trepov, the Tsar's main adviser on agrarian affairs, had told Witte that he would be glad to give up half his land if it would help him keep the rest. But as the revolutionary threat receded, the gentry became less inclined to compromise. The United Nobility—a landowners' organization with powerful supporters in the court, the State Council and the Civil Service—led the campaign against the Duma's reform proposals on the reasonable grounds that granting more land to the peasants would not solve the problem of their poverty, since this was caused by the inefficiencies of the village commune rather than by shortages of land.

Unwilling to consider its radical demands, the Tsar dissolved the Duma on 8 July. Outraged by the dissolution, which they saw as an 'attack on the parliamentary principle', the Kadets issued a manifesto from the Finnish town of Vyborg calling on 'the people' to unite in a mass campaign of civil disobedience, as they had done in the general strike of 1905. The Vyborg Manifesto was greeted by 'the people' with indifference. More than one hundred leading Kadets were brought to trial and suspended from the Duma for their part in it. Never again would the Kadets place their trust in the support of 'the people'. Nor would they claim to be their representatives. From this moment on, they would consciously become what they had been all along: the natural party of the middle class. Liberalism and the people went their separate ways.

Meanwhile, the Tsar appointed Petr Stolypin as Prime Minister—a man known for his resolute measures to restore law and order in the countryside as Governor of Saratov, one of the most violent provinces in 1905, but also for his ideas of agrarian and political reform to create stability in the longer term.

Few personalities in Russian history have been as controversial as Stolypin. The Left condemned him as a bloody defender of the tsarist order. He gave his name to the hangman's noose ('Stolypin neckties') used by the military field courts to quell the peasant revolution; and to the railway carriages in which the revolutionaries were transported to Siberia ('Stolypin carriages'). After 1917 the most hardened followers of the Tsar would come to denounce him as an upstart provincial bureaucrat whose dangerous reforms had only served to undermine the sacred principles of autocracy. But to the admirers of his authoritarian statesmanship—and Vladimir Putin is one of them—he was the only politician capable of saving Russia from the revolution and the Civil War. His reforms, they argue, if given enough time, would have transformed the country into a liberal capitalist society. But this is a very big 'if'. Time was the one thing Stolypin did not have. Was it really possible to stabilize a revolutionary situation through political reform? Could one man have saved the Tsar?

Stolypin belongs to a tradition of governance in Russia—it runs from Peter the Great to Putin—that sees the state as the main agency of social management and modernization. The aim of his reforms was not to create a democratic order but to use democratic elements to underpin the tsarist government. The same statist instrumentalism determined his relations with the Duma. He saw it as an appendage of the state, a public body to endorse government policies, but not to check or direct the administration. His constitutional model was more Prussian than English (Bismarck was his political hero).

The second Duma, which convened in February 1907, was tolerated by Stolypin only in so far as it did what he wanted. His administration had done its best to influence the elections and secure the return of its allies, the Octobrists, a 'party of state order' based on the political principles of the October Manifesto. But the 54 elected Octobrists, even if supported by the 98 Kadets and 60 other Centrist and Rightist deputies, were hardly enough to give the government a workable majority against the huge block of 222 socialists (including 65 SDs) now that all the parties of the Left, having been encouraged by the radical intentions of its deputies in 1906, had ended their boycott of the Duma. Nor could Stolypin rely on the peasant deputies to play a subservient role. One from his own Saratov province caused a great sensation during the debate on the land reforms when he said to a noble delegate: 'We know about your property, for we were your property once. My uncle was exchanged for a greyhound.'[2]

With little prospect of finding support for his reforms, Stolypin had no qualms about dissolving the Duma and changing the electoral law (by a decree on 3 June) so that when the next assembly convened it would be dominated by conservative elements. The representation of the gentry was increased at the expense of the peasants, workers and national minorities. When the third Duma assembled in November 1907 the pro-government parties (Octobrists and Rightists) controlled 287 of the 443 seats. The radicals called it a 'Duma of Lords and Lackeys'.

The 3 June decree was technically an infringement of the Fundamental Laws, and the liberals were quick to denounce it as a coup d'état. Even the Octobrists were uncomfortable with it. By his high-handed treatment of the Duma, Stolypin had undermined the one potential base of political support—the liberals—capable of bridging the divide between the tsarist regime and society. Justifying his break with the parliamentary principle in terms reminiscent of the arguments deployed to excuse dictatorships in the Third World today, Stolypin told the British ambassador that Russia could not be governed like Western European countries because 'political life and parliamentary ideals were enigmas to the enormous majority of the nation, ignorant and unlettered as they were'.[3]

Stolypin's land reform was his attempt to remedy that deficit. Its aim was to create a new class of peasant landowners, who, he hoped, by owning property, would feel they had a stake in the system and become involved in local zemstvo politics as supporters of the government. Stolypin called it a 'wager on the strong'.

The reform involved the dismantling of the village commune, the organizing institution of the peasant revolution on the land, by encouraging the stronger peasants to leave it and set up as farmers on their own. By a law of 9 November 1906, the head of a peasant family was given the right to convert his communal strips of arable land into private property on fully enclosed farms outside the village (*khutora*) or consolidated holdings within it (*otruba*). Further legislation followed to speed up the separations through agronomic measures and to help the separators purchase land with low-interest credit from the Peasant Land Bank. The state put its full weight behind the reforms. This was the first time it had ever really tried to effect a major change in the everyday life of the peasants and, unless its initiative succeeded, it would also be the last. Four ministries, hundreds of provincial and district land commissions, and thousands of officials, statisticians and agronomists were employed to implement the enclosure movement as quickly as possible. The regime had come to realize that its own survival would depend on the creation of a new agrarian order based on private property.

There were profound cultural reasons for the peasants to oppose the break-up of the commune, which had been the focus of their lives for centuries. The basic worry was that giving some peasants the right to own part of the communal land would deprive others of their customary rights of access to this land as their basic means of livelihood. What would happen if the peasant landowner bequeathed his property to his eldest son or sold it altogether? The rest of the family would be turned into paupers. Or if the richest peasants bought up all the land? Entire families would be unable to support themselves. There was also a widespread fear that the government surveyors, who had been instructed to encourage the enclosures, would reward the separators with more than their fair share of the best land.

And indeed the peasants had real cause to wonder just how the old patchwork of intermingled strips could be disentangled at all. On what terms was a good bit of land in one place to be exchanged for a poor one in another? How were they to divide the meadows, the woods and the rivers, which had always been held in common? And if the newly enclosed farms were to build their own roads, wouldn't these cut across existing boundaries and rights of way? The peasants were attached to their land in a very particular sense. No one had ever taught them how to calculate the area of a piece of land by multiplying its width by its length—their fields were divided 'by eye' or by pacing out the strips and making rough adjustments where their length or the quality of their soil was uneven—so they had no reliable means of satisfying themselves that two plots deemed the same by the government's surveyors, with their town-made suits, their rulers and their tripods, were in fact of equal size.

All these fears led the communes to resist the peasant-separators, often using force or intimidation to put them off. Of the 6 million applications for land consolidation recorded before 1915, over one third were subsequently withdrawn by the applicants themselves; and of the 1 million that were completed, two thirds had to be forced through by the authorities against the opposition of the communes. Overall, the land reforms must be deemed a failure. Between 1906 and the eve of the revolution approximately 15 per cent of the peasant households in European Russia consolidated land as private plots, bringing the total of peasant farms in hereditary tenure to only around 30 per cent. Yet for every household that enclosed its land there was another that had tried and failed, usually because of communal opposition or bureaucratic delays, with the result that the would-be separators lost interest.

Perhaps the land reforms were too ambitious to succeed. It turned out to be much harder to impose foreign capitalist ways on the Russian peasantry than the bureaucrats in St Petersburg had been prepared to acknowledge. The village commune was an old institution, in many ways defunct and inefficient, but in others still responsive to the basic needs of the peasants, living as they did on the margins of poverty, afraid of taking risks, and hostile to outsiders. Stolypin assumed that the peasants were poor because they had the commune: by getting them to break from it he could improve their lives. But the opposite was true: the commune existed *because* the peasants were poor, it served to distribute the burden of their poverty, and as long as they were poor there would be little incentive for them to leave it. For better or worse, the commune's egalitarian customs had come to embody the peasantry's basic notions of social justice and, as 1917 would prove, these were ideals for which they would fight long and hard.

As long as they were threatened by a peasant revolution on the land, the nobility supported Stolypin. But once they thought that threat had passed, they turned against the Prime Minister, whose broader reform programme was regarded by the court and its conservative allies in the military, the Church, nobility and nationalist circles as a challenge to the Tsar and the established order which threatened to lead Russia towards a liberal state they did not want.

Stolypin's political programme threatened to shift the balance of power from the court to the Imperial state. The Tsar saw the state as an extension of his personal rule (a patrimonial ideology rooted in medieval Muscovy). But Stolypin viewed it as an abstract agent of reform— above the dynasty or the aristocracy—whose purpose was to serve the empire's interests. For the Tsar and his conservative supporters the challenge represented by Stolypin's vision of the state loomed even larger because of the strength of his personality. As a statesman the Prime Minister was far more powerful than the feeble Nicholas, who was quite incapable of mastering the complex mechanisms of the modern state which Stolypin's programme would consolidate. If Stolypin was allowed to get his way, the Tsar's personal rule would be overshadowed by this bureaucratic state; the mystically sanctioned pyramid of power headed by the court and the aristocracy would be undermined.

The first sign of the court's opposition to Stolypin was over the Naval General Staff Bill in 1909. Proposed by the Octobrists in the Duma's Committee of Imperial Defence, which had a veto over the military budget, the bill threatened to refuse the navy credits unless the Naval General Staff came under the control of the Ministry of War rather than the court. Nicholas saw the ultimatum as an attempt by the Duma to wrest military command from the crown, and used his veto to block the bill. He was infuriated that Stolypin and his Council of Ministers had supported the bill, but stopped short of accepting his offer to resign.

The crisis united the defenders of autocracy against the Prime Minister. They managed to defeat virtually all his political reforms. His proposal to expand the state system of primary schools was defeated by reactionaries in the Church, who had their own parish schools. The same fate awaited his legislation to ease discrimination against the Jews and other religious minorities.

Stolypin's local-government reforms were bitterly opposed by the nobility because they challenged the gentry's domination of rural politics. Their intention was to give the peasants, as landowners, equal representation to the nobles in the zemstvos. They also proposed to abolish the peasant-class courts and bring the peasants fully into the system of civil law. Stolypin saw these measures as essential for the success of his land reforms. The new class of conservative peasant landowners which he hoped to create would not support the existing order unless they were made citizens with equal political and legal rights to those enjoyed by other classes. 'First of all,' he said, 'we have to create a citizen, a small landowner, and then the peasant problem will be solved.' He proposed to establish a new tier of zemstvo representation at the *volost'* (rural district) level, in which the franchise would be based on property rather than birth. But the gentry was afraid that the zemstvos would be swamped by the peasants, and accused Stolypin of trying to undermine 'provincial society' (i.e. themselves) through bureaucratic centralization. On this basis they organized against him in the Duma, the State Council and the United Nobility, forcing him to give up his reforms. Had Stolypin succeeded in broadening the social base of local government in the countryside, then perhaps in 1917 it would not have collapsed so disastrously and Soviet power might never have filled the subsequent political vacuum as successfully as it did.

As a result of the naval staff crisis and the gentry reaction, Stolypin lost support in the Duma, the Octobrists went into decline, and he became dependent on the Nationalists, formed in 1909 to represent the interests of the Russians in the empire's western borderlands.

The zemstvos had never been established in these western districts, because most of the landowners were Poles. But the Nationalists campaigned for a Western Zemstvo Bill, arguing that Russia's Imperial interests could be secured by a voting procedure based on nationality as well as property. The peasant smallholders in the region were mainly Russian, Ukrainian and Belorussians, all equally bearers of the Russian national idea, according to the Nationalists. If they were given the largest share of the vote in the zemstvos, as planned by the lower property franchise of the Western Zemstvo Bill, they might become model peasant citizens; an area dominated by Polish landowners would be ruled by the Russians.

The bill was passed by the Duma but defeated in the State Council, where the gentry's fundamentalists were unwilling to see the privileges of the noble estate sacrificed to ensure the domination of Russian interests; the fact that the Poles were aristocrats should in their view take precedence over the fact that the peasants were Russians. Their opposition was encouraged by Trepov and Durnovo, the reactionary Minister of the Interior, who were bitter rivals of Stolypin and favourites at the court. Stolypin threatened to resign unless the Tsar prorogued the Duma and passed the bill by emergency decree under Article 87. Nicholas agreed, albeit unhappily.

Stolypin had prevailed by sheer force of character. But his high-handed tactics had alienated almost everyone. The Tsar had been humiliated, and it was now far from clear whether the Prime Minister could count on his support. The liberals were outraged by Stolypin's treatment of the Duma. The Octobrists moved into partial opposition, leaving the Nationalists as Stolypin's only supporters.

Stolypin was assassinated by a student-revolutionary turned police informer called D. G. Bogrov in the Kiev Opera House on 1 September 1911. On hearing of his death, the Tsar said: 'Now there will be no more talk about reform.' The Empress was relieved to see the end of Stolypin, a resolute opponent of the mystic Rasputin, in whom she placed her faith as a healer for her haemophiliac son, the tsarevich Alexis, and whom she had promoted as a personal adviser to herself and Nicholas.[4] Some historians speculate that the assassination of Stolypin was approved or even organized by police agents with connections to the court.

Long before Bogrov's bullet killed him, Stolypin was politically dead. Had he been more skilful in 'the art of the possible', he might have gained more time for his reforms. But he adhered so rigidly to his principles that he lost sight of the need to negotiate and compromise with his opponents on both left and right. He alienated the old political élites by riding roughshod over their traditional privileges, as well as the liberals by suppressing the Duma when it stood in his way. This political inflexibility stemmed from his narrow bureaucratic outlook and dependence on the Tsar. He thought he could get his reforms by administrative fiat, and never moved outside the bureaucracy to mobilize a broader social base of support. He failed to create his own political party, which might have been possible if he had organized the peasant beneficiaries of his reforms. There was a Stolypin but no Stolypinites. And so when Stolypin died his reforms died with him.

According to some historians, the old regime's last real hope disappeared with him: his initiatives were its one chance to reform itself on parliamentary lines. But were these reforms succeeding in their aims? By 1911 they had made little headway in moving Russia towards a constitutional order. There had been some gains in civil liberties, and in press freedom, and the Duma had survived as something of a counter-weight to royal and executive authority. But this hardly meant that tsarist Russia was moving towards some sort of Western liberal 'normality'.

The nature of the tsarist regime was the single biggest guarantee of its own political irreformability. The autocratic ideology of Nicholas II was deeply hostile to the Western constitutional vision of Stolypin's programme of reforms; and the entrenched powers of the court, together with the vested interests of the Church and the landed aristocracy, were strong enough to prevent that programme being realized.

Perhaps we should also ask if any package of political reforms could have resolved the social problems that had led to the revolution of 1905. Could the land question—the main concern of the majority of the population—have been resolved without the confiscation of the gentry's land? Would the workers have been satisfied by the moderate proposals of the Duma to improve conditions in the factories and allow limited trade union rights? The answer to these questions must be 'no'.

After a relatively quiet period for industrial relations, between 1907 and 1911, there was a dramatic rise both in the number of strikes and in their militancy, beginning with a national wave of protests following the April 1912 massacre of demonstrating miners in Lena in Siberia, and culminating in July 1914 with a general strike in St Petersburg, where in the midst of a state visit by the French President barricades were erected by the workers and there was fighting in the streets. During these two years 3 million workers were involved in 9,000 industrial strikes, mostly organized under the Bolsheviks' militant slogans in preference to the Mensheviks'. Despite efforts at political reform, urban Russia on the eve of the First World War arguably found itself on the brink of a new and potentially more violent revolution than in 1905.

After Stolypin's assassination the government abandoned all reforms. The Duma was sidelined by the next Prime Minister, Vladimir Kokovtsov (1911–14), who took his lead from the court. Rightist elements pressured the Tsar to abolish the Duma, or at least to demote it to the status of a consultative body. It was only Western pressure and the fear of a popular reaction that restrained Nicholas.

Meanwhile the Tsar was courting the support of reactionary nationalists, who encouraged his illusion that the 'simple Russian people' loved their 'father-Tsar' (a belief embodied in the 'holy man' Rasputin, who was seen by Nicholas as 'just a simple peasant') and that nationalism could be used to rally mass support for the monarchy. The Tsar patronized the Union of the Russian People—an extreme nationalist and anti-Semitic party, whose paramilitary groups (the Black Hundreds) fought the 'foreign' revolutionaries in the streets and carried out pogroms against the Jews. But the nationalist card was a dangerous one for the regime to play. For the Duma parties also used it to define the nation's interests in opposition to the government.

The threat of war in Europe was growing. The two great Balkan empires, the Ottoman and Austro-Hungarian, were showing signs of cracking under growing pressure from Slav nationalist movements, leading to increasing tensions between Berlin and St Petersburg, not least because the Germans backed the Austrians in the defence of their Imperial interests in lands where the Russians saw their role as the protector of their fellow Slavs. Russia wanted what it had aimed to achieve throughout the nineteenth century: to capture Constantinople, the ancient Byzantine capital of their religious heritage; to control the Straits, a crucial military waterway between the Mediterranean and the Black Sea; and to oversee the dismantling of the Ottoman Empire in regions where the Russians claimed to represent the Christian Slavs.

For most of the nineteenth century Russia had pursued its interests in Europe through an alliance with Germany and the Austro-Hungarian Empire. The Romanov court had long been in favour of this pro-German policy, partly because of the strong dynastic ties between the ruling families and partly because of their mutual opposition to European liberalism. But after 1905 foreign policy could no longer be carried out regardless of public opinion. The Duma and the press called for a more aggressive policy in defence of Russia's Balkan interests, including support for Slav nationalists against rule from Vienna. Pan-Slav sentiment fuelled a new type of Germanophobic Russian nationalism, which had a revolutionary edge because of the perceived domination of German interests at the Romanov court (the Empress Alexandra was particularly unpopular because of her German origins). Nationalist opinion was increasingly frustrated by the government's conciliatory approach towards the German-backed Austrian aggressors in the Balkans.

By 1914, ideas of a war to defend the Balkan Slavs had spread into the court, the officer corps and much of the state itself. The Tsar too was coming to the view that a firm stand had to be taken against the Austrians, whose assertive defence of their interests in the Balkans was dragging Germany into a potential conflict with Russia. His Foreign Minister, S. D. Sazonov, was more cautious, knowing that the Russian military was not prepared for war with Germany, although he worked hard diplomatically to engineer a favourable alliance in support of Russia's military aims, should a European war become unavoidable. Others, like Durnovo, warned the Tsar that Russia was too weak to withstand the long war of attrition which was likely to result: a violent social revolution was bound to be the consequence. In a memorandum of February 1914 Durnovo outlined the revolution's likely course in remarkably prescient terms:

> The trouble will start with the blaming of the Government for all disasters . . . The defeated army, having lost its most dependable men, and carried away by the tide of primitive peasant desire for land, will find itself too demoralized to serve as a bulwark of law and order. The legislative institutions and the intellectual opposition parties, lacking real authority in the eyes of the people, will be powerless to stem the popular tide aroused by themselves, and Russia will be flung into hopeless anarchy.[5]

Nicholas faced a dilemma: if he went to war, he ran the risks of which Durnovo warned; but if he didn't, there could be an uprising of patriotic feeling against the Imperial family, which was seen as pro-German, possibly resulting in the loss of his political authority. There was little time to make a decision, for if Russia was to mobilize its forces, it would need a head start on its enemies, smaller countries with better railway systems that could mobilize their armies more quickly.

On 28 July, a month after the assassination of the Archduke Ferdinand by Serbian nationalists, the Austrians declared war against Serbia. The Tsar ordered the partial mobilization of his troops and appealed to the Kaiser to stop the Austrians. But Sazonov now called for a general mobilization, realizing that a German declaration of war against Russia was imminent (it came on 1 August). He warned Nicholas that 'unless he yielded to the popular demand for war and unsheathed the sword on Serbia's behalf, he would run the risk of a revolution and perhaps the loss of his throne'. Unhappily, the Tsar agreed. On 31 July, he ordered his forces to be mobilized for war.

4

WAR AND REVOLUTION

Whether or not there was a revolutionary situation in Russia on the eve of the First World War is a matter of debate. But no one doubts that the Russian Revolution was a product of that war in many ways. Military defeats turned society against the 'German' court and government, accused of treason and incompetence, so that it was seen as a patriotic act to remove them for the sake of national salvation. The February Revolution of 1917 would be a people's uprising against the monarchy and its military leadership, and it brought on to the streets a new sense of 'the nation' created by the war.

All this was a long way off in 1914. The Tsar's declaration of war first aroused a spirit of national unity. Workers' strikes came to a halt. Socialists united behind the defence of the Fatherland. There were mass arrests of the Bolsheviks and other extremists. The Duma dissolved itself, declaring on 8 August that it did not want to burden the government with 'unnecessary politics' at a time of war. Patriotic demonstrators attacked the German embassy, German shops and offices. In this wave of anti-German feeling (which was to become part of the popular uprising of February 1917) people changed their names to make them sound more Russian. Afraid of the revolutionary potential of this xenophobia, the government changed the German-sounding name of St Petersburg to the more Slavonic Petrograd.

But these patriotic signs were deceptive. The mass of the peasant soldiers had little sense of the empire they were fighting for, and only the slightest notion of what the war had to do with them. 'We are Tambov men,' a group of recruits was heard to say, 'the Germans will not get as far as that.'[1]

The Russian army was at least the equal of the German in manpower and matériel. Thanks to secret mobilizations before 1 August, it was ready in the field only three days after the Germans. The Schlieffen Plan (which had counted on the Russians taking three weeks longer so that Germany could knock out France before turning to the East) was thus confounded, and the Germans were bogged down in fighting on two fronts.

Under pressure from the French, the Russians attacked the Germans in East Prussia to force them to withdraw troops from the Western Front. A bold attack by Generals von Rennenkampf and Samsonov forced the Germans back, but then the Russians stopped and dispersed their forces to collect supplies and protect captured fortresses, which turned out to have no significance. This allowed the Germans to regroup their forces further south and destroy Samsonov's army in the Battle of Tannenberg. Moving their troops south again by rail, the Germans then defeated the Russians in the Battle of the Masurian Lakes (9–14 September), forcing von Rennenkampf to order a retreat. The Germans joked that the Russian general should be renamed 'Rennen vom Kampf' ('flight from battle').

From the autumn the Eastern Front began to stabilize as the war of mobility gave way to a war of position. Sweeping offensives like those of August were abandoned as the armies discovered the advantages of defensive warfare and dug themselves in. One entrenched machine-gunner was enough to repel a hundred infantrymen, and railways could bring up defenders much faster than the advancing troops could fill the gaps in the front line.

It was at this point that Russia's military weaknesses began to show. Russia was not prepared for a war of attrition, as Durnovo had warned. Other European powers managed to adapt to this new type of industrial warfare. But Russia was divided socially, its political system was too rigid, and its economy too weak to bear the strain of a long war.

Russia's single greatest asset, its seemingly inexhaustible supply of peasant soldiers, was not such an advantage as its allies had presumed when they had talked of the 'Russian steamroller' moving irresistibly towards Berlin. Russia had by far the largest population of any belligerent country. Yet it also was the first to suffer from manpower shortages. A large proportion of the Russian population was too young to be mobilized. Of the 27 million men who could be recruited, 48 per cent were exempt as only sons or as the sole male worker in their family. More serious still was the weakness of the Russian reserves. To save money the army had given little formal training to those beyond the First Levy. But there were so many casualties in the first months of the war that it soon found itself having to call on the poorly trained men of the Second Levy.

The lack of a clear command structure was one of the army's biggest weaknesses. Military authority was divided between the War Ministry, Supreme Headquarters (Stavka) at Baranovichi in Belorussia, and the Front commands, with each pursuing its own ends. The top commanders were drawn from a narrow circle of aristocratic cavalrymen and courtiers without much professional training or military experience. The Supreme Commander, the Grand Duke Nikolai, had never taken part in any serious fighting. General Sukhomlinov, the Minister of War, was a salon soldier. He had done very little to prepare the army for combat. The command committed endless blunders. It had learned nothing from the conflict with Japan. It conducted the war after the pattern of a nineteenth-century campaign, asking men to storm enemy artillery positions regardless of casualties, wasting resources on the obsolete cavalry, defending useless fortresses in the rear, and neglecting the technological needs of modern artillery warfare. It scorned the art of building trenches, which on the Russian side were so primitive that they were little more than graves.

As the war dragged on through the winter, the army began to experience terrible problems of matériel. Russia's transport network was too weak to cope with the massive deliveries of munitions, food, clothing, and medical care to the fronts. Munitions shortages were the most acute. The War Ministry had run down the armaments industry, assuming it could make do with existing stocks, and now had to order shells and guns abroad which took ages to arrive. Russia was cut off from its allies, France and Britain, who, because of the belligerence of the Turks, could not supply them easily with armaments (the Italians would receive allied aid more readily but fought less effectively with it). By the spring of 1915, whole battalions were being trained without rifles, while many second-line troops were relying on rifles picked up from the men who had been shot in front of them.

The army's morale and discipline began to fall apart. Unable to control their rebellious troops, some officers resorted to flogging them—a terrible reminder of the serf culture that still existed in the ranks (e.g. the obligation of the soldiers to address their officers by their honorific titles, to clean their boots, run private errands for them, and so on), which gave rise to an internal war between the peasant soldiers and their noble officers.

The tsarist command structure was also weakened by the rapid depletion of the officers corps as a result of casualties. The newly trained NCOs who took over the junior command posts were from the lower classes and their sympathies were with the troops. These NCOs were to be the leaders of the army revolution during 1917. Many of the Red Army's best commanders (e.g. Chapaev, Zhukov, Rokossovsky) had been NCOs in the tsarist army, much as the marshals of Napoleon's wars had begun as subalterns in the king's army. The sergeants of the First World War would become the marshals of the Second.

In May 1915, the Germans and the Austrians launched a massive offensive, breaking through the Russian lines right across the Eastern Front and forcing the Tsar's armies into headlong retreat. There was confusion and panic. As they fell back, the Russian troops destroyed buildings, bridges, military stores and crops to prevent them falling to the enemy.

The destruction often broke down into pillaging, especially of Jewish property, as the troops moved through the Pale of Settlement, where the Tsar's Jews were legally obliged to live. The summer months of unending retreat dealt a crippling blow to the troops' morale. A million men surrendered to the enemy. Huge numbers deserted to the rear, where many of them put their guns to a different use and lived from banditry.

Rumours quickly spread through the army's ranks about treason at the court. The German background of the Empress and the large number of German names at the court and in the government added credence to these conspiracy theories. So did the execution in March 1915 of Colonel Miasoyedov, one of Sukhomlinov's protégés, for spying for Germany. One NCO attempted to explain to his soldiers the reason for the retreat: 'there are many traitors and spies in the high command of our army, like the War Minister Sukhomlinov, whose fault it is that we don't have any shells, and Miasoyedov, who betrayed the fortresses to the enemy'. When he had finished a soldier-cook drew the conclusion: 'A fish begins to stink from the head. What kind of Tsar would surround himself with thieves and cheats? It's as clear as day that we're going to lose the war.'[2] For many soldiers this sort of discussion was the vital psychological moment of the revolution—the moment when their loyalty to the monarchy was finally broken. A government which made them fight a war they could not hope to win, which had failed to provide them with adequate weapons and supplies, and now was in league with the enemy was certainly not worthy of further sacrifices.

In a desperate attempt to restore morale and discipline Nicholas took over the Supreme Command. If the soldiers would not fight for 'Russia', then perhaps they would fight for the Tsar. It was the worst decision of his reign. It meant that he would take the blame for every defeat. His presence at the Front had a bad effect on the troops' morale. 'Everyone knew that Nicholas understood next to nothing about military matters,' noted General Brusilov, 'and, although the word "Tsar" still had a magical power over the troops, he utterly lacked the charisma to bring that magic to life. Faced with a group of soldiers, he was nervous and did not know what to say.'[3]

On his assumption of the command, Stavka was moved 200 miles eastward from Baranovichi to Mogilev—a dreary provincial town whose name derives from the word in Russian for a 'grave'.

The public blamed the government for the reverses at the Front. As in 1891, it responded to the crisis with its own initiatives to help the war effort which quickly turned political. The Zemstvo Union and its urban partner, the Union of Towns, known together as Zemgor, sprang into action, virtually running the military supply campaign in the absence of an effective government system. Led by Prince Lvov, a zemstvo activist since the 1890s, it quickly grew into a huge national infrastructure, an unofficial government, with 8,000 affiliated institutions, several hundred thousand employees, and a budget of 2 billion roubles, partly financed by the public and partly by the state.

The civic spirit of the February Revolution had its roots in the wartime activities of Zemgor and other voluntary organizations. One of these was the War Industries Committee, established by liberal businessmen in 1915 to break down the monopoly of the big munitions producers and win more influence for themselves and their allies in the Duma in the wartime regulation of industry. All but three of the ministers of the First Provisional Government of 1917 (which would be led by Prince Lvov) would emerge as national leaders through Zemgor or the War Industries Committee. There were close ties between these organizations. Lvov, for example, was the head of the Zemstvo Union, an ex-Duma deputy and a member of the War Industries Committee. Through their combined initiatives, these public bodies were able to form an effective political force. They enjoyed the support of several liberal-minded ministers who understood the need for political reform, as well as a number of senior generals, such as Brusilov, who valued their efforts for the war campaign.

Under growing pressure from these voices of reform, the Tsar agreed to reconvene the Duma on 19 July 1915. The liberal opposition now had a platform on which to demand what they called a 'ministry of national confidence' (a government appointed by the Tsar but approved by them). Two thirds of the deputies formed themselves into a Progressive

Bloc to strengthen this campaign. They urged the Tsar to appoint a new government capable of winning parliamentary support. The more radical deputies called for a government responsible to the Duma.

Among the Tsar's ministers there was a growing majority in favour of a compromise with the Progressive Bloc. They were alarmed that, with the Tsar's departure for the Front, the government was left at the mercy of the Empress and Rasputin. Alexandra persuaded Nicholas to reassert his autocratic power. On 2 September, the Duma was once again closed down by order of the Tsar—a move that sparked a two-day general strike in Petrograd but no further action by the liberals, who were frightened of a revolution on the streets. Nicholas summoned his disobedient ministers to Mogilev and gave them a dressing down. 'Show your fist,' the Empress told her mild husband. 'You are the Autocrat and they dare not forget it.'[4] She even urged him to comb his hair with Rasputin's comb in order to reinforce his will. The magic must have worked. For the ministers, having come determined to argue the case for reform, lost their nerve when confronted by the Tsar. The 'revolt of the ministers' was over, one by one they were dismissed, and the monarchy's last chance to save itself by political means had now been thrown away.

In all these changes in the government the influence of the Empress was at work. While the Tsar was at the Front, Alexandra became the real autocrat (in so far as there was one) in the capital. She liked to boast that she was the first woman in Russia to receive government ministers since Catherine the Great. Her ambitions were encouraged by her 'holy friend' Rasputin, who used her as a mouthpiece for his own pretensions to power. She would write to Nicholas with Rasputin's recommendations on food supply, transport, finance and land reform; she even tried to persuade her husband to base his military strategy on what the 'holy man' had 'seen in the night'.

By 1916, the influence of the Empress and Rasputin had become a major source of political tension between the public and the government. The idea of treason in high places gained momentum as rumours spread of the existence of a 'Black Bloc' at the court, which was said to be seeking a separate peace with Berlin. It was widely claimed that the Empress and Rasputin were working for the Germans; that they had a direct line to Berlin; and that the Tsar informed his uncle, the Kaiser Wilhelm, about the movement of his troops. The condemnation of the Romanov court as 'German' and 'corrupt' ultimately served to justify the Revolution as a patriotic act.

Similar credence was given to the rumours of sexual scandals at the court. It was said that the Empress was the mistress of Rasputin and the lesbian lover of Anna Vyrubova, her lady-in-waiting, who took part in orgies with them both. Alexandra's 'sexual corruption' became a kind of metaphor for the diseased condition of the monarchy. Similar porno-graphic tales about Marie Antoinette and the 'impotent Louis' had cir-culated on the eve of the French Revolution in 1789.

None of these rumours had any basis in fact (Vyrubova was a dim-witted spinster infatuated with the mystical powers of Rasputin and medically certified to be a virgin by a special commission appointed to investigate the charges against her in 1917). But the point of the rumours was not their truth or untruth: it was their power to mobilize an angry public against the monarchy. In a revolutionary crisis it is perceptions and beliefs that really count. Without this 'atmosphere'—created out of gossip, half-truths, facts and fabrications, bits of information from the press which were then distorted into fantasies—it is impossible to understand the 'revolutionary mood' or the ways in which the Revolu-tion turned on the interpretation of hearsay and events.

'Rumours filled the lives of all inhabitants,' recalled a resident of Petrograd. 'They were believed more readily than the newspapers, which were censored. The public was desperate for information, for almost anything, on political subjects, and any rumour about the war or Ger-man intrigues was bound to spread like wildfire.'[5] What gave these stories their revolutionary power and significance was how far they accorded with the 'general mood' (and with previous rumours that had shaped that mood). Once a rumour, however false, became the subject of common belief, it assumed the status of a political fact, informing the attitudes and actions of the public. All revolutions are based in part on myth.

Official efforts to counteract these rumours were feeble. The regime had no idea how to manage public information at a time when its survival depended on it. To propagandize their patriotic credentials the Imperial family arranged a photo opportunity for the Empress and her daughters dressed in Red Cross uniforms. They had visited the wounded at military hospitals in Petrograd at the beginning of the war. What they did not realize was that a consignment of nurses' uniforms had fallen into the hands of the city's prostitutes, who dressed in them to work the streets, and that the image of the nurse had changed as a result. The front-line soldiers looked upon the nurses ('sisters of comfort') as sex objects or as useless women ('sisters without mercy') who rode in the staff cars ('nurse carriers') but had no medicine or other means of helping them. Any mention of nurses automatically gave rise to dirty jokes among the ranks. The news, for example, in November 1915 that the Tsar was awarding medals to a group of nurses resulted in the rumour that they were being rewarded not just for their professional services but for other kinds of service too.

Concerned by the growing mood of discontent, the Tsar appointed a Duma man, the Octobrist A. D. Protopopov, as acting Minister of the Interior and allowed the Duma to reconvene. It was a belated effort to buy off the moderates of the Progressive Bloc with a manoeuvre to suggest that a government of national confidence would soon be appointed. But Duma circles were quickly disillusioned by Protopopov, who was in fact a protégé of Rasputin and did the court's bidding. When the Duma reopened, on 1 November, it was turned into a revolutionary tribune from which even the Kadets now denounced the government.

Political passions had been so inflamed by the rumours of treason that when the Kadet leader gave a speech denouncing the abuses of the government, asking after each: 'Is this treason or folly?', everyone concluded that Miliukov—a cautious politician with close connections to

Allied diplomats—must have evidence of actual treason. This had not been Miliukov's aim. To his own rhetorical question he himself would have answered: 'Folly.' Yet the public was so influenced by rumours of conspiracy that by the time it read his speech it was bound to conclude that treason there had been. Because the speech was banned from the press and had to be read in well-thumbed typescripts passed from hand to hand, people were even more inclined to reach this conclusion. Such was its revolutionary effect that in some versions of the typescript a particular social grievance would appear in the middle of the speech (e.g. claiming that in addition to its other abuses the government treated teachers unfairly). 'My speech acquired the reputation of a storm-signal for revolution,' Miliukov recalled. 'Such was not my intention, but the prevailing mood in the country served as a megaphone for my words.'[6]

The fact that all these rumours were circulated among the upper classes gave them even greater credence on the streets. 'What is said in high society,' wrote Vasily Gurko, the army's Chief of Staff, 'trickles down into the social circles of the two capitals, and subsequently, through the servants and caretakers, passes down to the masses, upon whom such rumours have a revolutionary effect.'[7] The rumours about Rasputin, in particular, circulated in the court and diplomatic circles, where 'dark forces' were blamed for the problems of the dynasty. The British and French ambassadors in Petrograd passed on as fact the import of these rumours to their respective governments.

Even members of the Imperial family were beginning to abandon Nicholas. There were several palace plots to replace him with his brother, the Grand Duke Mikhail, and appoint a government of national confidence. Historians disagree on these conspiracies, some seeing them as the opening acts of the February Revolution, others as nothing more than idle chit-chat. Neither is the case. The conspirators were serious in their intentions, but even if they had succeeded in carrying them out, they would have been quickly swept aside by the revolution on the streets.

The only plot to succeed was the murder of Rasputin, on 16 December

1916. Lured to the Petrograd palace of Prince Felix Yusupov to meet his beautiful wife, Rasputin was poisoned and shot several times by the conspirators. His body was thrown into the Neva, where it was washed up two days later. For several days thereafter, crowds of working-class women gathered at the spot to collect the 'holy water' from the river sanctified by Rasputin's flesh. News of his murder was greeted with joy in high society. One of the plotters, the Grand Duke Dmitry, was given a standing ovation when he appeared in the Mikhailovsky Theatre on 17 December. But any hope that Rasputin's murder might save the monarchy was illusory.

By this time the rumours of Rasputin's exploits had turned the soldiers against the Tsar. Whatever magical power his title might have had was lost for ever in the profane stories of royal corruption and treason which circulated in the ranks. German propaganda leaflets, dropped by aeroplane to the soldiers at the Front, reinforced their message with a picture of the Kaiser supported by the German people, while the Tsar was depicted resting against Rasputin's private parts. Among the soldiers it was widely held that the Empress was betraying military secrets to the Germans; that she was withholding shells, food and medical supplies from the army; and that she had brought the country to the brink of starvation by secretly exporting Russian bread to Germany. They said that she was forcing Nicholas to negotiate a separate peace, that the whole war had been a Romanov conspiracy to enslave Russia to Germany. The effect on the troops' morale and discipline was catastrophic, especially when these rumours came on top of months of supply shortages. Soldiers refused to take up their positions or to obey officers who sought to defend the Empress—particularly those with German names. 'What's the use of fighting if the Germans have already taken over?' many soldiers said. Military authority collapsed as soldiers talked and listened to the arguments of those familiar with socialist ideas about the reasons for their heavy losses in the war. They were radicalized by the realization that there was one war for the rich and another for the poor, whose lives were being wasted by an incompetent and treacherous regime.

The army was a school of revolution in this sense. It put millions of young peasant men into uniforms, took them far away from the narrow confines of their village world, and taught them how to handle guns and new technologies, to organize themselves collectively. It made them more literate, more socially aware, increased their sense of comradeship, their self-esteem and sense of power, and their willingness to use the gun to get things done. The skills they learned in the army would make them natural leaders of the revolution in the countryside. Soldiers returning from the army would take the lead in the land seizures of 1917. They would become the leaders of the rural Soviets. Later they would fight in the Civil War, when millions of peasants were schooled as revolutionaries in the Red Army. In this sense we should see the period of 1914–21 as one revolutionary continuum.

By the third year of the war, the army had conscripted 14 million men, mostly peasants. Hit by labour shortages, the big estates and commercial farms reduced their productive area by two thirds. The peasants, for their part, reduced their marketing of grain—the wartime decline of consumer industries meant that there was less for them to buy—and fed their livestock better, stocked up barns, or turned their grain into vodka, whose bottled production had been halted by the government in the interests of a sober war campaign. The cities of the north began to experience food shortages. Prices rocketed. Long queues appeared outside the bakeries and meat shops. After a long shift in their factories women stood in line. The bread queues became a sort of political forum where rumours and ideas were exchanged by hungry citizens. The workers' revolution was born here.

After a year of industrial peace the war between labour and capital resumed in 1915 with a series of strikes that soon gave way to larger and more political protests. They began with calls for bread but went on to demand an eight-hour day, an end to the war and the overthrow of the monarchy. The revolutionary parties played a secondary role in these protests. They had all been crippled by police repression in the war.

The Bolsheviks in Petrograd numbered fewer than 500 members. The provincial Party organizations had only a handful of members each. 'We of the older generation may not live to see the decisive battles of this coming revolution,' Lenin said in Zurich in a speech to commemorate the twelfth anniversary of Bloody Sunday on 9 January 1917.[8]

Nonetheless the Bolsheviks were gaining ideologically from the war. The Mensheviks and SRs were divided between those who supported the military effort on the grounds that Russia had the right to defend itself (the Defensists) and those who wanted to campaign internationally for an end to the 'imperialist war' (the Internationalists). These divisions were to cripple both the parties during 1917. They also tore apart the Second International, which had organized and united the European socialist parties since 1889. At their heart lay a fundamental difference of world-view between those who acknowledged the legitimacy of nation states and the inevitability of conflict between them and those who placed class divisions above national interests. The Bolsheviks alone were united in their opposition to the war. Unlike the Menshevik and SR Internationalists, who sought to bring the war to an end through peaceful demonstration and negotiation, Lenin called on the workers of the world to use their arms against their own governments, to end the war by turning it into a series of civil wars, or revolutions, across the whole of Europe (a 'war against war'). Many left-wing Mensheviks, such as Trotsky and Alexandra Kollontai, were converted to the Bolsheviks by Lenin's stress on international revolutionary action to end the war.

The Bolsheviks were also benefiting from the growing militancy of the workers. In the big industrial cities of the north workers were turning away from the Mensheviks and rejecting their calls to join the Labour Group, an adjunct of the War Industries Committees, which aimed to conciliate the workers and their employers in the interests of the war effort. In the spring of 1916 the Bolsheviks played a leading role in a big strike at the New Lessner machine-building plant in Petrograd. The Party's ranks swelled as a result. By the end of the year it numbered 3,000 members in the capital, and 10,000 nationwide.

The workers of the New Lessner and Renault factories in Petrograd came out on strike again in October. They fought with the police. The soldiers in the nearby barracks of the 181st Infantry Regiment came out in defence of the workers, throwing rocks and bricks at the police. Mounted Cossacks cleared the scene. The mutinous regiment was removed from the capital, and 130 soldiers were arrested. Over the next two days, 75,000 workers from sixty-three factories in the city joined the strike. Eventually order was restored. But the actions of the soldiers were an ominous sign of the army's reluctance to control the growing rebellion on the streets.

5

THE FEBRUARY REVOLUTION

It began with bread. For weeks there had been long queues at the bakeries in Petrograd. The problem was not lack of supplies. There was enough flour in the warehouses to feed the population for at least a week when what had started as a series of bread riots turned into a revolution. The problem was the freezing temperatures—the coldest winter Russia had experienced for several years—and the breakdown of the transport system, which interrupted the deliveries of flour and fuel to the capital. Factories closed. Thousands of laid-off workers milled around the streets. Women queued all night for a loaf of bread, only to be told in the early hours of the morning that there would be none for sale that day. Rumours spread. People said that 'capitalists'—which in the xenophobic wartime atmosphere was understood to be synonomous with German or Jewish merchants—were forcing up the prices by withholding stocks. On 19 February, the Petrograd authorities announced that rationing would begin on 1 March. In the panic buying that followed the shelves were laid bare, fights broke out, and several bakeries had their windows smashed.

On Thursday, 23 February, the temperature in the capital rose to a spring-like minus five degrees. It was International Women's Day, an important date in the socialist calendar, and towards noon a large demonstration of women, mostly shop and office workers, began to march towards the city centre to protest for equal rights. The mild weather brought out larger crowds than usual—people emerged from their winter hibernation to enjoy the sun and join the hunt for food—and the women were in good humour. But soon the mood began to change.

Women textile workers from the Vyborg factory district had come out in protest against shortages of bread. With their menfolk from the neighbouring metalworks, they marched towards the city centre with chants of 'Bread!' and 'Down with the Tsar!' By the end of the afternoon, 100,000 workers had come out on strike. There were clashes with the Cossacks and police before night descended and the crowds dispersed.

The next morning 150,000 workers marched again to the centre. They were armed with knives, hammers, spanners and pieces of iron, partly to fight the soldiers who had been brought in overnight to bar their way, and partly to help them loot the well-stocked foodshops of the Nevsky Prospekt. On Znamenskaya Square they were joined by people of all classes in a huge rally. In full view of the powerless police, orators addressed the crowd from the equestrian statue of Alexander III, which they engraved with the graffiti 'Hippopotamus', the people's nickname for this awesome but ridiculous monument to autocracy.

Encouraged by the absence of repressive measures, even larger crowds came out on 25 February. It was a general strike. The demonstrations now had a more political character. Red flags and banners began to appear. 'Down with the Tsar!' and 'Down with the War!' were their main demands. There were fights with the police, but the demonstrators also tried to win the soldiers over to their side. On the Nevsky Prospekt the protestors were blocked by a squadron of mounted Cossacks. A young girl appeared from the crowd and walked towards the Cossacks to present a bouquet of red roses to one of their officers, who leaned down from his horse to accept this offering of peace. It was a symbolic victory—one of those psychological moments on which revolutions turn: now the people knew that they could win.

Even at this point, the authorities could still have contained the situation, as long as they avoided open conflict with the protestors. If bread had been delivered to the shops, the demonstrations might have lost momentum, as food protests had done before. Alexander Shliapnikov, the leading Bolshevik in the capital, scoffed at the idea that this was the start of a revolution: 'Give the workers a pound of bread and the movement will peter out,' he told his fellow Bolsheviks on 25 February.[1] But any chances of containing the disorders were destroyed that evening, when the Tsar ordered General Khabalov, Chief of the Petrograd Military District, to 'put down the disorders tomorrow'.[2]

By Sunday morning, 26 February, the centre of the city had been turned into a militarized camp. Soldiers and police were everywhere. Around midday huge crowds of workers once again assembled in the factory districts and marched to the centre. As they converged on the Nevsky Prospekt, police and soldiers fired at them from several different points. The worst atrocity occurred on Znamenskaya Square, where more than fifty demonstrators were shot dead by a detachment of the Volynsky Regiment. An officer, who had been unable to get his young and obviously nervous soldiers to open fire on the crowd, grabbed a rifle from one of his men and began to shoot at the people. Among those killed were two soldiers from the regiment who had gone over to the people's side.

This shedding of blood—Russia's second Bloody Sunday—proved a critical turning-point. The demonstrators knew they were involved in a life-or-death struggle against the regime, and the killing of their comrades had emboldened them. As for the soldiers, they had to choose between their moral duty to the people and their oath of allegiance to the Tsar. If they followed the former, a full-scale revolution would occur. But if they chose the latter, then the regime might still manage to survive, as it had done in 1905.

After the shooting on the Nevsky Prospekt a group of the protestors broke into the barracks of the Pavlovsky Regiment, whose soldiers, shaken by the news, joined them in a mutiny. 'They are shooting at our mothers and our sisters!' was their rallying cry, as they broke into the arsenal of the barracks, grabbed some rifles, and began to march towards the Nevsky Prospekt, clashing with police along their way. Running out of ammunition, they were soon defeated by Khabalov's Cossacks and confined in their barracks. Nineteen ringleaders were arrested and imprisoned. But it was too late for repression by this time.

The training detachment of the Volynsky Regiment returned to their barracks with doubts and feelings of guilt after shooting at the protestors. One of the soldiers claimed to have recognized his own mother among the people they had killed. The following morning, when they were ordered to fire on the crowds again, they shot their commanding officer and came out to join the people's side in a mutiny, which was soon joined by other regiments.

The mutiny turned the demonstrations of the previous four days into a full-scale revolution. The tsarist authorities were virtually deprived of coercive power in the capital. They could no longer deal with the situation and were afraid to send in more troops from the Northern Front or provincial garrisons in case they also joined the mutiny: the army would be split, perhaps forcing Russia to leave the war. The rebel soldiers in the capital gave military strength and organization to the revolutionary crowds. They turned disordered protest into battles for the capture of strategic targets for the 'people's side': the arsenal, the telephone exchange, railway stations, the police headquarters and prisons.

There was no real leadership on the people's side. The socialist parties were all caught unawares, their main leaders in exile, in prison or abroad, and while many of their rank and file were in the crowds, they were in no position to direct them. The street generated its own leaders—students, workers, cadets and NCOs, socialists whose names have never made it into history books. People wore red armbands or ribbons in their buttonholes to show their support for 'the revolution'. Residents fed 'the revolutionaries' from their kitchens. Shopkeepers turned their shops into bases for the soldiers, and into shelters for the people when police were firing in the streets. Children ran about on errands for 'the leaders'—and veteran soldiers obeyed their commands. It was as if the people on the streets had suddenly become united by a vast network of invisible threads. And this secured their victory.

By the early afternoon of the 27th a crowd of 25,000 people—many of them soldiers from the nearby barracks—had gathered in front of the Tauride Palace, seat of the Duma and citadel of Russia's new democracy. They were looking for political leaders. The first to appear were the Mensheviks Khrustalev-Nosar, Chkheidze and Skobelev, who came out with the SR Kerensky to announce that a 'Provisional Executive Committee of the Soviet of Workers' deputies' had been established. They appealed to the workers to elect and send their representatives to an assembly of the Soviet scheduled for that evening.

Despite its name, there were not many workers among the fifty delegates and 200 observers packed into a smoke-filled room in the left wing of the Tauride Palace for that first chaotic session of the Soviet. Most of the workers were still on the streets, unaware of the Soviet's existence, and their voting places were taken by intellectuals. There was not a single factory delegate on the Soviet Executive, which was made up of six Mensheviks, two Bolsheviks, two SRs and five non-Party deputies. The meeting was disorderly. Debates were frequently interrupted by 'urgent announcements' and 'emergency reports' from delegations of soldiers. The assembly decided to establish a Petrograd Soviet of Workers' and Soldiers' Deputies.

For those socialists who had dreamed of a genuine workers' Soviet this was a setback. Organized in their regiments, the soldiers were in a far better position than the workers to elect their delegates to the Soviet. The blue of the workers' tunics was lost in the sea of grey uniforms when the first combined session of the Petrograd Soviet assembled in the Catherine Hall of the Tauride Palace on the evening of the 28th. Of the 3,000 delegates, more than two thirds were in army uniforms.

Meanwhile, in the right wing of the palace, the Duma leaders were meeting to decide whether they should place themselves at the head of the revolutionary crowds, whose cries from the streets were growing louder and more threatening all the time. Moderates like Miliukov cautioned that it would be illegal to usurp the powers of the Tsar. But such legal niceties were hardly the point now. This, after all, was a revolution; the only real power—the power of violence—now lay in the streets. As the chaos deepened and the Soviet emerged as a rival centre of political authority, the Duma leaders formed themselves into a Temporary Committee for the Restoration of Order and proclaimed themselves in charge.

The aim of the leaders in both wings of the Tauride Palace was to restore order in the capital. There was a real danger of the revolution degenerating into anarchy. Thousands of drunken workers and soldiers were rampaging through the city looting stores, breaking into houses and beating up and robbing well-dressed citizens. The fighting against the police was breaking down into chaotic violence. It was essential to get the soldiers to return to their barracks, but the mutineers were frightened that they would be punished by the officers and demanded guarantees of their immunity. The result was Order No. 1, which listed the demands and conditions for their return to the garrisons: the establishment of soldiers' committees to run the units and control the weaponry; the rights of citizens for off-duty soldiers; the end of honorific titles (such as 'Your Excellency') for the officers; and the obligation of the soldiers to obey their commanders only if their orders did not contradict the decrees of the Soviet. This crucial document, which did more than anything to destroy the discipline of the army, and thus in a sense brought the Bolsheviks to power, had taken only a few minutes for the soldiers to draw up together and pass by a vote in the Soviet assembly.

While the Soviet leaders wanted to restore order, they had no intention of assuming power themselves. They were afraid of a counter-revolution, and perhaps a civil war, if they tried to move directly to a socialist order. Rather, they wanted the Duma leaders to form a government. Most of them were Mensheviks and other socialists who thought that socialism would evolve within a democratic order. Their Marxist doctrine and reading of history taught them that in a backward peasant country such as Russia there would have to be a 'bourgeois-democratic revolution' before socialism could be built. What was needed now was freedom for the masses to organize themselves politically. Thus there arose what Trotsky later called the 'paradox' of February: that a revolution made in the streets resulted in a government made in the salons.

Agreement was reached on 1 March. The Duma leaders formed a Provisional Government and the Soviet agreed to support it as long as it adhered to a comprehensive list of democratic principles. This was the framework of the dual power system that lasted until October. Without the support of the Soviet, which alone had real authority, the Provisional Government was powerless. Yet the Soviet's conditions created so much room for popular initiative—and its new authority so much expectation of revolutionary change—that there was a crying need for stronger government to stop the drift to anarchy.

Informed about the mutiny in Petrograd, the Tsar at Stavka ordered General Ivanov, whom he now appointed to replace Khabalov as chief of the Petrograd Military District, to lead a force of punitive troops to the capital and establish a dictatorship there. From Mogilev, he set off by train to be reunited with his wife and children at Tsarksoe Selo, the imperial residence just south of Petrograd, but only got as far as Pskov. Because of the hasty arrangements, there was no formal ceremony to welcome Nicholas to the town, a republic in medieval times. The Commander of the Northern Front arrived late to meet him at the station. Too rushed to wear court uniform, he was wearing rubber boots.

On 1 March, General Alexeev, the Commander-in-Chief, called off the counter-revolutionary expedition. He was afraid of losing even more troops to the mutiny, and had concluded that the best hope for the restoration of order was the Duma government already in place. By the next day it was clear that nothing less than the Tsar's abdication would save the army and the war campaign. All his senior generals told him so in cables sent to his railway car in Pskov. Resigned to his fate, Nicholas agreed to abdicate in favour of his son. It is hard to say what was going through his mind at this decisive moment for the dynasty. Those who were with him on the imperial train were struck by his strange lack of emotion during this ordeal. Having made his decision, Nicholas went for his afternoon walk and appeared in the buffet car as usual for evening tea. 'The Tsar sat peacefully and calm,' recalled one of his aides-de-camp. 'He kept up conversation and only his eyes, which were sad, thoughtful and staring into the distance, and his nervous movements when he took a cigarette, betrayed his inner disturbance.'[3] Perhaps abdication came as a relief. It saved him from reneging on his coronation oath to 'uphold autocracy' and 'remit this oath in its integrity' to his son. Obsessed with this 'divine duty', he found it easier to abdicate than to turn himself into a constitutional king.

Throughout this crisis his main concern was to be reunited with his family. After he was told that his son, Alexei, could not live long because of his haemophilia and that once he had renounced the throne he himself would have to leave Russia, Nicholas resolved to abdicate for his son as well and hand the crown to the Grand Duke Mikhail. But when this was announced to the crowds in Petrograd there were angry demonstrations with banners calling for the overthrow of the monarchy. Not a man to risk danger, Mikhail was persuaded to step down.

The end of the monarchy was marked by scenes of rejoicing throughout the empire. Rapturous crowds assembled in the streets of Petrograd and Moscow. Red flags were hoisted on to the roofs and hung from the windows of buildings. In Helsingfors, Kiev, Tiflis and other capitals, where the downfall of the Tsar was associated with the liberation of the nation, national flags were often displayed alongside them. Symbols of the monarchy—Romanov emblems, coats of arms, double-headed eagles—were torn down by the crowds.

In the countryside people at first spoke in muted voices about the 'big events' in the capital, but soon the peasants too were celebrating the end of the monarchy. A survey by the Duma based upon the reports of its provincial agents for the first three months of the revolution summarized this process:

the widespread myth that the Russian peasant is devoted to the Tsar and that he 'cannot live' without him has been destroyed by the universal joy and relief of the peasants upon discovering that in reality they can live without the Tsar... Now the peasants say: 'the Tsar brought himself down and brought us to ruin.'[4]

The February Revolution was a revolution against monarchy. The new democracy to which it gave birth defined itself by the negation of all things monarchical. In the rhetoric of its leaders the Tsar was associated with the dark oppression of old Russia, while his removal equalled freedom and enlightenment. The symbols of the revolution—on newspaper mastheads, posters and banners—were a broken chain, the radiant sun, and a toppled throne and crown.

The monarchy was dead. All its institutions of support—the bureaucracy, the police, the army command and the Church—collapsed almost overnight. No one really tried to revive it. None of the counter-revolutionary leaders in the Civil War embraced monarchism as a cause, despite the efforts of the many monarchists in their ranks, because they realized that it would be suicide for them to do so. As Trotsky put it with his usual bluntness, 'the country had so radically vomited up the monarchy that it could not ever crawl down the people's throat again'.[5]

Kept under house arrest at Tsarskoe Selo, in August 1917 the Imperial family was evacuated to Siberia out of fears for their personal safety. It had been intended to send the Tsar and his family to England, but George V withdrew his invitation for fear of alienating the Labour Party, so they were sent to the provincial backwater of Tobolsk, far from the revolutionary crowds. There they lived in comfortable conditions until the spring of 1918, when they were sent to Ekaterinburg by the Bolsheviks after rumours of a monarchist plot to rescue the Imperial family. They were executed on the night of 16–17 July. Nicholas and Alexandra and all five of their children were shot at close range by a Bolshevik firing squad in the basement of the Ipatev House in Ekaterinburg. The public reaction to the announcement of the ex-Tsar's death was remarkably subdued. Bruce Lockhart, the British agent, noted that 'the population of Moscow received the news with amazing indifference'.[6] The Tsar had been dead politically since February 1917.

To the crowds outside the Tauride Palace the names of their new rulers, the Provisional Government, were little known. Most of them had been named in the various 'ministries of confidence' proposed by the liberal opposition circles since 1915. All were from the propertied élite. When the name of the new Prime Minister, Prince Lvov, was announced to the crowds outside the Tauride Palace, a soldier shouted: 'You mean all we did was exchange a tsar for a prince, and that's it?'[7]

Only the name of Alexander Kerensky, the Minister of Justice, met with the approval of the crowd. The only socialist and member of the Soviet in the Provisional Government, he had come to stand for the people's hopes. In the first euphoric weeks of freedom these hopes were expressed in the 'Kerensky cult'. The darling of the radical intelligentsia, Kerensky was hailed as the 'poet of the nation', as the 'uncrowned king of the hearts and minds of Russia', and as the 'first love of the revolution'. He was a brilliant orator. His speeches were full of pathos, theatrical gestures and even fainting fits at climactic moments, all of which was calculated to tug at the heart-strings of his listeners. In a land where power was conceived monarchically it was unsurprising that a new cult of the leader should be born so soon after the removal of the Tsar.

The Minister of Justice was the busiest man in the Provisional Government. He oversaw a dazzling series of reforms—granting freedoms of assembly, press and speech, lifting legal restrictions on religion, race and gender—which, as Lenin put it, made Russia overnight the 'freest country in the world'. Political reform was the main aim of the government. The outlook of its leaders was shaped by the liberal constitutional values of the intelligentsia. They saw themselves as a wartime government of national confidence and salvation, above class or party interests. Their purpose was to see the country through to the ending of the war and the election of a Constituent Assembly, which alone could legally resolve the fundamental issues of the revolution, such as land reform and the demands of the national minorities. Their idea, in effect, was to ask the people to wait for their problems to be legally resolved by a parliament which did not yet exist. If they had acted more quickly to convene the Constituent Assembly, they might have created a democratic mandate for themselves; but they got bogged down in preparations for the elections and it was not until November, after the Bolsheviks had come to power, that the vote could be held.

Political reforms were not enough to satisfy the revolutionary expectations of the people in 1917. The leaders of the Provisional Government compared themselves to the French revolutionaries of 1789. They looked for precedents for their policies, and for models for their institutions, in the revolutionary history of France. But Russia could not be another France. The constitutional phase of the Revolution had been played out between 1905 and 1917. Political reform had nothing left to give. Only a fundamental social revolution, without precedent in European history, could resolve the power question—the question asked by Lenin in his memorable phrase of 'kto kogo' (who would prevail over whom?)— thrown up by the downfall of the old regime.

The February Revolution created a new culture of democracy. It was suddenly considered politically correct to call oneself a 'democrat'. But the abstract Western language of democracy was soon absorbed into Russian ideas about social class. The common people thought about themselves more and more in terms of class. Instead of 'citizen' (grazhdanin), a form of address for anyone regardless of their class, they increasingly identified themselves by the term 'comrade' (tovarishch) reserved for 'the toiling masses' (trudiakhshchisia) and other categories of the 'proletariat'. The word 'democracy' (demokratiia) was popularly used as a social definition rather than a political principle. It was understood to mean the 'common people', whose opposite was not 'dictatorship' but the 'bourgeoisie' (*burzhooi*). This was not just a question of semantics. The common people saw 'democracy' in terms of 'us' and 'them'.

The revolution of 1917 should be understood as a general crisis of authority. There was a rejection of not just the state but all figures of authority—judges, policemen, government officials, army and navy officers, priests, teachers, employers, landowners, village elders, patriarchal fathers and husbands. There were revolutions going on in virtually every sphere of life.

The Soviet was the only real political authority. Yet even the Soviet had limited control over the revolution in the remote provinces, where towns and villages behaved as if they were independent of the state. The politics of 1917 should thus be understood not so much as a conflict of dual power—the division between the Provisional Government and the Soviet which has so preoccupied historians—but as a deeper problem of the fragmentation of power.

As in 1905, the village commune was the organizing agent of the revolution on the land. The peasants elected their own ad hoc committees (some of them called 'Soviets'), which were really no more than the commune in a more revolutionary form. By and large these peasant organs ignored the calls of the Provisional Government to wait for the Constituent Assembly to resolve the land question. They passed their own 'laws' to legitimize the peasant seizures of the gentry's property.

The mass confiscation of the gentry's land began in the spring. Peasants marched on the manors, carted away the contents of their barns, and destroyed or vandalized anything (paintings, books and sculptures) that smacked of excessive wealth. Sometimes they burned the manor houses and killed their inhabitants.

This 'war on the manors' was given pseudo-legal endorsement by district and provincial peasant assemblies and at a national level by the First All-Russian Peasant Assembly on 4–25 May. Nothing did more to undermine the government's authority in the countryside. The SR party activists, who dominated the executives of these assemblies, appealed for patience on the land question. But the radical mood of the delegates forced them to sanction the seizures. The peasants believed that the resolutions of these assemblies carried the status of 'laws'.

As with the peasants, so with the workers—their expectations spiralled out of all control in the spring of 1917. It was impossible for the Provisional Government to satisfy them. Over half a million workers went on strike between April and July. Their demands were not just economic but political. The eight-hour day, in particular, was seen by workers as a symbol of their rights and dignity as 'citizens'. Strikers demanded to be treated with respect by employers, to be addressed with the formal 'you' (*vyi*) as opposed to the familiar 'you' (*tyi*) reserved for children, animals and serfs. During protests they frequently appeared in suits with collared shirts and ties to assert their equality with other citizens. Women demanded equal pay to men.

Workers' organizations grew rapidly. The trade unions and Soviets resumed from where they had left off in 1905–6. But these were overtaken by two innovations of 1917: the factory committees, which supervised the management (they called it 'workers' control') to prevent closures and lay-offs (a tactic threatened by the capitalists to 'make the workers come to their senses'); and the Red Guards, which were formed to defend the factories. Both organizations were dominated by the Bolsheviks. The arming of the workers was a vital aspect of their growing solidarity. By July, there were 20,000 armed workers in the Red Guards of Petrograd alone.

Soldiers too had their own organizations—the soldiers' committees, established by Order No. 1, which supervised relations with the officers and discussed their military commands. Some soldiers refused to fight for more than eight hours a day, claiming the same rights as the workers. Many refused to salute their officers, or replaced them with their own elected officers on the grounds that the revolution had been made by the soldiers and so power should belong to them. This assertion of 'soldier power' was essential to the spirit of 'trench Bolshevism' that swept through the armed forces during 1917. The term was used by officers to describe those soldiers who were not necessarily Bolsheviks (there were few Party members in the front-line units) but who wanted peace at any cost so that they could go back to their villages. The Bolsheviks were the only major party that would give them that without delay, and many of the soldiers identified with them for this reason.

As the guardian of the state, the Provisional Government saw it as its duty to protect Russia's Imperial boundaries until the conclusion of the war and the resolution of the nationalities question by the Constituent Assembly. This did not rule out the possibility of conceding, as an interim measure, rights of local self-rule and cultural freedoms to the non-Russian territories. But it did prohibit giving in to nationalist demands for independence, especially in Poland and Ukraine, where it was feared that these could serve as a Trojan Horse for the Germans and the Austrians, whose armies occupied the western borderlands. Russia's enemies were indeed keen to help the nationalists attain their independence in order to control these weak new states and use them in the war against Russia.

For much of 1917 the nationalists' demands were not for independence but for more autonomy within a federal Russian state. Only in Poland and Finland were there demands for independence from the start. In most territories the social question was more pressing than the national one. Nationalism was strongest in those areas where it was underpinned by class interests. The peasants wanted land, they preferred politicians who spoke to them in their own language, and would support the nationalists where they helped them in their struggle against foreign landowners. Demands for independence only grew as the Provisional Government (supported by the Soviet leaders) refused to negotiate over more autonomy. In Finland and Ukraine the nationalist-dominated parliaments declared their independence by the end of June. The Polish case was the one exception to this rule—the nationalist demand for independence here receiving the support of the Provisional Government from as early as March—because, with Poland occupied by the Germans and the Austrians, there was nothing to be lost by promising to give the Poles their freedom and, on the contrary, the possibility of winning the support of the Polish population for the military campaign.

Lenin arrived at Petrograd's Finland Station shortly before midnight on 3 April. The square outside was packed with automobiles and tank-like armoured cars; mounted searchlights swept over the faces of the workers and soldiers who had turned out to welcome him with red flags. A military band played a thunderous 'Marseillaise' when his 'sealed' train—a single carriage exempt from border inspections—at last arrived from Switzerland. The Germans had arranged his return to Petrograd in the hope that his anti-war activities would undermine the Russian war effort.

Lenin was a stranger to Russia. Apart from a six-month stay in 1905–6, he had spent the previous seventeen years in exile in Europe. The man who was set to become the country's dictator had very little recent knowledge of the way its people lived.

He was already thinking of a second revolution—a revolution of his own. He outlined it in a ten-point programme—his famous April Theses—on the journey from Zurich and began to agitate for it on his arrival at the Finland Station. The message was simple: no support for the Provisional Government; a clean break with the Mensheviks and the Defensists of the Second International; the arming of the workers; the transfer of all powers to the Soviets; and the conclusion of an immediate peace. The Bolsheviks were stunned. Many thought the Theses were the 'ravings of a madman'. Lenin had turned the SD programme on its head. Instead of accepting the need for a 'bourgeois stage' of the revolution he was calling for a 'proletarian revolution' in one step.

The Theses had their roots in the lessons Lenin learned from 1905 (that the Russian bourgeoisie was too weak to lead a democratic revolution) as well as in the war (which had led him to conclude that, since the whole of Europe was on the brink of a socialist revolution, the Russian Revolution did not have to limit itself to 'bourgeois-democratic objectives' because it would be quickly internationalized). However, the practical implications of the Theses—that the Bolsheviks should not support the February Revolution but organize the masses against the Provisional Government—went far beyond anything that all but the most extreme left-wing Bolsheviks had considered possible.

Gradually Lenin brought the Party round to his Theses. The dominance of his personality was one factor. So was his assurance that he had in mind a 'lengthy period of agitation' rather than an imminent uprising against the Provisional Government. But the main factor working in his favour was the massive enrolment into the Party of workers and soldiers who were less interested in theory and more radical than their leaders. Knowing little about Marxist dogma, they could not understand the need to go through a 'bourgeois revolution'. Why did their leaders want to reach socialism in two stages when they could get there in one? Hadn't enough blood been spilled in February? And why should they let the bourgeoisie take power, if this was only going to make it harder to remove them later on?

The April Crisis brought home Lenin's message to the rank and file. The crisis arose when Miliukov, the Foreign Minister, told the British press that the Soviet peace campaign, calling on the peoples of the belligerent nations to protest against the 'imperialist war', would not alter Russia's commitment to its Imperial allies. Miliukov's behaviour suggested Lenin might be right that peace could not be gained through the Provisional Government. On 20–21 April, thousands of armed workers and soldiers came out on the streets of Petrograd to demonstrate against the war and the 'bourgeois ministers'. Fights broke out between the protestors and a counter-demonstration of right-wing patriots.

Fearful of a civil war, the Soviet leaders formed a coalition with the liberals to bolster the authority of the Provisional Government. The socialists (Mensheviks, SRs and Trudoviks) took only six of the sixteen cabinet posts (a minority in deference to the theory that they should not be in the government at all), including Agriculture (Chernov), Labour (Skobelev) and War (Kerensky). The leading Soviet figure in the coalition was the Georgian Menshevik Irakli Tsereteli (Post and Telegraphs). He had shaped the policy of Revolutionary Defensism (to go on with the war in defence of Russia and the Revolution) on which the coalition would be based between May and October.

The war was the most divisive issue for the Provisional Government. The politics of 1917 were basically a battle between those on the Left who saw the revolution as a means of ending the war and those on the Right (including the Kadets) who saw the war as a means of ending the revolution.

Allied pressure had been mounting on the Russians to launch an offensive in the summer. The fighting capacity of the Russian army was in serious doubt. But the coalition leaders convinced themselves that the soldiers would be willing to fight to defend the Revolution and that this would restore national unity and discipline. They compared Russia's situation with that of France on the eve of the war against Austria in 1792. It seemed to them that a revolutionary war would give birth to a new civic patriotism, just as the defence of *la patrie* had given rise to the national chorus of '*Aux armes, citoyens*'. Defeat by Germany would mean the restoration of the Romanov ('German') dynasty.

Much of this patriotic hope was focused on Kerensky, who toured the Front to raise the troops' morale. Dressed in semi-military uniform, he wore his right arm in a sling, although there was no record that it had been wounded, to add theatrical effect to his speeches calling on the troops to fight for their freedom. The adulation he received from those soldiers who were picked to meet him created the impression that the rank and file were eager for battle. In fact, as the date of the offensive approached, the flood of deserters rose sharply.

The attack began on 16 June. The Women's Battalion of Death, a volunteer unit, led the way to shame the men into fighting. The main attack was aimed towards Lvov in the south, while supporting offensives were also launched on the Western and Northern Fronts. For two days the advance continued. The German lines were broken and a glorious 'triumph for Liberty!' was heralded in the patriotic press. But then the advance stopped, the Germans launched a counter-offensive, and the Russians fled in panic. The main reason for the fiasco was the simple reluctance of the troops to fight. Soldiers turned their guns against their commanding officers rather than go into battle. Their retreat degenerated into chaos as they looted liquor stores and rampaged through mainly Jewish settlements.

The collapse of the offensive dealt a fatal blow to the authority of the Provisional Government. The coalition fell apart. There was a three-week interregnum while the socialists and Kadets tried to patch together a new coalition, during which there was a vacuum of power. This was the context of the July uprising.

It began in the First Machine-Gun Regiment, the most menacing bastion of anti-government power in Petrograd, whose barracks on the Vyborg side nestled among the most strike-prone factories in the capital. On 20 June, the regiment was ordered to send 500 machine guns with their crews to the Front. It was the first time a unit of the Petrograd garrison had been ordered to the Front since the February Revolution. Order No. 1 had guaranteed a right for the 250,000 soldiers of the garrison to stay in Petrograd for its defence against 'counter-revolutionary' threats.

Accusing the Provisional Government of using the offensive to break up the garrison, the First Machine-Gun Regiment resolved to overthrow it if it continued with its 'counter-revolutionary' order. The Bolshevik Military Organization in the garrison encouraged an uprising. But the Party's Central Committee was more cautious, fearing that its failure would lead to an anti-Bolshevik backlash. It was unclear if Lenin could control his hot-headed followers in the garrison.

On 3 July, a solid mass of soldiers and workers marched through the city in armed ranks. The bulk of the crowd moved towards the Tauride Palace, where the Soviet leaders were debating whether to form a socialist government or another coalition with the Kadets. From the streets there were chants of 'All power to the Soviets!' But as night fell the crowds dispersed. With further demonstrations scheduled for the following day, the Bolshevik Central Committee agreed to support them, although it is unclear if it meant to use them for a seizure of power.

Lenin was uncharacteristically hesitant the next day, 4 July, when 20,000 Kronstadt sailors massed in front of Bolshevik headquarters in the Kshesinskaya Mansion, the palace of the last Tsar's favourite balle- rina, looking for instructions to start the uprising. Lenin did not want to speak. When he was finally persuaded to make an appearance on the balcony, he gave an uncertain speech, lasting barely a minute, in which he expressed his confidence in the coming of Soviet power but left the sailors without specific orders on how to bring it about. It was a telling moment, one of the few in Lenin's long career when he was faced with the task of leading a revolutionary crowd that was standing before him— and lost his nerve.

Confused by the lack of a clear call for the insurrection to begin, the Kronstadters set off for the Tauride Palace. On the Nevsky they merged with another vast crowd of workers from the Putilov metal factory. As the column turned into the Liteiny Prospekt, shots were fired by the Cossacks and cadets from the roof-tops and windows of the buildings, causing the marchers to scatter in panic. Some fired back. Others ran for cover, breaking down the doors and windows of the shops. When the shooting ceased, the leaders of the demonstration tried to restore order by re-forming ranks, but the equilibrium of the crowd had been upset, dozens had been killed, and, as they marched through the afflu- ent residential streets approaching the Tauride Palace, their columns broke down into a riotous mob, looting shops and houses and attacking well-dressed passers-by.

With a large crowd of armed and angry men surrounding the Tauride Palace there was nothing to prevent them carrying out a coup d'état. To the Soviet leaders inside the palace debating the question of power, it seemed 'completely obvious' that they were about to be stormed. But an order for attack never came from Lenin, and without one the insurgents were uncertain what to do. The hand of God, in the form of the weather, also played a part in the collapse of the uprising. At 5 p.m. the storm clouds broke and there was a torrential rainstorm. Most of the demonstrators ran for cover and did not bother to come back. But those who remained became impatient in the rain and began to fire in frustration at the palace. Some of the Kronstadt sailors climbed in through the windows, seized Chernov and took him out to an open car, shouting at him angrily: 'Take power, you son of a bitch, when it's handed to you!' The dishevelled and terrified SR leader was released when Trotsky appeared from the Soviet assembly and intervened with his famous speech calling on the 'Comrade Kronstadters, pride and glory of the Russian revolution', not to harm their cause by 'petty acts of violence against individuals'.[8]

One final scene symbolized the powerlessness of the crowd. At around 7 p.m. a group of workers from the Putilov plant broke into the palace and, flourishing their rifles, demanded power for the Soviets. But the Soviet chairman, Chkheidze, calmly handed to their hysterical leader a manifesto, printed by the Soviet the evening before, in which it was said that the demonstrators should go home or be condemned as traitors to the revolution. 'Here, please take this,' Chkheidze said to him in an imperious tone. 'It says here what you and your Putilov comrades should do. Please read it carefully and don't interrupt our business.'[9] The confused workman took the manifesto and left the hall with the rest of the Putilovites. No doubt he was angry and frustrated; yet he was unable to resist, not for lack of coercive power, but for lack of confidence. Centuries of serfdom and subservience had not prepared him to stand up to his political masters—and in that lay the tragedy of the Russian people as a whole. This was one of the most revealing scenes of the whole revolution—one of those rare episodes when the hidden relations of power are illuminated on the surface of events and the broader course of history becomes clear.

The crowds dispersed. The 'uprising' was over. Forces loyal to the Provisional Government arrived to defend the Tauride Palace. Leaflets were released by the Ministry of Justice accusing the Bolsheviks of working for the Germans (because Lenin had been sent by them on the 'sealed train' to foment opposition to the war effort) and blaming them for the reverses at the Front. Warrants for the arrest of their main leaders were published. Troops cleared the Party's headquarters in the Kshesinskaya Mansion. The capital succumbed to anti-Bolshevik hysteria.

Known or suspected Bolsheviks were attacked in the streets by Black Hundred elements. Hundreds of Bolsheviks were arrested. But Lenin fled into hiding. Refusing to stand trial for 'treason', he argued that the state was in the hands of a counter-revolutionary 'military dictatorship' which was already engaged in a 'civil war' against the proletariat. 'It is not a question of "courts" but of *an episode in the civil war* . . . All hopes for a peaceful development of the Russian revolution have vanished for good,' he wrote on 8–10 July.[10]

He now moved to the idea of an armed uprising for the seizure of power.

6

LENIN'S REVOLUTION

Kerensky became Prime Minister on 8 July. As the only major politician with popular support yet acceptable to the military command, he was seen as the man to reunite the country and halt the drift towards a civil war. The programme of the new coalition government (formed on 25 July) was no longer based on the democratic principles agreed with the Soviet as the basis of the dual power structure in February. On the Kadets' insistence, Kerensky passed tough new restrictions on public gatherings, restored the death penalty at the Front, agreed to roll back the influence of the soldiers' committees to restore military discipline, and appointed General Kornilov as the new Commander-in-Chief.

Kornilov was hailed as a national saviour by business leaders, officers and right-wing groups. With their backing he pushed for further reactionary measures, including the restoration of the death penalty for civilians, the militarization of the railways and defence industries, and a ban on workers' organizations. A clear threat to the Soviet, the measures would amount to martial law. Kerensky vacillated but eventually, on 24 August, he agreed, leading Kornilov to expect the establishment of a military dictatorship headed by Kerensky or himself. Hearing rumours of a Bolshevik uprising to prevent this coup, the Commander-in-Chief despatched a Cossack force to occupy the capital and disarm the garrison.

At this point Kerensky turned against Kornilov. His own fortunes had been falling fast and he saw his *volte-face* as a way to revive them. Condemning Kornilov as a 'counter-revolutionary' and traitor to the government, Kerensky dismissed him as Commander-in-Chief and called on the people to defend Petrograd. The Soviet established an all-party committee to mobilize an armed force for the defence of the capital. The Bolsheviks were rehabilitated after their suppression in the aftermath of the July Days. Several of their leaders were released, including Trotsky.

Only the Bolsheviks had the ability to bring out the workers and soldiers. In the northern industrial regions ad hoc revolutionary committees were formed to fight the 'counter-revolution'. Red Guards organized the defence of the factories. The Kronstadt sailors, who had last come to Petrograd during the July Days to overthrow the Provisional Government, arrived once again—this time to defend it against Kornilov. There was no need for fighting in the end. On their way to Petrograd the Cossacks were met by a Soviet delegation from the northern Caucasus, who talked them into laying down their arms. The civil war was put off to another day.

Kornilov was imprisoned with thirty other officers in the Bykhov Monastery near Mogilev for having been involved in a 'counter-revolutionary conspiracy'. Viewed by the Right as political martyrs, the 'Kornilovites' were later to become the founding nucleus of the Volunteer Army, the major White (or anti-Bolshevik) force fighting the Red Army in the Civil War.

In the end, the 'Kornilov Affair' undermined rather than strengthened Kerensky's position. Condemned by the Right for betraying Kornilov, the Prime Minister was also widely suspected on the Left of having been involved in his 'counter-revolutionary' action. Kerensky's insistence on continuing the coalition with the Kadets (who had clearly played a role in the Kornilov movement) added to these left-wing suspicions. 'The prestige of Kerensky and the Provisional Government,' wrote Kerensky's wife, 'was completely destroyed by the Kornilov

Affair; and he was left almost without supporters.'[1] The people's hero of the spring had become their anti-hero by autumn.

The mass of the soldiers suspected that their officers had supported Kornilov. For this reason there was a dramatic deterioration in army discipline from the end of August. Soldiers' assemblies passed resolutions calling for peace and power to the Soviets. The rate of desertion rose sharply: tens of thousands left their units every day. Most of the deserters were peasants, eager to return to their villages, where the harvest season was now in full swing. Armed and organized, these peasant soldiers led the attacks on the manors which became more frequent from September.

In the big industrial cities there was a similar process of radicalization in the wake of the Kornilov crisis. The Bolsheviks were the principal beneficiaries of this, winning their first majority in the Petrograd Soviet on 31 August. The Soviets of Riga, Saratov and Moscow fell to them soon afterwards. The rising fortunes of the Bolsheviks were due mainly to the fact that they were the only major political party which stood uncompromisingly for 'All power to the Soviets'.

This point bears emphasizing, for one of the most basic misconceptions about the October Revolution is that the Bolsheviks were swept to power on a tide of mass support for the Party. They were not. The October insurrection was a coup d'état, actively supported by a small minority of the population, but it took place in the midst of a social revolution, which was focused on the popular ideal of Soviet power. After the Kornilov crisis there was a sudden outpouring of resolutions from factories, villages and army units calling for a Soviet government. But almost without exception they called on all the socialist parties to participate in its establishment, and often showed a marked impatience with their factional disputes.

The real significance of the Kornilov Affair was that it reinforced the popular belief in a 'counter-revolutionary' threat against the Soviet—a threat the Bolsheviks would invoke to mobilize the Red Guards and other militants in October. In this sense the Kornilov Affair was a dress rehearsal for the Bolshevik seizure of power. The Bolshevik Military Organization emerged from the underground—where it had been since July—with renewed strength from its participation in the struggle against Kornilov. The Red Guards were also reinforced: 40,000 of them had been armed in the crisis. As Trotsky later wrote, 'the army that rose against Kornilov was the army-to-be of the October revolution'.[2]

The Kornilov Affair made up Lenin's mind that the time had come for an uprising against the Provisional Government. But this did not happen straight away. Before the Democratic Conference on 14 September, when the power question was supposed to be resolved, he supported the efforts of his Bolshevik comrades to persuade the SRs and the Mensheviks to leave the coalition with the liberals and join them in an all-socialist government. The cooperation of the left-wing parties in the defeat of Kornilov had opened up the prospect of attaining Soviet power by political means. Kamenev was the Bolshevik in charge of this initiative. Unlike Lenin, Kamenev believed that the Party should campaign for power within the Soviet movement and the democratic institutions of the February Revolution. As he saw it, the country was not ripe for a Bolshevik uprising, and any attempt to stage one was bound to end in terror, civil war and the defeat of the Party.

But Lenin reverted to his campaign for an armed uprising once the SRs and the Mensheviks failed to break with the Kadets at the Democratic Conference. Instead, under Kerensky's leadership, they renewed their coalition with the liberals on 24 September—a move that led to the collapse of their share of the vote in the city Duma elections of that week. In Moscow, the vote for the SRs declined from 56 per cent in the June elections to just 14 per cent; the Mensheviks fell from 12 to 4 per cent; while the Bolsheviks, who had polled 11 per cent in June, swept to victory with 51 per cent in September. The Kadets, meanwhile, increased their share from 17 to 31 per cent. The result underlined the polarization of the country—it was dubbed the 'civil war election'—as voters rallied to the extreme parties with an overt class appeal.

From his new hiding place in Finland, Lenin bombarded the Central Committee with a series of increasingly impatient letters calling for the armed uprising to begin. The Bolsheviks, he argued, 'can and *must* take state power into their own hands'. Can—because the Party had already won a majority in the Moscow and Petrograd Soviets and this was 'enough to carry the people with it' in a civil war. Must—because if it waited for the convocation of the Constituent Assembly to win power through the ballot box, 'Kerensky and Co.' would take pre-emptive action against the Soviets, either by giving up Petrograd to the Germans or by establishing a military dictatorship. Reminding his comrades of Marx's dictum that 'insurrection is an art', Lenin concluded that 'it would be naive to wait for a "formal" majority for the Bolsheviks. No revolution ever waits for *that*.'[3]

The Central Committee ignored Lenin's instructions. It was still committed to Kamenev's parliamentary tactics and resolved to wait until the Second All-Russian Soviet Congress, due to convene on 20 October, for the transfer of power to the Soviets. Moving to the resort town of Vyborg, 120 kilometres from the capital, Lenin intensified his barrage of violent messages to the Party organizations, urging them to start an armed insurrection at once—*before* the Congress. 'If we "wait" for the Congress of Soviets,' Lenin wrote on 29 September, 'we shall *ruin* the revolution.'[4]

Lenin's impatience was political. If the transfer of power took place by a vote of the Congress, the result would almost certainly be a Soviet coalition made up of all the socialist parties. The Bolsheviks would have to share power with at least the left wing (and possibly all) of the SRs and Mensheviks. This would be a victory for Kamenev, Lenin's arch-rival in the Party, who would probably emerge as the central figure in any Soviet coalition government. By seizing power before the Congress Lenin would retain the political initiative, forcing the rest of the socialist parties to endorse the Bolshevik action and join his government, or go into opposition, leaving the Bolsheviks in power on their own. Lenin's revolution was as much against the other Soviet-based parties as it was against the Provisional Government.

Running out of patience with his comrades, Lenin returned to Petrograd and convened a secret meeting of the Central Committee on 10 October at which he forced through the crucial decision by ten votes against two (Kamenev and Zinoviev) to prepare an uprising. When it would take place was not yet clear.

Most of the Bolshevik leaders were against any action before the Soviet Congress. A meeting of the Central Committee on 16 October was told by the Bolshevik Military Organization and other activists that the Petrograd soldiers and workers would not come out on the Party's call alone but 'would have to be positively stung by something for a rising, that is: the withdrawal of troops [i.e., the break-up of the garrison by Kerensky]'.[5] But Lenin was insistent on the need for immediate preparations and discounted the cautious mood of the Petrograd masses: in a coup d'état, which is how he conceived the seizure of power, only a small force was needed, provided it was well armed and disciplined enough. He was even prepared to carry out the coup as a military invasion of Petrograd by Bolshevik supporters in the Baltic garrisons.

Such was Lenin's towering influence that he got his way at the meeting on 16 October and (by 19 votes to 2) a vote was passed by the Central Committee backing his proposal for an uprising in the immediate future. Unable to support the resolution, Kamenev and Zinoviev submitted their resignations from the Central Committee and, on 18 October, aired their opposition to an insurrection in a newspaper article.

With the Bolshevik conspiracy now public knowledge, the Soviet leaders resolved to delay the Soviet Congress until 25 October. They hoped that the extra five days would give them the chance to muster their supporters from the far-flung provinces. But they merely gave the Bolsheviks the extra time they needed to prepare the uprising. The delay also lent credibility to the Bolsheviks' claim that the Soviet Congress might not be allowed to meet at all, helping them to bring out their supporters on the streets to defend it. Rumours of a 'counter-revolution' were further strengthened when Kerensky announced his foolish plans to transfer the bulk of the Petrograd garrison to the Northern Front. It was to prevent the garrison's removal that the Military

Revolutionary Committee (MRC)—the leading organizational force of the Bolshevik uprising—was formed on 20 October. Threatened by a transfer to the Front, the bulk of the soldiers refused to obey the General Staff and switched their allegiance to the MRC, which on 21 October proclaimed itself the ruling authority of the garrison. The MRC take-over of the garrison was the first act of the uprising.

It is one of the ironies of the Bolshevik insurrection that hardly any of its leaders had wanted it to happen how and when it did. Until late in the evening of 24 October the majority of the Central Committee and the MRC had not envisaged the overthrow of the Provisional Government before the opening of the Soviet Congress in the white-colonnaded ballroom of the Smolny Institute—a vast ochre-coloured classical palace that had once been a school for noble girls—the following day. Their armed supporters had occupied the streets solely to defend the capital from a counter-revolutionary attack.

Lenin's intervention was decisive. Disguised in a wig and cap with a bandage wrapped around his head, he left his hiding place in Petrograd and set off for the Bolsheviks' headquarters in one of the former classrooms (Room 36) of the Smolny Institute to force the start of the uprising. On his way across town, near the Tauride Palace, he was stopped by a government patrol, but they mistook him for a harmless drunk and let him pass. One can only ask how different history might have been if Lenin had been arrested?

Arriving at the Smolny, Lenin bullied the Central Committee into giving the command for the insurrection to begin. A map of the city was brought out and the Bolshevik leaders pored over it, drawing up the main lines of attack. Lenin suggested making a list of the Bolshevik government to be presented to the Soviet Congress. The question arose as to what to call themselves. The term 'Provisional Government' had been discredited; calling themselves 'ministers' seemed bourgeois. It was Trotsky who came up with the name of 'people's commissars' in emulation of the Jacobins. Everyone liked the suggestion. 'Yes, that's very good,' said Lenin, 'it smells of revolution. And we can call the government itself "the Council of People's Commissars".'[6]

Few historical events have been more distorted by myth than those of 25 October 1917. The common perception of the Bolshevik uprising as a heroic fight by the masses owes more to *October*—Sergei Eisenstein's propaganda film of 1927—than to historical fact. The Great October Socialist Revolution, as it became known in the Soviet Union, was in fact such a small-scale action, being in reality no more than a coup, that it passed unnoticed by the vast majority of the inhabitants of Petrograd. Theatres, restaurants and tram cars functioned much as normal while the Bolsheviks came to power.

The legendary 'storming' of the Winter Palace, where the remnants of Kerensky's cabinet were bunkered without hope of salvation in the Malachite Hall, was more like a house arrest. Led by the Bolshevik Vladimir Antonov-Ovseenko, it caused less damage to the palace than its re-enactment by Eisenstein's film crew. Most of the forces defending it had already left for home, hungry and dejected, before the assault began. The number of active participants in the insurrection was not large (not many were needed)—probably something in the region of 10,000–15,000 workers, soldiers and sailors in Palace Square. Not all of them were actually involved in the 'storming', although many more would later claim that they had taken part. Once the palace had been seized, larger crowds of people did become involved, mainly to join in the looting of the palace and its huge wine stores.

The seizure of the Winter Palace was announced to the Soviet Congress in the smoke-filled great hall of the Smolny Institute. The 670 delegates—mostly workers and soldiers in their tunics and greatcoats—had unanimously passed a resolution proposed by the Menshevik Martov to form a socialist government based on all the parties in the Soviet. When the seizure of power was announced shortly afterwards, most of the Menshevik and SR delegates announced that they would have nothing to do with this 'criminal venture' and walked out of the Congress in protest, while the Bolshevik delegates, perhaps half those in the hall, whistled, stamped their feet, and hurled abuse at them.

Lenin's planned provocation—the pre-emptive coup—had worked. By walking out of the Congress, the Mensheviks and SRs 'gave the Bolsheviks a monopoly of the Soviet, of the masses, and of the revolution', in the words of Nikolai Sukhanov, one of the first Mensheviks to acknowledge their mistake. 'By our own irrational decision, we ensured the victory of Lenin's whole "line"!'[7]

The immediate effect was to split the Mensheviks and SRs. Trotsky seized the initiative. Denouncing Martov's resolution for a coalition with the 'wretched groups who have left us', he pronounced this memorable sentence on those Menshevik and SR delegates who remained in the great hall: 'You are miserable bankrupts, your role is played out; go where you ought to go—into the dustbin of history!' In a moment of rage, which he must have agonized over for the rest of his life, Martov shouted: 'Then we'll leave!' and walked out of the hall.[8]

It was past two o'clock in the morning and it only remained for Trotsky to propose a resolution condemning the 'treacherous' attempts of the Mensheviks and SRs to undermine Soviet power. The mass of the delegates, who probably did not comprehend the significance of what they were doing, raised their hands to support it. The effect of their action was to give a Soviet stamp of approval to the Bolshevik dictatorship.

Few people thought that the new regime could last. 'Caliphs for an hour' was the verdict of much of the press. The SR leader, Gots, gave the Bolsheviks 'no more than a few days'; Gorky gave them two weeks; Tsereteli three. Many Bolsheviks were no more optimistic. 'Things are so unstable,' the Commissar of Education, Lunacharsky, wrote to his wife on 29 October, 'that every time I break from a letter, I don't even know if it will be my last. I could at any moment be thrown into jail.'[9]

The Bolsheviks had a tenuous hold on the capital—where all the major ministries and government departments, the State Bank and Post and Telegraphs went on strike in protest against their seizure of power— but no grip whatsoever on the provinces. They had no means of feeding

Petrograd, having lost control of the railways. It seemed likely that they would share the fate of the Paris Commune—the prototype of their 'dictatorship of the proletariat'—which was too isolated from the rest of France to withstand the attacks of the French army in 1871.

The most immediate military threat came from Kerensky. Having fled the Winter Palace on the 25th, he had rallied eighteen Cossack companies from the Northern Front to fight against the Bolsheviks in Petrograd, where a small force of cadets and officers was supposed to rise up in support of their attack. In Moscow, meanwhile, garrison forces loyal to Kerensky fought against the Bolsheviks for ten days. The heaviest fighting took place around the Kremlin, and many of the city's architectural treasures were damaged.

These first exchanges of the Civil War were complicated by the intervention of Vikzhel, the Railwaymen's Union. Made up of workers from all the socialist parties, Vikzhel tried to stop the fighting and force the Bolsheviks to inter-party talks to form a socialist coalition government by threatening to bring the railways to a halt. Lenin's government could not survive if food and fuel supplies to the capital were cut. It depended on the railways for its military campaign against Kerensky's forces in Moscow and Petrograd. The Bolsheviks opened talks with the Mensheviks and SRs on 29 October. But Lenin was opposed to any compromise. As soon as he was sure of victory against Kerensky's troops, he undermined the inter-party talks, which finally broke down on 6 November. The seizure of power had irrevocably split the socialist movement in Russia.

Although the seizure of power had been carried out in the name of the Soviet Congress, Lenin had no intention of ruling through the Congress, or its permanent executive, where the Left SRs, the Anarchists and a small group of Menshevik Internationalists acted as a parliamentary brake on the Council of People's Commissars (Sovnarkom), the driving force of his dictatorship. On 4 November, Sovnarkom decreed for itself the right to pass legislation without approval from the Soviet—a clear breach of the principle of Soviet power—and from that point it ruled by fiat without consulting it. On 12 December, the Soviet executive met for the first time in a fortnight: during its recess Sovnarkom had begun peace talks with the Central Powers, declared war on Ukraine, and imposed martial law in Moscow and Petrograd.

From his first days in power Lenin set out to destroy all those 'counter-revolutionary' parties opposed to his seizure of power. On 27 October, Sovnarkom banned the opposition press. Kadet, Menshevik and SR leaders were arrested by the MRC. By the end of November the prisons were so full of these new 'politicals' that the Bolsheviks began to release criminals to make more room.

Slowly but surely, the shape of the new police state was starting to emerge. On 5 December, the MRC was abolished and, two days later, its duties were transferred to the Cheka (Extraordinary Commission for Struggle against Counter-Revolution and Sabotage), the new security organ that would one day become the KGB. At the Sovnarkom meeting at which it was established the Cheka boss, Dzerzhinsky, described its mission as a fight to the death against the revolution's 'enemies' on the 'internal front' of a civil war:

> We need to send to that front—the most dangerous and cruel of fronts—determined, hard, dedicated comrades ready to do anything in defence of the Revolution. Do not think that I seek forms of revolutionary justice; we are not now in need of justice. It is war now—face to face, a fight to the finish. Life or death![10]

The opposition parties pinned their hopes on the Constituent Assembly. It was surely the true organ of democracy—elected by universal adult suffrage and representing every citizen, regardless of class, whereas the Soviets represented only workers, peasants and soldiers—and it seemed unlikely that the Bolsheviks would dare to challenge it. In fact the Bolsheviks were divided.

Lenin had always been contemptuous of formal democratic principles. He had made it clear in his April Theses that he viewed Soviet power as a higher form of democracy than the Constituent Assembly. There was no place for the 'bourgeoisie' in the Soviets and, in his view, no place for them either in the Dictatorship of the Proletariat. But the

Bolshevik seizure of power had been partly justified as a measure to ensure the convocation of the Constituent Assembly—Lenin had been arguing since July that 'Kerensky & Co.' would not let it meet—and he could not go back on his promise without losing face.

The moderates in his party, moreover, were committed to competing for power in the November elections to the assembly. Some, like Kamenev, even favoured the idea of combining Soviet power at the local level with the Constituent Assembly as a national parliament. It would have made an interesting hybrid form of direct democracy suited to the revolutionary situation of Russia at the time and perhaps capable of preventing the country's downward spiral into civil war with all its consequences for the violent evolution of the Soviet regime.

The November election was a national referendum on the Bolsheviks. Its verdict was unclear. The SRs received the largest vote (38 per cent), but the ballot papers had not distinguished between the Left SRs, who supported the October seizure of power, and the Right SRs, who did not. The split in the Party had taken place too recently for the printing changes to be made. The Bolsheviks polled just 10 million votes (24 per cent), most of them cast by the soldiers and workers of the industrial north. In the agricultural south they did badly.

Lenin at once declared the results unfair, not just because of the SR split but because the October uprising had 'brought the class struggle to a head' and shifted mass opinion to the left since the election. 'Naturally, the interests of this revolution stand higher than the formal rights of the Constituent Assembly', a 'bourgeois parliament', which had to be abolished in a 'civil war', Lenin insisted.[11]

Petrograd was in a state of siege on 5 January, the opening day of the Constituent Assembly. The Bolsheviks had forbidden public gatherings and flooded the city with troops, who fired on a crowd of 50,000 demonstrators organized by the Union for the Defence of the Constituent Assembly. At least ten were killed and dozens wounded. It was the first time government troops had fired on an unarmed crowd since the February Days.

In the Catherine Hall of the Tauride Palace, where the assembly met at 4 p.m., the atmosphere was tense. There were almost as many troops as there were delegates. They stood at the back of the hall and sat up in the galleries, drinking vodka and shouting abuse at the SR deputies. Lenin watched the scene from the old government loge, where the tsarist ministers had sat during the sessions of the Duma. He gave the impression of a general at the moment before the start of a decisive battle.

Under Chernov's chairmanship the SRs started a debate—they wanted to rush through decrees on land and peace to leave behind a legislative legacy—but nobody could hear above the soldiers' heckling. After a while, the Bolsheviks declared the assembly to be in the hands of 'counter-revolutionaries' and walked out, followed later by the Left SRs. Then, at 4 a.m., the Red Guards brought proceedings to a close. One of them, a sailor, climbed up on the tribune and, tapping Chernov on the shoulder, announced that everyone should leave the hall 'because the guard is tired'. Chernov kept the session going for a few more minutes but finally agreed to adjourn it when the guards made threats. The delegates filed out and the Tauride Palace was then locked, bringing the twelve-year history of Russia's democratic citadel to an end. When the deputies returned the following day, they were barred from entering and presented with a Sovnarkom decree dissolving the Constituent Assembly.

There was no popular reaction against the closure of Russia's national parliament. Among the peasantry, the traditional base of support for the SR Party, there was indifference. The SRs had mistakenly believed that the peasants shared their veneration for the Constituent Assembly. To the educated peasants the assembly was perhaps a symbol of 'the revolution'. But to the mass of the peasants, whose political outlook was confined to their own village, it was a distant parliament, dominated by the urban parties and associated with the discredited Duma. They had their own village Soviets, which stood closer to their own ideals, being in effect no more than their own village assemblies in a more revolutionary form. 'What do we need some Constituent Assembly for, when we already have our Soviets, where our own deputies can meet and decide everything,' an SR propagandist heard a group of peasant soldiers say.[12]

Through their Soviets the peasantry divided the gentry's land and property among themselves. They did so in line with their own egalitarian norms of social justice, and did not need the sanction of the Decree on Land passed at the Soviet Congress on 26 October. No central power could tell them what to do. In most areas the commune allocated strips of confiscated arable land according to the number of 'eaters' in each household. The landowners themselves were usually left a plot if they worked it with their own labour, as the peasants did. The rights of land and labour, which lay at the heart of the village commune, were understood as basic human rights.

After their defeat in the capital the Right SRs returned to their old provincial strongholds to rally support for the restoration of democracy. It was to prove a painful lesson in the new realities of provincial life. In town after town the moderate socialists had lost control of the Soviets to the extreme Left. In the northern and central industrial regions, where the Bolsheviks and Left SRs could count on the support of the workers and garrison soldiers, as well as a large proportion of the semi-industrial peasants, most of the provincial Soviets were in Bolshevik hands, usually through the ballot box, by the end of October, and only in Novgorod, Pskov and Tver did any serious fighting take place. Further south, in the agricultural provinces, the transfer of power was longer and more bloody with fighting in the streets of the main towns.

The establishment of Soviet power was often accompanied by the confiscation of 'bourgeois' property. Lenin encouraged local Bolshevik leaders to organize the 'looting of the looters' as a form of social justice by revenge. Soviet officials, bearing flimsy warrants, would go round bourgeois houses confiscating valuables and money 'for the revolution'. The Soviets levied taxes on the *burzhooi* and imprisoned hostages to force payment. Thus began the Bolshevik Terror.

Retribution and revenge were powerful revolutionary impulses. For the vast majority of the Russian people the ending of all social privilege was the basic principle of the revolution. By giving institutional form to this war on privilege, the Bolsheviks were able to draw on the revolutionary energies of those numerous elements from the poor who derived satisfaction from seeing the rich and mighty destroyed, regardless of whether it brought about any improvement in their own lot. The Soviet policy of forcing the old wealthy classes to share their spacious houses with the urban poor or to do such menial jobs as clearing snow or rubbish from the streets had a popular appeal. As Trotsky put it, 'For centuries our fathers and grandfathers have been cleaning up the dirt and filth of the ruling classes, but now we will make them clean up our dirt. We must make life so uncomfortable for them that they will lose their desire to remain bourgeois.'[13]

The Bolsheviks portrayed the *burzhooi* as 'parasites' and 'enemies of the people'. They encouraged terror on a massive scale to destroy the bourgeoisie. In 'How to Organize Competition?', written in December 1917, Lenin suggested that each town and village should be left to develop its own means

> to clean the land of Russia of all vermin, of fleas—the rogues, of bugs—the rich, and so forth and so forth. In one place half a score of rich, a dozen rogues, half a dozen workers who shirk their work . . . will be put in prison. In another place they will be put to cleaning latrines. In a third place they will be provided with 'yellow tickets' after they have served their time, so that everyone shall keep an eye on them, as *harmful* persons, until they reform. In a fourth, one out of every ten idlers will be shot on the spot.[14]

The slogan 'Death to the Bourgeoisie!' was written on the walls of the Cheka.

Dispossessed and degraded, these 'former people' struggled to survive. They were forced to sell their last possessions just to feed themselves. Baroness Meyendorff sold a diamond brooch for 5,000 roubles—enough to buy a bag of flour. Mighty scions of the aristocracy were reduced to petty street vendors. Many sold off everything and went abroad—around 2 million Russian émigrés were in Berlin, Paris and New York by the early 1920s—or fled south to the Ukraine and Kuban, where the White Guards of the counter-revolution had their main bases of power. Made up of volunteers from the Imperial army, Cossacks, and landowners' and bourgeois' sons, the White Guards were united by their fight against the Bolsheviks. Their only clear aim was to put the clock back to before October 1917.

Of all the early Bolshevik decrees none had the same emotional appeal as the Decree on Peace passed at the Soviet Congress on 26 October. When Lenin read out the decree—a bombastic 'Proclamation to the Peoples of All the Belligerent Nations' proposing a 'just and democratic peace' on the old Soviet formula of no annexations or indemnities— there was an overwhelming wave of emotion in the Smolny hall. 'Suddenly,' recalled John Reed in *Ten Days That Shook the World*, 'we found ourselves on our feet, mumbling together into the smooth lifting unison of the Internationale . . . "The war is ended!" said a young workman near me, his face shining.'[15]

But there was no end to the war at all. The Decree on Peace was an expression of hope, not a statement of reality. The Bolsheviks used it as propaganda to fan the flames of revolution in the West. It was the only means they had to end the war—or rather to transform it, as Lenin had suggested, into a series of civil wars in which the workers of the world would unite against their belligerent governments. The belief in the imminence of a world socialist revolution was central to Bolshevik thinking. As Marxists, it was inconceivable to them that the revolution could survive for long in a backward peasant country such as Russia without the support of the proletariat in the advanced industrial societies. The seizure of power had been carried out on the assumption that a European revolution was just around the corner. Every report of a strike or mutiny in the West was hailed as a sign that it was 'starting'.

But what if this revolution failed to come about? The Bolsheviks would then find themselves without an army (millions of soldiers took the Decree on Peace as an excuse to demobilize themselves) and would be defenceless against a German invasion. To those on the left of the Party, such as Bukharin, a separate peace with imperialist Germany would represent a betrayal of the international cause. They favoured the idea of fighting a 'revolutionary war' (possibly with no more than Red Guards) against the German invaders, arguing that it would inspire revolutions in the West. Lenin, by contrast, was increasingly doubtful about the chances of sustaining such a fight. Facing the lack of an army, the Bolsheviks had no choice but to conclude a separate peace, which would give them the 'breathing spell' they needed to consolidate their power base. Moreover, in so far as a separate peace in the East would enable the Central Powers to prolong their campaign on the Western Front, such a policy was likely to increase the revolutionary possibilities. Lenin did not want to end the war in Europe: he wanted it to last as long as possible to make revolutions more likely. The Bolsheviks were masters of using wars for revolutionary purposes.

On 16 November, a Soviet delegation left for the Belorussian town of Brest-Litovsk to negotiate an armistice with the Germans. In mid-December Trotsky was sent to drag out the peace talks in the hope of a revolution starting in the West before any document was signed. The Germans' patience soon ran out. They opened talks with the Ukrainians, who were ready to accept a German protectorate to win their independence from Bolshevik Russia, and used this threat to pressure the Russians to accept their tough demands (including the separation of Poland from Russia and the German annexation of Lithuania and most of Latvia). Trotsky called for an adjournment and returned to Petrograd to confer with the rest of the Bolshevik leaders.

At the decisive meeting of the Central Committee, on 11 January, the largest faction supported Bukharin's call for a revolutionary war. Trotsky suggested playing for more time. But Lenin insisted that they had no choice but to sign a separate peace, in which case it was better done sooner than later. There was no point putting the whole of the revolution at risk on the chance that a German revolution might break out, he argued. 'Germany is only just pregnant with revolution, and we have already given birth to a completely healthy child.'[16]

With only Zinoviev and four others behind him in the Central Committee, including the shadowy figure of Stalin (at this time no more than a 'grey blur' according to Sukhanov), Lenin was forced to ally with Trotsky to win a majority against Bukharin. Trotsky was sent back to Brest-Litovsk to spin out the talks. But on 9 February the Germans signed a treaty with the Ukrainians, and a week later recommenced hostilities against Russia. Within five days the Germans had advanced 150 miles towards Petrograd—as much as the German army had advanced in the three previous years.

Lenin was furious. By refusing to sign the German treaty, his opponents in the Central Committee had merely enabled the enemy to advance. After a heated debate he at last got his way in the Central Committee on 18 February. A cable was sent to Berlin accepting the German conditions. For several days, however, the enemy continued to advance towards the Soviet capital. German planes dropped bombs on Petrograd. Lenin was convinced the Germans were planning to occupy the city and remove the Bolsheviks. He reversed his earlier position and called for a revolutionary war. Military help was requested from the Allies, who were more concerned to keep the Russians in the war than they were with the nature of their government and on that basis offered aid. The Bolsheviks began to evacuate the capital to Moscow. Panic broke out in Petrograd.

On 23 February, the Germans delivered their final offer for peace. Berlin now demanded all the territory which its troops had seized in the past five days. In the Central Committee Lenin insisted that they had no choice but to accept the harsh peace terms. 'If you do not sign them, you will be signing the death sentence of Soviet power in three weeks', he argued.[17] It was agreed to accept the German proposals. The Bukharin faction resigned in protest from the Central Committee.

The peace treaty was finally signed on 3 March. None of the Party leaders wanted to go to Brest-Litovsk and put their name to a treaty which was seen throughout the country as a 'shameful peace'. The Left

SRs resigned from the Soviet government in protest, leaving the Bolsheviks in power on their own.

Under the terms of the Brest-Litovsk Treaty, Russia was obliged to give up nearly all its territories on the European continent. Poland, Finland, Estonia and Lithuania achieved a sort of independence under German protection. Soviet troops were evacuated from Ukraine. In the final reckoning, the Soviet Republic lost 34 per cent of its population (55 million people), 32 per cent of its agricultural land, 54 per cent of its industrial enterprises and 89 per cent of its coalmines (peat and wood now became its biggest source of fuel). As a European power, Russia was reduced to a status on a par with seventeenth-century Muscovy. But Lenin's revolution had been saved.

7

CIVIL WAR AND THE MAKING
OF THE SOVIET SYSTEM

Because of the Treaty of Brest-Litovsk a large force of Czech and Slovak soldiers—prisoners of war and deserters from the Austro-Hungarian army—became stranded on Soviet soil. As nationalists determined to fight for their country's independence from the Austro-Hungarian Empire, they had sided with the Russians in the war. But now they wanted to continue their struggle as part of the Czech army fighting in France. Rather than run the risk of crossing enemy lines, they decided to travel eastwards, right around the world, intending to reach Europe via Vladivostok and the United States. On 26 March an agreement was reached with the Soviet authorities at Penza, whereby the 35,000 soldiers of the Czech Legion were allowed to travel on the Trans-Siberian Railway as 'free citizens' with a specified number of weapons for self-defence.

By mid-May, they had got as far as Cheliabinsk in the Urals when they became involved in fighting with the local Soviets and their Red Guards, who had tried to confiscate their guns. Deciding to fight their way through the free-for-all of Soviet Siberia, the Legion broke up into groups and captured one town after another from the poorly armed and disciplined Red Guards, who ran away in panic at the first sight of the well-organized Czechs. On 8 June, a force of 8,000 Czechs took the Volga town of Samara, a stronghold of the Right SRs, whose leaders had fled there after the closure of the Constituent Assembly and formed a government, the Komuch (Committee of Members of the Constituent Assembly), which the Czechs now installed in power. The Right SRs had promised that they would secure French and British help to overthrow the Bolsheviks and get Russia to rejoin the war against Germany and Austria. Thus began a new phase of the Civil War—organized on military lines by Red and White armies—in which fourteen Allied powers would ultimately become involved.

Fighting had already started on the Don River, in south Russia, where Kornilov and his White Guards, having fled the Bykhov Monastery, had formed a Volunteer Army of 4,000 men, mostly officers, who briefly captured Rostov from the Reds before retreating south across the ice-bound steppe to the Kuban in February. Kornilov was killed in an attack on Ekaterinodar on 13 April. Taking over the command, General Denikin led the Whites back to the Don, where they found the Cossack farmers in revolt against the Bolsheviks, who were seizing food at gunpoint and wreaking havoc in the Cossack settlements. By June, 40,000 Cossacks had joined General Krasnov's Don Army. With the Whites they were in a strong position to strike north towards the Volga and link up with the Czechs to attack Moscow.

The story of the Civil War is often told as a conflict in which the Bolsheviks were forced to fight by the Whites and the Allied intervention in Russia. In this left-wing version of events the Reds were not to blame for the 'extraordinary measures' they were forced to take in the Civil War— the rule by fiat and terror, the requisitionings, mass conscriptions and so on—because they had to act decisively and quickly to defend their revolution against counter-revolutionaries. But this misses the whole point of the Civil War and its relationship to the revolution for Lenin and his followers.

In their view the Civil War was a necessary phase of the class struggle. They embraced it as a continuation of the revolution in a more intensive and military form. 'Our Party is for civil war!' Trotsky told the

Soviet on 4 June. 'Long live civil war! Civil war for the sake of the . . . workers and the Red Army, civil war in the name of direct and ruthless struggle against counter-revolution.'[1]

Lenin was prepared for a civil war and perhaps even welcomed it as a chance to build his party's power base. The effects of such a conflict would be predictable: the polarization of the country into 'revolution-ary' and 'counter-revolutionary' sides; the extension of the state's mili-tary and political power; and the use of terror to suppress dissent. In Lenin's view all these things were necessary for the victory of the Dicta-torship of the Proletariat. He often said that the defeat of the Paris Commune was explained by the failure of the Communards to launch a civil war.

The ease of the Czech victories made it clear to Trotsky, now Commis-sar of War, that the Red Army had to be reformed on the model of the tsarist conscript army, with regular units replacing the Red Guards, professional officers and a centralized hierarchy of command. There was a lot of opposition to these policies among the Party's rank and file. Whereas the Red Guards were seen as an army of the working class, mass conscription was bound to build an army dominated by the peas-antry, a hostile social force in the view of the Bolsheviks. The rank and file were particularly opposed to Trotsky's conscription of ex-tsarist officers (75,000 would be recruited by the Bolsheviks in the Civil War). They saw it as a return to the old military order and as a hindrance to their own promotion as 'Red officers'. The so-called Military Opposi-tion crystallized around this lower-class mistrust and resentment of the professional officers and other 'bourgeois specialists'. But Trotsky ridi-culed his critics' arguments: revolutionary zeal was no substitute for military expertise.

Mass conscription was introduced in June. Factory workers and Party activists were the first to be called up. Without a military infra-structure in the countryside, mobilizing peasants turned out to be far more difficult than expected. Of the 275,000 peasant recruits anticipated from the first call-up, only 40,000 actually appeared. Peasants did not want to leave their villages at harvest time. There were peasant uprisings against conscriptions and mass desertions from the Red Army.

As Soviet power in the countryside was strengthened, the rate of peasant conscription improved. The Red Army grew to 1 million men by the spring of 1919; to 3 million by 1920; and 5 million by the end of the Civil War in 1920. In many ways the Red Army was too big to be effective. It grew faster than the devastated Soviet economy was able to supply it with guns, food and clothes. The soldiers lost morale and deserted in their thousands, taking their weapons, so that new recruits had to be thrown into battle without proper training, which only made them even more likely to desert. The Red Army was thus drawn into a vicious circle of mass conscription, supply shortages and desertion, which in turn led to the draconian system of War Communism, the first attempt by the Bolsheviks at a command economy, whose main purpose was to channel all production towards the demands of the army.

War Communism began with a grain monopoly. But it broadened to include a comprehensive range of state controls on the economy. It aimed to abolish private trade, to nationalize all large-scale industry, to militarize labour in essential industries, and at its height, in 1920, to replace money with universal rationing by the state. Because it was a model for the Stalinist economy it is important to explain its origins and decide where it fits into the revolution's history.

One view is that War Communism was a pragmatic response to Civil War exigencies—a temporary diversion from the mixed economy that Lenin had supposedly outlined in the spring of 1918 and to which he would return in the New Economic Policy of 1921. This view suggests that the 'soft' version of socialism pursued by the Bolsheviks during these two phases was the real face of Leninism, as opposed to the 'hard' or anti-market socialism of the Civil War and Stalinist eras. A different view is that War Communism was rooted in Lenin's ideology— an attempt to impose socialism by decree which the Bolsheviks abandoned only when they were forced to by mass protests in 1921.

Neither side is right. War Communism was not just a response to the Civil War. It was a means of fighting civil war, a set of policies to make class war against the peasantry and other social 'enemies'. This explains why its policies were kept in place for a year after the White armies had been defeated. Nor could it be said that the Bolsheviks had a clear ideology. They were divided over policies—the Left wanting to move directly towards the abolition of the capitalist system, while Lenin talked of using capitalist methods for the reconstruction of the economy. These divisions resurfaced repeatedly throughout the years of the Civil War so that the policies of War Communism had to be constantly chopped and changed in the interests of Party unity.

War Communism was essentially the Bolsheviks' political response to the urban food crisis and the exodus of workers from the hungry cities where they had their power base. During the first six months of the Bolshevik regime around 1 million workers left the big industrial cities and moved to the countryside to live closer to food supplies. The metal industries of Petrograd were the worst hit—their workforce falling from a quarter of a million to barely 50,000 during these six months. The Bolsheviks' once mighty strongholds, the New Lessner and Erickson plants, each of which had more than 7,000 workers in October, had fewer than 200 between them by April. The Bolshevik Party, in the words of Shliapnikov, was becoming 'the vanguard of a non-existent class'.[2]

The root of the crisis was the peasantry's reluctance to sell foodstuffs for paper money when there was nothing they could buy with it. The peasants reduced production, stored their surpluses, used their grain to fatten up their cattle, or sold it to black-market traders from the towns. Townsmen travelled to the countryside to trade with the peasants. They left with bags of clothes and household goods to sell or exchange in the rural markets and returned with bags of food. Workers traded tools they had stolen from their factories, or manufactured simple items, such as axes, ploughs, primus stoves or cigarette lighters to barter with the peasants. The railways were paralysed by these armies of 'bagmen'. The Orel Station, a major junction between Moscow and the agricultural south, had 3,000 bagmen pass through it every day. Many of them travelled in armed brigades which hijacked trains.

The Bolsheviks announced their grain monopoly on 9 May. All the peasants' surplus harvest became state property. Armed brigades went into the villages to requisition grain. Where they found none (because there were no surpluses) they assumed that it was being hidden by the 'kulaks'—the phantom class of 'capitalist' peasants invented by the Bolsheviks—and a 'war for grain' began.

The battle cry was given by Lenin in a speech of shocking violence: 'the kulaks are the rabid foes of the Soviet government . . . These bloodsuckers have grown rich on the hunger of the people . . . Ruthless war on the kulaks! Death to all of them!'[3] The brigades beat and tortured villagers until the required amount of grain was given up—often at the expense of vital seed stocks for the next harvest. The peasants tried to hide their precious grain from the brigades. There were hundreds of peasant uprisings against the requisitioning.

The Bolsheviks reacted by tightening their policies. In January 1919 they replaced the grain monopoly with a general Food Levy (*prodrazverstka*) which extended the monopoly to all foodstuffs and took away the powers of the local food committees to set the levies in accordance with the harvest estimates: henceforth Moscow would take what it needed from the peasantry without any calculation as to whether it was taking their last stocks of food and seed.

The purpose of the Food Levy was not just to meet the growing needs of the Red Army. By stamping out the bag trade, it also helped to keep the workers at their factories. The control of labour was the essence of War Communism—'the right of the dictatorship', as Trotsky put it, 'to send every worker to the place where he is needed in accordance with the state plan'.[4] One step towards this planned economy was the nationalization of large-scale industry on 28 June 1918. State-appointed managers replaced the authority of the factory committees and trade unions (put in charge of the factories by the Decree on Workers' Control in November 1917), which had brought chaos to industrial relations and encouraged the workers' protest movement against the Bolsheviks during the spring of 1918. The Decree on Nationalization was passed three days before a planned general strike in Petrograd, allowing the new factory bosses to threaten workers with dismissal if they went ahead with the action.

The rationing system was the final element of War Communism. Left-wing Bolsheviks saw the ration coupon as the founding deed of the Communist order—an alternative to money, whose disappearance they mistakenly believed would mean the end of the capitalist system. Through the rationing system the Bolshevik dictatorship further tightened its grip on society. The class of one's ration defined one's place in the new social hierarchy. Red Army soldiers and bureaucrats got the first-class ration (which was meagre but adequate); most workers received the second-class ration (which was rather less than adequate); while the *burzhooi*, at the bottom of the pile, had to make to do with the third-class ration (which, in Zinoviev's memorable phrase, was 'just enough bread so as not to forget the smell of it').[5]

The totalitarian state had its origins in War Communism, which attempted to control every aspect of the economy and society. For this reason the Soviet bureaucracy ballooned spectacularly during the Civil War. The old problem of the tsarist state—its inability to impose itself on the majority of the country—was not shared by the Soviet regime. By 1920, 5.4 million people worked for the government. There were twice as many officials as there were workers in Soviet Russia, and these officials were the main social base of the new regime. This was not a Dictatorship of the Proletariat but a Dictatorship of the Bureaucracy.

Joining the Party was the surest way to gain promotion through the ranks of the bureaucracy. From 1917 to 1920, 1.4 million people joined the Party, nearly all from lower-class and peasant backgrounds, and many through the Red Army, which taught millions of conscripts how to think and act like 'Bolsheviks', the foot-soldiers of a disciplined revolutionary vanguard. The leadership was worried that this mass influx would reduce the Party's quality. Levels of literacy were very low (in 1920 only 8 per cent of Party members had more than four years of primary schooling). As for the political literacy of the rank and file, it was rudimentary: at a Party school for journalists none of the students could say who the British or French leaders were, and some believed that imperialism was a republic somewhere in England. But in other ways this lack of education was an advantage for the Party leaders, for it underpinned their followers' political obedience. The poorly educated rank and file mouthed the Party's slogans but left all critical thinking to the Politburo and the Central Committee.

As the Party grew it also came to dominate the local Soviets. This involved a transformation of the Soviets—from local revolutionary bodies controlled by an assembly to bureaucratic organs of the Party-state where all real power was exercised by the Bolsheviks, who dominated the executives. In many of the higher-level Soviets, especially in areas deemed important in the Civil War, the executives were not elected: the Central Committee in Moscow simply sent in commissars to run the Soviets. In the rural (*volost'*) Soviets the executives were elected. Here the Bolsheviks' success was partly due to the open system of voting and intimidation of voters. But it was also due to the support of the younger and more literate peasants who had left the village in the First World War and returned in the Civil War. Newly skilled in military techniques and organization, and well versed in socialist ideas, these were the peasants who would join the Bolsheviks, and dominate the rural Soviets by the end of the Civil War. In the Volga region, for example, where this has been studied in detail, two thirds of the *volost'* Soviet executive members were literate peasant males under the age of thirty-five and registered as Bolsheviks in the autumn of 1919, compared with just one third the previous spring. In this sense the dictatorship depended on a cultural revolution in the countryside. Throughout the peasant world Communist regimes have been built on the ambition of literate peasant sons to join the official class.

Odd though it may seem, it was as late as September 1918—and then only because he nearly died—that Lenin became widely known in Soviet Russia. During the first ten months of Soviet power he was rarely seen by the public. 'Nobody even knew Lenin's face,' his wife, Nadezhda Krup-skaya, recalled.[6]

All that changed on 30 August, when the Bolshevik leader was wounded by two shots fired by a terrorist assassin called Fanny Kaplan while visiting a Moscow factory. Lenin's quick recovery was declared a miracle in the Soviet press. He was hailed as a Christ-like figure, pro-tected by supernatural powers, who was not afraid to sacrifice his life for the good of the people. Portraits of Lenin began to appear in the streets. He was seen for the first time in a documentary film, *Vladimir Ilich's Kremlin Stroll*, widely shown that autumn to dispel the growing rumour that he had been killed. It was the start of the Lenin cult—a cult designed by the Bolsheviks, against Lenin's will, to promote their leader as the 'people's Tsar'.

Thus too began the Red Terror. Although Kaplan had always denied it, she was accused of working for the SRs and the capitalist powers. She was living proof of the regime's paranoiac theory that it was surrounded by a well-connected ring of internal and external enemies—demonstrated by the Allies' support for the Whites and counter-revolutionary uprisings—and that to survive it had to fight a constant civil war. This same logic would drive the Soviet terror throughout the Stalin years.

The press demanded mass reprisals for the attempt on Lenin's life. Thousands of 'bourgeois hostages' were arrested. A tour of the Cheka jails would reveal a vast array of different people—politicians, merchants, traders, officers, priests, professors, prostitutes, dissident workers and peasants—in short, a cross-section of society. People were arrested for no more than being near the scene of a 'bourgeois provocation' (a shoot-ing or a crime). One old man was arrested because during a general raid the Cheka found on his person a photograph of a man in court uni-form: it was the picture of a deceased relative taken in the 1870s.

The ingenuity of the Cheka's torture methods was on a par with the Spanish Inquisition's. Each local Cheka had its speciality. In Kharkov they went in for the 'glove trick'—putting the victim's hands in boiling water until the blistered skin could be peeled off. In Kiev they fixed a cage with rats to the victim's torso and heated it so that the rodents ate their way through the victim's body to escape.

The Red Terror gave rise to protests from all quarters of society. Within the Party too there were critics of its excesses. But the 'hard men' in the leadership—Lenin, Stalin and Trotsky—stood by the Cheka. Lenin had no patience for those who were squeamish about using terror in a civil war. 'How can you make a revolution without firing squads?' he had asked on hearing that the Second Soviet Congress had passed a resolution proposed by Kamenev to abolish the death penalty on 26 October 1917. 'Do you expect to dispose of your enemies by disarming yourself? What other means of repression are there? Prisons? Who attaches significance to that in a civil war?'[7]

In *Terrorism and Communism* (1920)—a book studied closely by Stalin—Trotsky maintained that terror was essential to push for victory in the class war:

> The Red Terror is a weapon utilized against a class, doomed to destruction, which does not wish to perish. If the White Terror can only retard the historical rise of the proletariat, the Red Terror hastens the destruction of the bourgeoisie. This hastening—a pure question of acceleration—is at certain periods of decisive importance. Without the Red Terror, the Russian bourgeoisie, together with the world bourgeoisie, would throttle us long before the coming of the revolution in Europe. One must be blind not to see this, or a swindler to deny it. The man who recognizes the revolutionary historic importance of the very fact of the existence of the Soviet system must also sanction the Red Terror.[8]

Terror was an integral element of the Bolshevik regime from the beginning. Nobody will ever know the number of its victims in these years, but it may have been as many as those killed in the battles of the Civil War—a figure in excess of 1 million—if one counts the mass killings of peasants and Cossack farmers by the Red Army.

The Czech Legion fell apart after the capture of Samara. It had no reason to continue fighting after the ending of the First World War in November 1918. Without an effective force to resist the Red Army, it was only a matter of time before the Komuch lost its hold on the Volga region. The SRs fled to Omsk, where their brief Directory government was overthrown by the Rightist officers of the Siberian army who invited Admiral Kolchak to become the Supreme Leader of the anti-Bolshevik movement. Kolchak received the backing of the British, the French and the Americans, who remained committed to removing the Bolsheviks from power on political grounds, even though, with the World War now over, there were no longer any military reasons for the Allied intervention in Russia.

Kolchak's White army of 100,000 men advanced to the Volga, where the Bolsheviks were struggling to cope with a large peasant uprising behind their lines in the spring of 1919. In a desperate counter-offensive the Reds pushed Kolchak's forces back to Ufa by mid-June, after which the cities of the Urals and beyond were taken by the Reds in quick succession as the Whites lost cohesion and retreated through Siberia. Finally captured in Irkutsk, Kolchak was executed by the Bolsheviks in February 1920.

Meanwhile, at the height of the Kolchak offensive, Denikin's forces struck into the Donbas coal region and south-east Ukraine, where the Cossacks were in rebellion against a Red campaign of mass terror to clear them off the land ('decossackization'). With military support from the British and the French, now committed to the anti-Bolshevik campaign on explicitly political grounds, the Whites advanced easily into Ukraine. The Reds were suffering from a crisis of supplies and lost more than 1 million deserters on the Southern Front between March and October. The rear was engulfed in peasant uprisings, as the Reds resorted to the requisitioning of horses and supplies, the conscription of reinforcements and the repression of villages suspected of hiding deserters. In the south-east corner of Ukraine the Reds were heavily reliant on

Nestor Makhno's peasant partisans, who fought under the black flag of the Anarchists but were no match for the better-supplied and better-disciplined White troops.

On 3 July, Denikin issued his Moscow Directive, the order for a general attack on the Soviet capital. It was an all-or-nothing gamble, counting on the speed of the White cavalry to exploit the temporary weakness of the Reds, but at the risk of leaving the White rear unprotected in the form of trained reserves, sound administration and lines of supply.

The Whites pushed north and took Orel, only 250 miles from Moscow, on 14 October. But Denikin's forces had overstretched themselves. In the rear they had left themselves without enough troops to defend their bases against Makhno's Anarchist partisans and Ukrainian nationalists, and at the height of the Moscow offensive they were forced to withdraw troops to deal with them. Without regular supplies, the troops broke down into looting peasant farms. But the Whites' main problem was the peasants' fear of them as an avenging army of the landowners. The peasants were afraid that a White victory would reverse the revolution on the land. Denikin's officers were mostly squires' sons. On the land question the Whites had made it clear that they would not go beyond the Kadet programme, under which the gentry's surplus land would be sold off to the peasants at a future date. Under these proposals the peasants would have to give back three quarters of the land they had taken from the gentry during the revolution.

As the Whites advanced towards Moscow, the peasants rallied behind the Red Flag. Between June and September a quarter of a million deserters returned to the Red Army from the two military districts of Orel and Moscow alone. These were regions where the local peasantry had gained substantial amounts of land during 1917. However much the peasants might have detested the Bolshevik regime, with its violent requisitionings and commissars, they would side with the Reds against the Whites to defend their revolution on the land.

With 200,000 troops the Reds launched a counter-offensive, forcing the Whites, who had half as many men, to retreat south, losing discipline as they did so. The remnants of Denikin's army ended up in

Novorossisk, the main Allied port on the Black Sea, from which 50,000 troops were hurriedly evacuated to the Crimea in March 1920. There were desperate scenes as soldiers and civilians struggled to get on board the Allied ships. Priority was given to the troops, but not all of these could be rescued and 60,000 soldiers were left at the mercy of the Bolsheviks (most of them were later shot or sent to labour camps). For Denikin's critics, the botched evacuation was the final straw. A generals' revolt forced his resignation in favour of Baron Wrangel, a critic of the Moscow Directive, who led one last stand against the Bolsheviks in the Crimea during 1920. But this was only to delay for a few months the inevitable defeat of the Whites.

What were the reasons for their failure? The White émigré communities in Constantinople, Paris and Berlin would agonize for years over this question.

Historians sympathetic to their cause have often stressed the 'objective factors' that stacked the odds against them. The Reds had an overwhelming superiority of numbers. They controlled the vast terrain of central Russia with its prestigious capitals, most of the country's industry, if not fuel, and the core of its railway network, which enabled them to shift their forces from one front to another. The Whites, by contrast, were divided between several different fronts, which made it difficult to coordinate their operations, and they had to rely on the Allies for much of their supplies. All these factors played a part. But at the root of their defeat was a failure of politics. The Whites proved unable and unwilling to frame policies capable of winning mass support. They had no propaganda to compare with the Bolsheviks', no political symbols of their own to challenge the Red Flag or the Red Star. They were divided politically. Any movement that included right-wing monarchists and socialist republicans would have problems reaching political agreement. But it was practically impossible for the Whites to agree on policies. They did not even try. Their sole idea was to put the clock back to before October 1917. They failed to adapt to the new revolutionary situation. Their refusal to accept the national independence movements was disastrous. It lost them the potentially invaluable support of the Poles and

Ukrainians and complicated their relations with the Cossacks, who wanted more autonomy from Russia than the White leaders were prepared to give. But the main cause of their undoing was their failure to accept the peasant revolution on the land.

The peasants supported the Reds against the Whites only for as long as the revolution was threatened. Once the Whites had been defeated the peasants turned against the Bolsheviks, whose requisitionings had brought much of rural Russia to the brink of starvation. By the autumn of 1920, the whole of the country was inflamed with peasant wars. Angry peasants were taking up arms and chasing the Bolsheviks out of the villages; they were forming bands to fight the requisitioning brigades; and joining larger peasant armies, such as Makhno's in Ukraine or Antonov's rebel force in the central Russian province of Tambov, to destroy the Soviet infrastructure in the countryside. Everywhere their aims were basically the same: to restore the peasant self-rule of 1917–18. Some expressed this in the confused slogans: 'Soviets without Communists!' or 'Long live the Bolsheviks! Death to the Communists!' Many peasants were under the illusion that the Bolsheviks and the Communists were two separate parties: the Party's change of name in March 1918 had yet to be communicated to the remote villages. The peasants believed that the 'Bolsheviks' had brought them peace and land, whereas the 'Communists' had brought them civil war and the requisitioning of their grain.

By 1921, Bolshevik power had ceased to exist in much of the countryside. The consignment of grain to the cities had been brought to a halt within the rebel strongholds. As the urban food crisis deepened, workers went on strike.

The strikes that swept across Russia during February 1921 were no less revolutionary than the peasant rebellions. Given the punishments which strikers could expect (instant dismissal, arrest and imprisonment, even execution), it was a desperate act to go on strike. Whereas earlier strikes had been a means of bargaining with the regime, those of 1921 were an attempt to bring it down.

Workers were angered by the Bolsheviks' attempts to subordinate trade unions to the Party-state. As Commissar for Transport, Trotsky planned to break up the railway union (which had been opposed to the October insurrection) and replace it with a general transport union subordinated to the state. His plans enraged not only workers but Bolshevik trade unionists, who saw it as part of a broader campaign to end all independent union rights. In 1920, a Workers' Opposition had emerged within the Party to defend the rights of the unions in management and resist the growing power of centrally appointed factory managers, bureaucrats and 'bourgeois specialists', resented by the workers as a 'new ruling class'.

Moscow was the first industrial city to rebel. Workers went on strike. They called for an end to the Communists' privileges, and the restoration of free trade, civil liberties and the Constituent Assembly. The strikes spread to Petrograd, where similar demands were made. On 27 February, the fourth anniversary of the revolution, the following proclamation appeared in the streets of Petrograd. It was a call for a new revolution:

> The workers and peasants need freedom. They do not want to live by the decrees of the Bolsheviks. They want to control their own destinies.
>
> We demand the liberation of all arrested socialists and non-Party working men; abolition of martial law; freedom of speech, press and assembly for all who labour; free elections of factory committees, trade unions and soviets.
>
> Call meetings, pass resolutions, send delegates to the authorities, bring about the realization of your demands.[9]

That day the revolt spread to the Kronstadt naval base. In 1917 Trotsky had called the Kronstadt sailors the 'pride and glory of the Russian revolution'. They had played a key role in bringing the Bolsheviks to power. But now the sailors were demanding the overthrow of their dictatorship. They elected a new Kronstadt Soviet without Communists.

They demanded freedom of speech and assembly, 'equal rations for all the working people', and an end to the brutal treatment of the peasantry, from which many of the sailors came. Trotsky took command of the suppression of the mutiny. On 7 March, the assault began with a bombardment of the naval base.

This was the crisis situation in which the Tenth Party Congress assembled in Moscow on 8 March. Determined to defeat the Workers' Opposition, Lenin got a vote condemning it, and then forced a secret resolution (one of the most fateful in the history of the Communist Party) banning factions. Henceforth the Central Committee was to rule the Party on the same dictatorial lines as the Party ruled the country; no one could challenge its decisions without exposing themselves to the charge of factionalism. Stalin's rise to power was a product of the ban.

Equally important was the second landmark resolution of the congress, the replacement of food requisitioning by a tax in kind. This abandoned the central plank of War Communism and laid the foundations of the New Economic Policy (NEP) by allowing the peasants to sell their surplus foodstuffs on the free market once the tax in kind was paid. Fearful that the delegates would denounce the NEP as a restoration of capitalism, Lenin insisted that it was needed to quell the peasant uprisings (which he said were 'far more dangerous than all the Denikins . . . and Kolchaks put together')[10] and build a new alliance (*smychka*) with the peasantry.

Meanwhile the Bolsheviks focused on suppressing the popular revolts. On 10 March, 300 Party leaders left the Congress for the Kronstadt Front. After several days of artillery shelling and bombing from the air, 50,000 crack troops crossed the ice at night to storm the naval base. They took it at the cost of 10,000 lives. During the following weeks, 2,500 Kronstadt sailors were shot without trial; hundreds of others were later sent on Lenin's orders to Solovki, the first big Soviet prison camp in the former monastery of a White Sea island, where many died a slower death from hunger, illness and exhaustion. In Petrograd and Moscow the strikes lost momentum after the arrest of their leaders and the restoration of free trade. But the peasant uprisings were harder to suppress, despite the introduction of the tax in kind. In the Volga region, where the requisitionings had resulted in a famine crisis, the peasants fought with more determination because they were now fighting for their lives. Ruthless terror was used against the rebel areas in Tambov and other provinces. Villages were burned. Tens of thousands of hostages were taken, and thousands more were shot, before the resistance was subdued. On the 'internal front' the Bolsheviks had won their civil war. But now they had to learn to rule.

The Civil War was a formative experience for the Bolsheviks. It became their model of success, the 'heroic period' of the revolution when 'any fortress could be stormed'. It shaped their political habits for a generation—until 1941, when another example of military success supplanted it. When Stalin spoke of a 'Bolshevik approach' or of doing things at a 'Bolshevik tempo'—in the Five Year Plans for example—he had in mind the Party's methods in the Civil War. From the Civil War the Bolsheviks inherited their cult of sacrifice; their military style of government, with its constant 'battles' and 'campaigns' on 'fronts'; their insistence on the need to struggle permanently against the revolution's enemies, foreign and internal, which they saw everywhere; their mistrust of the peasants; and their prototype of the planned economy with its militarization of labour and utopian vision of the state as the maker of a new society.

8

LENIN, TROTSKY AND STALIN

The first indications of Lenin's illness appeared in 1921 when he complained of headaches and exhaustion. Some doctors put it down to lead poisoning from Fanny Kaplan's bullets, which were still lodged in Lenin's arm and neck. But others suspected more systemic problems. Their suspicions were confirmed on 25 May 1922, when Lenin suffered a major stroke, leaving his right side virtually paralysed and depriving him for a while of speech.

During that summer, as he recovered at his country house in Gorki, Lenin concerned himself with the question of his succession. He clearly favoured a collective leadership to succeed him. He was particularly worried by the personal rivalry that had developed during the civil war between Trotsky and Stalin.

Both men had qualities that made them natural leaders but neither one was right to succeed him. Trotsky was a brilliant orator and administrator. As the supreme leader of the Red Army, he more than anyone had won the Civil War. But his pride and arrogance—not to speak of his Menshevik past or his Jewish intellectual looks—made him unpopular in the Party. Trotsky was not a natural 'comrade'. He would rather be the general of his own army than a colonel in a collective command. He was an 'outsider' to the rank and file. Although a member of the Politburo, he had never held a lower Party post.

Stalin, by contrast, seemed at first more qualified to manage a collective leadership. During the Civil War he had taken on a number of responsibilities—he was the Commissar for Nationalities, the Commissar of Rabkrin (Workers' and Peasant Inspectorate), a member of the Politburo and the Orgburo (Organizational Bureau), and the Chairman of the Secretariat—so that he had gained a reputation for modest and industrious mediocrity. Short in size and rough in manner with a pock-marked face and Georgian accent, Stalin was made to feel inferior among the Party's more cosmopolitan and intellectual leaders, and one day he would take revenge on them. A secretively vengeful man, he never forgave or forgot a slight from a comrade—a gangster habit he had picked up from the semi-criminal and vendetta-ridden world of the revolutionary underground in the Caucasus. He was especially resentful of those Bolsheviks who minimized his role in 1917, none more so than Trotsky, who portrayed his nemesis as an intellectual non-entity. In *My Life* (1930) Trotsky wrote of Stalin at the time of Lenin's death in 1924:

> He is gifted with practicality, a strong will, and persistence in carrying out his aims. His political horizon is restricted, his theoretical equipment primitive . . . His mind is stubbornly empirical and devoid of creative imagination. To the leading group of the party (in the wider circles he was not known at all) he always seemed a man destined to play second and third fiddle.[1]

All the Party leaders made the same mistake—a fatal one for those who would be wiped out by the terror of the 1930s—of underestimating Stalin's power as a result of the patronage he had accrued from holding all his posts. Lenin was as guilty as the rest. On Stalin's urging, he made him the first General Secretary of the Party in April 1922. It was arguably the worst mistake in the revolution's history.

Stalin's power grew from his control of the Party apparatus in the provinces. As the Chairman of the Secretariat, and the only Politburo member in the Orgburo, he could promote his supporters and obstruct the careers of his opponents. During 1922 alone more than 10,000 provincial officials were appointed by the Orgburo and Secretariat. They were to be Stalin's main supporters in his struggles for the leadership against Trotsky, Zinoviev, Kamenev and Bukharin. Most, like Stalin, came from very humble origins. Mistrustful of intellectuals like Trotsky and Bukharin, they preferred to place their trust in Stalin's practical wisdom, with his simple calls for unity and discipline, when it came to matters of revolutionary ideology.

During Lenin's absence the government was run by the triumvirate (Stalin, Kamenev and Zinoviev), which had emerged as an anti-Trotsky bloc. The three met before Party meetings to coordinate their strategy and instruct their followers on how to vote. Kamenev was fond of Stalin: they had been together in exile in Siberia before 1917. As for Zinoviev, he did not care much for Stalin. But his personal dislike of Trotsky was so all-consuming that he would have sided with the Devil so long as it secured his enemy's defeat. Both men thought they were using Stalin to promote their own claims to the leadership over those of Trotsky, whom they considered the more serious threat.

By September Lenin had recovered and returned to work. He became suspicious of the triumvirate, which was acting like a ruling clique behind his back, and asked Trotsky to join him in a 'bloc against bureau-cracy' (i.e. Stalin and his power base). But then, on 15 December, Lenin suffered a second stroke. Using his powers as the General Secretary, Sta-lin took charge of Lenin's doctors and restricted his visitors. Confined to his wheelchair, and allowed to dictate for only '5 to 10 minutes a day', Lenin was his prisoner. His two main secretaries, Nadezhda Allilueva (Stalin's wife) and Lydia Fotieva, reported to Stalin everything he said.

Between 23 December and 4 January Lenin dictated a series of frag-mentary notes for the forthcoming Twelfth Party Congress which became known as his Testament. Lenin ordered them to be kept secret but his secretaries showed them to Stalin. Throughout these writings there is a sense of deep concern, anxiety, about the way the revolution had turned out. Lenin was concerned with three issues—and in each Stalin was, it seemed, the main problem.

The first of these was the nationalities question and what sort of

union treaty should be signed. It centred on the question of the Bolsheviks' relations with Georgia. Despite his Georgian origins, Stalin was
the foremost of those Bolsheviks criticized by Lenin in the Civil War
for their Great Russian chauvinism towards the national minorities.
Once the Red Army had reconquered Russia's old Imperial borderlands
in Ukraine, Central Asia and the Caucasus, Stalin, as the Commissar of
Nationalities, proposed that the non-Russian republics should join Russia as autonomous regions, effectively depriving them of the right to
secede from the union. Lenin believed they ought to have this right as
sovereign republics because he thought they would want to be a part of
the Soviet federation in any case. As he saw it, the revolution trumped
all national interests.

Stalin's plans were bitterly opposed by the Georgian Bolsheviks,
whose power base depended on their having gained a measure of autonomy from Moscow for their country. The entire Central Committee of
the Georgian Communist Party resigned in protest against Stalin's
policy. Lenin intervened. He was outraged when he learned that in an
argument Sergo Ordzhonikidze, the head of Moscow's Caucasian Bureau
and Stalin's close ally, had beaten up a Georgian Bolshevik. It made him
see Stalin and the Georgian issue in a different light. In his notes for the
congress Lenin called Stalin a 'rascal and a tyrant' who could only bully
and subjugate small nations, whereas what was needed was 'profound
caution, sensitivity, and a readiness to compromise' with their legitimate national aspirations, especially if the Soviet Union was not to
become a new empire and was to pose as a friend and liberator of the
oppressed nations in the colonial world.[2]

Because of Lenin's illness, Stalin got his way. The founding Treaty
of the Soviet Union was basically centralist in character, allowing the
republics to develop cultural forms of 'nationhood' within a political
framework set by the Communist Party of the Soviet Union (CPSU)
in Moscow. The Politburo purged the Georgian Bolsheviks as 'national
deviationists'—a label Stalin would use against many leaders in the
non-Russian regions in the years to come.

Lenin's second concern in his Testament was to make the Party's leading organs more accountable. He proposed to 'democratize' the Central Committee by adding 50–100 new members from the lower Party organs and to open up the Politburo to the scrutiny of the Central Committee. It is doubtful whether these belated efforts to bridge the widening gap between the Party bosses and the rank and file would have resolved the fundamental problem of the Bolshevik dictatorship—its bureaucratism and alienation from the working masses whom it claimed to represent. As Lenin himself wrote in the Testament, the real problem was that the revolution had taken place in a backward peasant country that lacked the necessary 'requisites of civilization' to establish a genuinely socialist government based on the administration of the masses by themselves (the closest he would come to acknowledging that the Mensheviks might have been right). Still, the Bolsheviks needed to relinquish the violent habits of the Civil War and learn how to govern more effectively through the complex mechanisms of the 'state machine'.

The final issue of Lenin's Testament—and the most explosive—was the question of the succession. As if to underline his preference for a collective leadership, Lenin pointed out the faults of the major Party leaders. Kamenev and Zinoviev were compromised by their stand against him in October 1917. Bukharin was the 'favourite of the whole Party but his theoretical views could only be classified as Marxist with reserve'. Trotsky was 'perhaps the most capable man in the Central Committee' but 'displayed excessive self-assurance'. Yet it was for Stalin that Lenin's most devastating criticisms were reserved:

> Stalin is too rude and this defect, although quite tolerable in . . . dealings between Communists, becomes intolerable in a General Secretary. For this reason I suggest that the comrades think about a way to remove Stalin from that post and replace him with someone who has . . . greater tolerance, greater loyalty, greater courtesy and consideration to comrades, less capriciousness, etc.[3]

Lenin was making it clear that Stalin had to go.

His resolve was strengthened on 5 March, when he found out about an incident in December which had been kept from him. Stalin had subjected Krupskaya 'to a storm of coarse abuse' and had even threatened her with an investigation for breaking Party rules after she had taken a dictated letter from Lenin to Trotsky congratulating him on a debating victory against the triumvirate. Lenin was devastated by the incident. He dictated a letter to Stalin demanding an apology for his 'rudeness' and threatening to break off relations. Stalin, who had become completely arrogant with power, could hardly mask his contempt for the dying Lenin in his reply, reminding him that Krupskaya 'is not just your wife but my old Party comrade'.[4]

Lenin's condition worsened overnight. Three days later he suffered his third stroke. It deprived him of speech. Until his death, ten months later, he could only utter single syllables: *vot-vot* ('here-here') and *s'ezd-s'ezd* ('congress-congress').

The Twelfth Party Congress finally convened in April 1923. The Testament was not read out to the delegates as Lenin had intended. The triumvirate saw to that. Trotsky did not fight the decision. He knew he was too weak in the Central Committee.

Instead he posed as the champion of the rank and file against the 'police regime' of the leadership. On 8 October, he wrote an 'Open Letter to the Central Committee' in which he accused it of suppressing democracy in the Party (a hypocritical stance given his own supercentralism in the Civil War) and claimed that this explained the recent workers' strikes in Soviet Russia and the failure of the revolutionary movement in Germany, where workers too were disillusioned with the Communists. Support for Trotsky came from a 'Group of 46' leading Bolsheviks, including Piatakov and Smirnov, whose Declaration formed the basis of the Left Opposition against the triumvirate between 1923 and 1927. Yet this gave Trotsky's enemies the evidence they needed to accuse him of 'factionalism' (a heinous crime since Lenin's ban on factions in March 1921). They also accused him of 'Bonapartism', a charge that relied on his reputation for high-handedness.

At the October Party Plenum Trotsky defended himself by recounting how he had rejected Lenin's offer of high office—once in October 1917 (as Commissar of the Interior) and again in 1922 (as Deputy Chairman of Sovnarkom)—on the grounds that it was unwise to have a Jew in such a senior post given the problem of anti-Semitism in Russia. On the first occasion Lenin had dismissed his objection, but on the second he agreed. Trotsky was calling on Lenin's authority to imply that the opposition to him in the Party was because he was a Jew. It was a tragic moment for Trotsky—not just as a revolutionary but also as a man—that at this vital moment in his life, standing condemned before the Party, he should have to fall back on his Jewish roots. For a man who had never felt himself a Jew, it was a mark of how alone he was.

Trotsky's emotional appeal made little impression on the delegates—most of whom had been picked by Stalin. By 102 votes to two the Plenum passed a motion of censure against Trotsky for 'factionalism'. Kamenev and Zinoviev pressed for his expulsion from the Party, but Stalin (always eager to appear as the voice of moderation) opposed this and the motion was turned down. Stalin, in any case, had no need to hurry. Trotsky was finished as a major political force in the Soviet Union. The Left Opposition remained a noisy critic of the triumvirate but it was impotent against the Party apparatus, which was increasingly in Stalin's hands.

This was confirmed at a meeting prior to the Thirteenth Party Congress, a few months after Lenin's death in January 1924, when, on Krupskaya's insistence, her husband's Testament was read out to the Central Committee and other senior delegates. Stalin offered to resign but Zinoviev and Kamenev persuaded the meeting to disregard Lenin's advice to remove him from the post of General Secretary on the grounds that, whatever offence Stalin had been guilty of, it was not grave, and he had since made amends. Trotsky did not speak at the meeting, no doubt sensing that he had no chance of convincing people otherwise. It was decided to read the Testament to each regional delegation separately but not to discuss it at the congress. In effect the Testament was deprived of the effect which Lenin had intended it to have in removing Stalin from

the leadership. Instead the congress turned into a chorus of denunciation against Trotsky based on calls for Party unity behind Stalin's leadership. Trotsky was unable to resist. He left the congress a defeated man.

Removed from ministerial office in January 1925, Trotsky was
expelled from the Party on 12 November 1927. He had organized an
independent demonstration commemorating the tenth anniversary of
the October seizure of power which had been broken up by the police.
Most of his supporters were excluded too, following a resolution by the
Fifteenth Party Congress in December 1927 in which it was declared
that 'opposition' views were incompatible with Party membership. Zinoviev and Kamenev were expelled from the Party at this time as well.
Having fallen out with Stalin in 1925, they had joined forces with
Trotsky's Left Opposition and several leading figures of the former
Workers' Opposition to establish a United Opposition demanding greater
freedom of expression in the Party (in effect an end to the ban on factions) in 1926. Expelled for constituting a faction, they later both admitted their mistake and were readmitted to the Party. But for Trotsky
there was no way back. Exiled to Kazakhstan, he was deported from the
Soviet Union in 1929.

When did Stalin 'come to power'? It is difficult to say with exacti-
tude because of the confusion Lenin left behind over the question of his
succession. Lenin's leadership was based on his personal authority—the
Bolsheviks were *his* party—and he needed no official post to sanction
that power. After his death it was not immediately possible for any single
leader to assume that same authority. Stalin made an early claim as his
sole successor when he made a speech at a memorial meeting just one
week after Lenin's death pledging to complete the revolution Lenin had
begun. But in truth Stalin was obliged to operate in a collective leadership. It was not until the 1930s that he broke its last restraints on his
dictatorship.

Lenin's death revived the cult of his personality, on which the regime
would increasingly depend for its own sense of legitimacy. Monuments

to Lenin were erected everywhere. Giant portraits of the leader appeared in the streets. Petrograd was renamed Leningrad. Factories, offices and schools set up 'Lenin Corners'—shrines with photographs and artefacts to illustrate his achievements. As Lenin the man died, so Lenin the God was born. Work began on the first edition of Lenin's collected works (the *Leninskii sbornik*), the holy scriptures of the October Revolution.

'Lenin is dead, Leninism lives,' declared Zinoviev at Lenin's funeral. The term 'Leninism' was thus used for the first time. The triumvirate sought to present themselves as its true defenders against Trotsky, the 'anti-Leninist'. From this point, the leadership would invoke 'Leninism' to justify its policies—whatever they may be—and condemn its critics as 'anti-Leninist'. Lenin's actual ideas had always been evolving and changing. They were often contradictory. Like the Bible, his writings could be used to support many different things, and those who followed him would choose those parts that suited them. Stalin, Khrushchev, Brezhnev, Gorbachev—they were all 'Leninists'. But if there was one unchanging principle—the fundamental basis of the Bolshevik dictatorship for three quarters of a century—it was 'Party unity': the Leninist imperative for every Party member to fuse his personality in the collective and submit to the judgement of the leadership. It was on this absolutist principle that any questioning of the Party line was deemed 'anti-Leninist'.

Lenin had wanted to be buried next to his mother's grave in Petrograd. But Stalin insisted on having the corpse embalmed. If he was to keep alive the cult of Lenin, there had to be a body on display, one which, like the relics of the saints, was immune to corruption. Lenin's pickled body was placed in a wooden crypt—later replaced by the granite mausoleum which exists today by the Kremlin wall on Red Square. It was opened to the public in August 1924.

His brain was removed from his body and transferred to the newly opened Lenin Institute. It was sliced up into 30,000 segments, each stored between glass plates in monitored conditions, so that future generations of scientists would be able to study it and discover the 'substance of his genius'.

What would have happened if Lenin had survived a few more years? Would Stalin have come to power? Would the revolution have followed the same path?

The basic elements of the Stalinist regime—the one-party state, the system of terror and the cult of the leader—were in place by 1924. The Party apparatus was already, for the most part, an obedient tool in Stalin's hands. Lenin had allowed all this to come about. His belated efforts at political reform were not going to change the nature of the Bolshevik dictatorship, nor the political attitudes of the Party's rank and file, which had been firmly set by the Civil War.

But there were major differences between Lenin's regime and Stalin's. Fewer people were killed under Lenin for a start. Despite his ban on factions, the Party still made room for fierce but comradely debates while Lenin was alive—and would continue to disagree on policies until the early 1930s, when Stalin imposed a rigid Party line with lethal consequences for those who challenged it. Lenin had no hesitation killing opponents of the revolution but he never had his Party comrades imprisoned or killed for their political opinions.

Above all, it was in his policies towards the peasantry that Lenin differed from Stalin. Lenin would never have allowed the collectivization of agriculture to be carried out in the violent way it was under Stalin's leadership. His vision of the revolution in the NEP was more peasant-friendly, more pluralist and patient, if no less utopian in the longer term, than the 'great break' promised by Stalin when he overturned the NEP in 1928–9. Ultimately, then, the question about Lenin and the revolution's fate rests on the chances of the NEP, and it is to this that we now turn.

9

THE REVOLUTION'S GOLDEN AGE?

The restoration of the market brought back life to the Soviet economy. Private trade responded instantly to the chronic shortages that had built up over seven years of war, revolution and the Civil War. By 1921 everyone was living in patched-up clothes and shoes, cooking with broken utensils. People set up booths and stalls; flea-markets flourished; peasants sold their foodstuffs in town markets; and 'bagging' to and from the countryside once again became a mass phenomenon. Licensed by new laws, private cafés, shops and restaurants, even small-scale manufacturers appeared like mushrooms after the rain. Foreign observers were astounded by the transformation. Moscow and Petrograd, dying cities in the Civil War, sprang back into life, with noisy traders, busy cabbies and bright shop signs livening up the streets just as they had done before 1917. 'The NEP turned Moscow into a vast market place,' wrote Emma Goldman, the American anarchist, in 1924:

Shops and stores sprang up overnight, mysteriously stacked with delicacies Russia had not seen for years. Large quantities of butter, cheese and meat were displayed for sale; pastry, rare fruit, and sweets of every variety were to be purchased. . . . Men, women and children with pinched faces and hungry eyes stood about gazing into the windows and discussing the great miracle: what was but yesterday considered a heinous offence was now flaunted before them in an open and legal manner.[1]

How could these hungry people buy such goods? For many Bol-sheviks the return of private trade was a betrayal of the revolution. It seemed to them that it would lead to a widening gap between rich and poor. 'We young Communists had all grown up in the belief that money was done away with once and for all,' recalled one Bolshevik. 'If money was reappearing, wouldn't rich people reappear too? Weren't we on the slippery slope that led back to capitalism? We put these questions to ourselves with feelings of anxiety.'[2] Their doubts were reinforced by the rise of unemployment in the first years of the NEP. While laid-off work-ers lived on the bread line, the peasants, they assumed, were getting rich. 'Is this what we made the revolution for?' Goldman heard a Red soldier say.[3] Among the workers there was a widespread feeling that the NEP was sacrificing their class interests to the peasantry, that it would allow the 'kulaks' to come back, and with them the capitalist system would return. Tens of thousands of Bolshevik workers tore up their Party cards in disgust with the NEP: they renamed it the 'New Exploi-tation of the Proletariat'.

Much of this plebeian anger was directed against the 'NEPmen', the new class of businessmen who thrived with the return of private trade. In the popular imagination, shaped by Soviet propaganda and cartoons, the 'NEPmen' dressed their wives and mistresses in diamonds and furs, drove around in huge imported cars, and boasted loudly in expensive hotel bars of the dollar fortunes they had wasted at the newly opened race tracks and casinos. The legendary spending of these *nouveaux riches*, set against the backdrop of urban poverty, gave rise to bitter resentment among those who thought the revolution should end ine-quality.

For Lenin the NEP was more than a temporary concession to the mar-ket in order to get the country back on its feet. It was a radical if ill-formulated effort to redefine the role of socialism in peasant Russia, where, largely as a result of his own party's coup d'état in 1917, the 'bourgeois revolution' had not been completed. Only 'in countries of developed capitalism' was it possible to make an 'immediate transition to socialism', Lenin had told the Tenth Party Congress. Soviet Russia was thus confronted with the task of 'building Communism with bourgeois hands', which for the Bolsheviks meant letting peasants create wealth through the market.

Lenin saw the NEP as a necessary concession to the peasantry to save the *smychka*—the worker–peasant alliance on which the revolution would depend. That alliance would be built on the exchange of manufactured goods and food. By allowing the peasants to sell their surplus freely after they had paid the 20 per cent tax in kind, the NEP aimed to stimulate their market sales. This would feed the towns and through taxation raise the capital for state investment in the manufacturing of basic household items the peasants wanted for their grain. By taxing this exchange and exporting food, the state would pay for the imported tools and machines it needed to industrialize.

The NEP was presented as a strategic retreat. 'We are taking one step backwards, to take two steps forward later on,' Lenin had assured its many doubters in 1921. But how long it should last was left unclear. The Bolshevik leader talked of 'not less than a decade and probably more'— suggesting that the NEP was to be adopted 'not as a form of political trickery' to save the revolution from popular revolts but 'seriously' and 'for an entire historical epoch'.[4] He saw the NEP as a long-term programme to advance towards socialism through a mixed economy. Responding to fears that it might allow capitalism to return, he argued that as long as the state controlled the 'commanding heights of the economy' (e.g. steel, coal, the railways), there was no danger in allowing small-scale private farming, trade and handicrafts to satisfy consumer needs.

For the Party that emerged from the Civil War this was a radically different vision of the revolution from the one it had fought for. War Communism had promised to arrive at Communism fast by stamping out all signs of private trade. In a backward peasant country such as Russia it was easy for the Bolsheviks to reach for state coercion—the dragooning of the population into labour teams—as a way to close the gap with the more advanced industrial societies. But the NEP meant going more slowly—'on the peasant cart' as Bukharin put it—towards the revolution's goal. The slow pace of the NEP raised serious concerns. What would happen if the revolution lost all forward momentum? If in slowing down it allowed inertia to creep in? Wouldn't it succumb to the bourgeois habits and mentalities of the old society which remained so dominant and threatened to seduce the Party's rank and file? Wasn't there a danger of the revolution being undermined by its internal enemies—the 'kulaks' and petty capitalists—as they grew rich from private trade? Would the country industrialize fast enough to defend itself if war broke out against the capitalist states?

Urban opposition to the NEP was sharpened by the occasional breakdown of the market mechanism—which was bound to happen after years of war and revolution—resulting in shortages of food in the state shops. The root of the problem was the absence of consumer goods to trade with the peasants. Industry was badly damaged by the Civil War. It took longer to recover than the peasant farms, which had bumper harvests in 1922 and 1923. The result was a widening gap (what Trotsky termed the 'scissors crisis') between deflated agricultural prices and steeply rising prices for consumer goods. As the price of manufactures rose, the peasantry reduced its grain sales to the state depots. The procurement rates paid by the state were too low for the peasants to afford the household items they needed—some of which they could make for themselves in their own cottage industries (ploughs, ropes, shoes, candles, soap and simple wooden furniture). Instead of selling grain at low prices, the peasants fed it to their cattle, stored it in their barns, and sold it to the private traders and bagmen.

To combat the breakdown of the food supply the government resorted to civil-war-style requisitioning, reduced industrial costs to boost productivity, and, in response to working-class resentment of the 'NEPmen', closed down 300,000 shops and market stalls. By April 1924 the immediate crisis had been solved. But the breakdown of the market remained a potential problem for the NEP.

The Bolsheviks were divided about how to deal with the issue. Those on the left of the Party favoured keeping agricultural prices low and taking grain by force if necessary to increase industrial production; whereas those on the right argued for higher procurement prices, even if this entailed slowing down the rate of capital accumulation for industrialization, to preserve the *smychka* and the market mechanism as the basis of the state's relations with the peasantry.

They were also disunited on the international context of the NEP. When the Bolsheviks had taken power they had all assumed that the Revolution would soon spread to the more advanced industrial societies. In their view socialism was unsustainable in Russia on its own because it lacked the industries it needed to defend itself against the 'imperialist' powers. By the end of 1923 it was becoming clear that revolutions were unlikely in Europe. The immediate post-war instability had passed. In Italy the Fascists had come to power to restore order. In Germany the strikes backed by the Communists had failed to develop into larger uprisings. Abandoning the idea of exporting the revolution as an immediate goal, Stalin advanced the policy of 'socialism in one country'. It was a dramatic turnaround in the Party's revolutionary strategy. Instead of waiting, as had been universally assumed, for support to come from the industrial states, the Soviet Union would now have to become self-sufficient and defend itself by building industries with capital extracted from its own economy. It would export grain and raw materials to pay for tools and machines imported from the West. Developed by Bukharin, the idea was adopted as the Party's policy in 1926. But it was condemned by the Left Opposition as a fundamental break from Marxist ideology, which ruled out building socialism in a single country isolated from the world.

The NEP allowed for a mixed economy in which the state and socialized sectors would compete with the private. Under the NEP a socialist
economy would be brought about by state regulation, fiscal measures
and agronomic aid to encourage the peasants to join collective farms
and agricultural cooperatives.

Lenin attached great importance to the role of the cooperatives. He
thought they were the key to the building of a socialist society in a peasant country such as Russia because they were the 'simplest, easiest
and most acceptable' mode of socialist distribution and exchange for
the peasants. Supported by the state, the cooperatives could offer the
peasants a guaranteed rate of exchange between their produce and consumer goods. They could provide credit to buy tools or help the peasants to improve their land with fertilizers, irrigation or agronomic aid
to rationalize their landholding and solve the problem of their narrow
strips in the commune. In this way the cooperatives were meant to wean
the peasants off the private traders and integrate them in a socialized
sector where the state could influence their farming practices. It was a
measure of the NEP's success that half the peasant farms belonged to an
agricultural co-operative by 1927. As a result there was a steady rise in
productivity: the 1913 levels of agricultural production were regained
by 1926; the harvest yields of the mid-twenties were 17 per cent higher
than those of the 1900s, the so-called 'golden age' of Russian agriculture.

If the NEP had lasted as long as Lenin had intended, it might have
served as an example of socialist development in the Third World.
Based on its buoyant agricultural sector, the Soviet economy grew
rapidly between 1921 and 1928. Industry did well, arguably achieving
higher rates of growth than in the 1930s. If the NEP had continued, the
country would have been in a far stronger position to resist the Nazi
invasion in 1941 than it was as a result of Stalin's economic policies
after 1928. Instead, the NEP was overturned by mass collectivization
which permanently crippled Soviet agriculture and destroyed millions
of peasant lives.

The NEP had always involved plans for agricultural collectivization.

Ideologically the Bolsheviks were committed to the long-term goal of transforming the communes into large collective farms (kolkhozes) where all the land could be farmed together, production could be mechanized, and the state could guarantee its food supply through fixed contracts with these farms. But this was to be a gradual and voluntary process in which the peasants were to be encouraged to form collective farms through state financial and agronomic aid. After 1927 greater pressure was exerted through taxation policies. But there was no question of forcing any peasants to join the collectives. In fact force was not needed. The peasants anyway were attracted to the small collectives known as TOZes, where the land was farmed in common but the livestock and the tools remained their private property. The TOZes grew in number from 6,000 in 1927 to 35,000 in 1929. With more time, they would have formed a significant collective-farming sector within the NEP. With agronomic aid from the cooperatives, they would have become efficient modern farms led by the strongest peasants—the 'kulaks'. But Stalin would have none of that. He wanted larger collectives where all the land, the tools and livestock were collectivized, and forced the peasants to join these. The result was a national catastrophe.

The NEP entailed a reprieve for the remnants of 'bourgeois culture' which the revolution promised to eliminate but could not yet do without. It brought a halt to the war against the professional class—the 'bourgeois specialists', technicians, engineers and scientists—whose expertise was needed by the Soviet economy. It also meant a relaxation in the war against religion: churches were no longer closed or the clergy persecuted as they had been before (or would be afterwards). Under Lunacharsky, the Commissar of Enlightenment, the Bolsheviks adopted a permissive cultural policy. The artistic avant-garde of Russia's 'Silver Age', the first two decades of the century, continued to flourish in the third, when many artists took inspiration from the revolution's promise to create a new and more spiritual world.

The NEP, however, did not mean a halt in the war against bourgeois customs and mentalities (what they called *byt*). With the ending of the Civil War, the Bolsheviks prepared for a longer struggle on this cultural front. They saw the revolution's goal as the creation of a higher type of human being—more collective, more actively engaged in public life— and set about the liberation of this personality from the individualism of the old society. The Communist utopia would be built by engineering this New Soviet Man.

From Marx the Bolsheviks had learned that consciousness was formed by the environment. So they set about their task of human engineering by formulating social policies to alter modes of thinking and behaviour.

The family was the first arena where they engaged. They viewed the 'bourgeois family' as socially harmful—a stronghold of religion, patriarchal oppression and 'egotistic love' that would disappear as Soviet Russia developed into a fully socialist system with state nurseries, laundries and canteens. *The ABC of Communism* (1919) envisaged a future society in which adults would jointly care for all the children in their community.

Meanwhile the Bolsheviks adopted policies to weaken family ties. They took marriage away from the control of the Church and turned divorce into a matter of simple registration, resulting in the highest rates of divorce in the world. To tackle the housing shortages they organized communal apartments (*kommunalki*), accommodating typically a family per room with one shared kitchen and toilet. By getting people to live communally, the Bolsheviks believed they could make them more collective in nature: private space and property would disappear; family life would be replaced by Communist fraternity and organization; and the individual would be subjected to the mutual surveillance and control of the community.

During the mid-1920s new types of housing were designed with this in mind. Constructivist architects designed 'commune houses' where all the property, including even clothes, would be shared by the inhabitants, domestic tasks like cooking and childcare would be assigned to teams on a rotating basis, and everybody would sleep in one big dormitory, divided by gender, with private rooms for sex. Few houses of this sort were built—they were too ambitious to be finished in the brief time Constructivist ideas were politically acceptable—but they loomed large in the utopian imagination and in dystopian novels such as Zamyatin's *We* (1920).

For the Bolsheviks education was the key to the creation of a socialist society. Through the schools and Communist youth leagues they aimed to indoctrinate the young in the new collective way of life. 'Children, like soft wax, are very malleable and should become good Communists,' declared one theorist. 'We must rescue these children from the nefarious influence of family life . . . we must nationalise them.'[5] The cultivation of socialist values was the guiding principle of the Soviet school curriculum. There was an emphasis on teaching children science and economy through practical activities. Schools were organized as microcosms of the Soviet state: work plans and achievements were displayed in graphs and pie-charts on the walls; pupils were encouraged to set up councils and monitors to police the teachers for 'anti-Soviet' views; there were even classroom 'trials' of children who had broken the school rules. To instil an ethos of obedience some schools introduced a system of politicized drilling, with marches, songs and oaths of allegiance to the Soviet leadership.

Children played at being 'revolutionaries'. One of the most popular courtyard games of the 1920s was Reds and Whites, a Soviet Cowboys and Indians in which the events of the Civil War were played out by the children, often using air-guns marketed especially for the game. Another was Search and Requisition, in which one group would play the role of a requisitioning brigade and another act as 'kulaks' hiding grain. Such games encouraged children to accept the Soviet division of the world into 'comrades' and 'enemies', and to accept violence for a just end.

Politically, the education system was geared towards producing activists. Children were indoctrinated in the practices and rituals of the Soviet system so that they would grow up to become committed Communists. The Party needed to expand its membership, especially in country areas, where the number of active Bolsheviks was a minuscule proportion of the population. This generation—the first to be schooled in the Soviet system—was ripe for recruitment.

At the age of ten Soviet children joined the Pioneers, established in 1922 on the model of the Scout movement, where they swore an oath 'to stand firmly for the cause of our Communist Party'. One in five children belonged to the organization by 1925, and the number grew in later years. Pioneers did a lot of marching and singing, gymnastics and sport. With their special uniforms (a white shirt and red scarf), banners, flags and songs, they gave children a strong sense of belonging. Those excluded from the Pioneers (as many were because of 'bourgeois' origins) were made to feel inferior.

At fifteen, children could progress from the Pioneers to the Komsomol, the Communist Youth League. Not all made the grade. In 1925 the Komsomol had a million members—about 4 per cent of the fifteen- to 23-year-olds. To join the Komsomol was to start a Communist career. The organization functioned as a reserve army of enthusiasts, providing volunteers for Party work as well as spies and informers ready to denounce corruption and abuse. It had a broad appeal to a generation too young to have fought in the Civil War but brought up in the cult of activism inspired by its memory in the 1920s and '30s. Many people joined the Komsomol not because they were Communists, but because they had no other channel for their social energy.

'Bolshevism has abolished private life,' wrote Walter Benjamin on a visit to Moscow in 1927. 'The bureaucracy, political activity, the press are so powerful that no time remains for interests that do not converge with them. Nor any space.'[6] People were obliged in many ways to live completely public lives. The revolution did not tolerate a 'private life' free from public scrutiny. There were no party politics but everything people did in private was 'political'—from what they read and thought to whether they were violent in the family home—and as such was subject to the censure of the collective. The ultimate aim of the revolution was to create a transparent society in which people would police themselves through mutual surveillance and the denunciation of 'anti-Soviet' behaviour.

Some historians think it succeeded—that by the 1930s it had managed to create an 'illiberal Soviet subject' who lost his own identity and values in the public culture of the state. In this interpretation it was practically impossible for the individual to think or feel outside the terms defined by the public discourse of the Bolsheviks and any dissenting thoughts or emotions were likely to be felt as a 'crisis of the self' demanding to be purged from the personality.[7] Perhaps this was so for some people—the young and impressionable who had been indoctrinated through schools and clubs, adults who behaved like this from fear—but they were surely a minority. Indeed one could argue just the opposite—that constant public scrutiny drove people to withdraw into themselves and live behind a mask of Soviet conformity to preserve their own identity. They learned to live two different lives—one in public, where they mouthed the language of the revolution and acted out the part of loyal Soviet citizens; the other in the privacy of their own homes, or the internal exile of their heads, where they were free to speak their doubts, or tell a joke.

The Bolsheviks were frightened of this hidden sphere of freedom. They could not tell what people were thinking behind their masks. Even their own comrades could be hiding anti-Soviet thoughts. The purges began here—in the Bolsheviks' need to unmask potential enemies.

The debate about the NEP came down to a question about time. How long would it take for the Soviet Union to industrialize through the mechanisms which the NEP allowed—accumulating capital by taxing peasant farms and market sales, fixing prices to favour industry, and exporting grain to pay for new machinery? Would it be fast enough to build the defence industries the Soviet Union needed before the outbreak of a war with the capitalist states?

The question about time was related to the broader issue of the regime's relations with the peasantry. What should it do if the market mechanism broke down once again and there were grain shortages, especially if these occurred when there was a danger of a war? Should it pay the peasants more and have less for investment in industry? Or return to requisitioning and endanger the alliance with the peasantry?

As the Party's main supporter of the NEP, Bukharin favoured raising the procurement prices, even if this meant that industrialization progressed at the pace of a peasant cart. Assessing the situation in 1926, he claimed that industry had managed to regain its pre-war levels and would continue to do well under the NEP. He was confident that the USSR faced neither an external threat (foreign trade was easing relations with the capitalist states) nor an internal one (the danger of the 'kulak' and 'private profiteer' was being counteracted by the rapid growth of the cooperatives).

Two events occurred in 1927 to turn Bolshevik opinion against the NEP. The first was another breakdown in the supply of grain to the cities. A poor harvest coincided with a shortage of consumer goods, and as the price of manufactures rose the peasants reduced their sales of grain. The state's procurements from the peasantry that autumn were half what they had been the previous year. The second incident was a war scare. The press reported false rumours that the British were about to launch an 'imperialist war' against the Soviet Union. Stalin exploited these reports to attack the United Opposition, accusing its leaders, Trotsky and Zinoviev, of undermining the unity of the Soviet state at a time of grave danger. The two issues—the 'kulak' grain strike and the threat of war with the capitalist states—were connected in his view.

Trotsky and Zinoviev opposed raising the procurement price. They favoured a temporary return to requisitioning to secure the stocks of food needed by the state to boost production of consumer goods. That in turn would give the peasants more incentive to sell their grain. At this point Stalin sided with Bukharin against Trotsky and Zinoviev, who were defeated at the Fifteenth Party Congress in December 1927. But after that he turned against Bukharin and the NEP. His Machiavellian tactics show a complete disregard for ideology in the pursuit of power.

Returning to the violent language of the Civil War, Stalin called for a new battle for grain to industrialize the Soviet Union in a Five Year Plan. The war scare played into his hands, enabling him to push for the NEP to be abandoned on the grounds that it was too slow as a means of industrial armament, and too uncertain as a means of procuring food in the event of war.

Stalin's Five Year Plan was based on a radicalized vision of the revolution as an unending 'class struggle' with foreign and internal 'enemies'. He spoke in violent terms about rooting out the final remnants of the capitalist economy (petty trade and peasant farming), which, he claimed, had blocked the country's progress to socialist industrialization. In his political battles with Bukharin during 1928–9, he accused his rival of subscribing to the 'dangerous' view that the class struggle would lessen over time and that 'capitalist elements' could be reconciled with a socialist economy. This assumption, Stalin argued, would only lead the Soviet state to lower its defences against its enemies, thus allowing them to infiltrate the system and subvert it from within. In a precursor to the twisted logic by which he rationalized the spiral of state violence leading to the Great Terror, Stalin reasoned, on the contrary, that the resistance of the bourgeoisie was bound to intensify as the country moved closer to socialism, so that ever-growing vigour was required to 'root out and crush the opposition of the exploiters'.

Stalin's call for a return to the class struggle of the Civil War appealed to a broad section of the Party's rank and file, among whom there was a growing sense that the NEP represented a retreat from the revolution's goals. His rhetoric of industrial progress had a powerful appeal to all those lower-class Bolsheviks who as young men had fled the peasant world of icons and cockroaches, and who saw the revolution as an overturning of this legacy of poverty. Most of them had joined the Party in the Civil War and had been promoted by Stalin. They were practical people, without much grasp of Marxist theory, whose allegiance to the Bolsheviks was intimately linked with their own identity as 'proletarians'. They identified with Stalin's simple vision of the Five Year Plan as a new revolutionary offensive to overcome the country's backwardness and make it a great industrial power in the world.

Stalin's fighting words also had a special attraction to younger Communists—those born in the first two decades of the century—who were too young to have fought in the Civil War but who had been educated in the 'cult of struggle' based on stories about it. One Bolshevik (born in 1909) maintained in his memoirs that the militant world-view of his contemporaries had prepared them to accept Stalin's arguments about the need for 'renewed class war' against the 'bourgeois specialists', 'NEPmen', 'kulaks' and other 'hirelings of the bourgeoisie'. Young Communists had become frustrated with the NEP. 'The Komsomols of my generation—those who met the October Revolution at the age of ten or younger—took offence at our fate,' explained one Stalinist. 'When our consciousness was formed and we joined the Komsomol, when we went to work in factories, we lamented that nothing would be left for us to do, because the revolution was gone, because the severe [but] romantic years of civil war would not come back, and because the older generation had left to our lot [only] a boring, prosaic life that was devoid of struggle and excitement.'[8]

Here was the cohort of enthusiasts that would be the pioneers of Stalin's 'revolution from above', the beginning of the revolution's second generational phase.

Stalin responded to the grain crisis by returning to the methods of the Civil War. Requisitioning was backed up by a series of 'emergency measures'—including the notorious Article 107 of the Criminal Code which allowed the brigades to arrest any peasants and confiscate their property if they were suspected of withholding grain. Known as the 'Urals-Siberian method', the relative success of this 1928 campaign, albeit at the cost of many tens of thousands of ruined peasants' farms, persuaded Stalin to press ahead with more coercive measures to break the 'kulak grain strike' and secure the necessary food for the industrial revolution promised by the Five Year Plan. The 'battle for grain' was leading Stalin and his supporters towards crash collectivization.

10

THE GREAT BREAK

On the twelfth anniversary of the October Revolution, Stalin wrote an article in *Pravda*, 'The Year of the Great Break', in which he heralded the Five Year Plan as the start of the last great revolutionary struggle against 'capitalist elements' in the USSR, which would end in the foundation of a Communist industrial society. 'We are advancing full steam ahead along the path of industrialization—to socialism, leaving behind the age-old "Russian" backwardness,' he wrote on 7 November 1929.

> We are becoming a country of metal, a country of automobiles, a country of tractors. And when we have put the USSR on an automobile, and the peasant on a tractor, let the worthy capitalists, who boast so much of their 'civilization', try to overtake us! We shall see which countries may then be classified as backward and which as advanced.

What Stalin meant by the 'great break', as he explained to Gorky, was the 'total breaking up of the old society and the feverish building of the new'.[1]

This utopian vision of the country's transformation was the inspiration of the Five Year Plan (1928–32), Stalin's industrial and cultural revolution, in which his regime—and the lasting institutions of the Soviet system—were founded.

The plan's targets were utopian. Its original production goals, supported by Bukharin and his allies on the Party's Right, had been optimistic but not impossible. But they were raised dramatically by Stalin in 1929. Industrial investment was to triple, coal and steel production to double, and pig-iron production to quadruple by 1932. In a wave of frenzied optimism the Soviet press advanced the Stalinist slogan 'The Five Year Plan in Four!' Time itself was speeding up.

The Five Year Plan promised to create a society of universal abundance for the proletariat. Soviet propaganda persuaded people that hard work and sacrifice would be rewarded in the future, when everybody would enjoy the fruits of their collective labour. A young worker of these times recalled:

We Soviet people consciously denied ourselves a lot. 'Today we don't have things that we really need. Well, so what? We shall have them tomorrow.' That was the power of our belief in the Party's cause! Young people of my generation were happy in this belief.[2]

But when the Five Year Plan had been completed, this paradise had not been reached, and another plan was introduced. By the carrot and the stick the Soviet people were driven by the state to go on working for the Communist utopia, which was always imminent but never came. The Five Year Plan became the basic model of Soviet development. It was Stalin's legacy.

The 'great break' began with collectivization, the foundation of the Five Year Plan. Far more than the events of 1917–21, the collectivization of agriculture was the real revolution in the countryside. It destroyed a way of life that had developed over many centuries—a life based on the family farm, the peasant commune, the village and its church, all of which were to be swept away as legacies of 'backwardness'. Millions of people were uprooted from their homes and dispersed across the Soviet Union. This nomadic population became the main labour force of Stalin's industrial revolution, filling the great cities and building-sites, the labour camps and 'special settlements' of the Gulag.

Collectivization was driven less by economics than by politics and a general mistrust of the peasantry. Marxist ideology had taught the Bolsheviks to see the peasant way of life as incompatible with a Communist society. Peasants were too tied to patriarchal customs, too imbued with the individualistic principles of free trade and private property, despite the commune, and too wedded to the family and its smallholding, ever to be fully socialized. Almost independent in their villages, they could hold the state to ransom by withholding grain. Stalin's revolution aimed to break that 'kulak threat' by controlling food at the point of its production in collective farms.

From 1929, Stalin spoke with growing enthusiasm about the potential of large and mechanized collective farms. Statistics showed that the few such farms already in existence had a much larger marketable surplus than the small agricultural surpluses produced by the peasant family farms. But these big collectives were hardly representative. Most collectives were smaller, not unlike the TOZes, and had no tractor, no mechanic to maintain it if they did, and no agronomist to make the necessary land improvements to produce such higher yields.

Beginning that summer, thousands of enthusiasts were sent into the countryside to agitate for the collective farms. Most of the peasants were afraid to give up a centuries-old way of life, to make such a leap into the unknown. The collectivizers resorted to coercive measures. Reinforced by army and police units, they went into the villages with strict instructions not to come back without organizing a collective farm. 'Throw your bourgeois humanitarianism out of the window and act like Bolsheviks worthy of Comrade Stalin,' they were told. 'Beat down the kulak agent wherever he raises his head. It's war—it's them or us! The last decayed remnant of capitalist farming must be wiped out at any cost!'[3]

During just the first two months of 1930, roughly half the Soviet peasantry (around 60 million people in 100,000 villages) was herded into the collective farms. The collectivizers used various tactics of intimidation at the village meetings where the decisive vote was taken to form a collective. In one Siberian village, for example, where the peasants were reluctant to accept the motion to collectivize, troops were brought in and those opposed were asked to speak—when no one dared, it was declared that the motion had been 'passed unanimously'. In other villages the meeting was attended by a small hand-picked minority, but the result of the vote was made binding on the population as a whole.

Peasants who spoke out against collectivization were threatened and harassed, sometimes beaten, and arrested; many were expelled as 'kulaks' from their homes and driven out of the village. The war against the 'kulaks' was not a side-effect but the driving force of collectivization, which was conducted as a war against the revolution's enemies. It had two main aims: to remove potential opposition; and to serve as an example to the other villagers, encouraging them to join the collective farms in order not to suffer the same fate. As Stalin saw it, there was nothing to be gained from trying to neutralize the 'kulaks,' nor from attempting to involve them as farm leaders or even labourers in the kolkhozes, as some Bolsheviks had suggested. 'When the head is cut off,' Stalin argued, 'you do not weep about the hair.'[4]

In January 1930, a Politburo commission drew up a target of 60,000 'malicious kulaks' to be sent to labour camps and 150,000 other 'kulak' households to be exiled to the north, Siberia, the Urals and Kazakhstan. The figures were part of an overall plan for 1 million 'kulak' households (about 6 million people) to be dispossessed and sent to labour camps or 'special settlements'. The fulfilment of the quotas was assigned to OGPU (the political police), which raised the target to between 3 and 5 per cent of all peasant households and then handed quotas down to local OGPU and Party organizations (which frequently exceeded them to demonstrate their vigilance). The rural Soviet, Komsomol and Party activists drew up lists of 'kulaks' for arrest in each village. In many the peasants chose the 'kulaks' from their own number (isolated farmers, widows and old people were particularly vulnerable). In some they drew lots to decide.

It is difficult to give accurate statistics for the number repressed as 'kulaks'. At the height of the campaign the country roads were jammed with long convoys of deportees, each one carrying the last of their possessions or pulling them by cart. One eye-witness in the Sumy region of Ukraine saw lines 'stretching as far as the eye could see in both directions, with people from new villages continually joining', as the column marched towards the collecting points on the railway.[5] By 1932, there were 1.4 million 'kulaks' in the 'special settlements', mostly in the Urals and Siberia, and even larger numbers in labour camps attached to Gulag factories and construction sites, or simply living on the run. Stalin called this social holocaust the 'liquidation of the kulaks as a class'.

The men and women who fought this brutal war against the peasantry were mostly soldiers and workers without the education to question state orders. Hatred of the 'kulak parasites' and 'bloodsuckers' had been drummed into them. 'We were trained to see the kulaks, not as human beings, but as vermin, lice, which had to be destroyed,' recalled the leader of a Komsomol brigade in the Kuban.[6]

Others were 'Enthusiasts'. Inspired by the revolutionary passions stirred up by the propaganda for the Five Year Plan, they thought they were advancing to a Communist society, and believed that any sacrifice was justified to reach that end. In the words of one of the '25,000-ers', the urban army of enthusiasts sent into the countryside to help with the campaign: 'Constant struggle, struggle and more struggle! This was how we had been taught to think—that nothing was achieved without struggle, which was a norm of social life.'[7]

According to this militant world-view, the creation of a new society would necessarily involve a life-or-death struggle with its 'enemies'. The 'anti-kulak' terror could thus be justified with Communist beliefs and hopes. Lev Kopelev, then a member of the Komsomol who took part in brutal actions against the Ukrainian peasants, recalled years later (when he was a dissident) that he was appalled by the children's screams; but he told himself not to 'give in to debilitating pity. We were realizing historical necessity. We were performing our revolutionary duty. We were obtaining grain for the socialist fatherland. For the Five Year Plan.'[8]

The 'anti-kulak' violence was also justified as a necessary measure against village uprisings. The Soviet police registered 44,779 'serious disturbances' against collectivization during 1929–30. Communists and rural activists were attacked in their thousands. In many villages women led the protests in the defence of their church, which had been targeted as a 'kulak' institution by the Bolsheviks and generally either destroyed or turned into a farm building. The country was returning to the peasant wars of 1921. But now the regime was too strong for the rebels to succeed. Aware of their impotence, many peasants took up passive resistance. They ran away from the collective farms, committed acts of arson, and slaughtered their own livestock to prevent them being taken for the collectives. The number of cattle in the Soviet Union fell by half from 1928 to 1933.

Faced with the ruin of the agricultural sector, Stalin called for a temporary halt to the campaign. In an article in *Pravda* ('Dizzy With Success') on 2 March 1930, he accused local officials of excessive zeal in setting up kolkhozes by decree. Millions of peasants saw this as a licence to leave the collectives, and they voted with their feet. The population of the collective farms fell from 58 to 24 per cent of peasant households between March and June.

But in September Stalin launched a second, even more ambitious offensive to collectivize at least 80 per cent of the peasantry (up from 50 per cent the first time around) by the end of 1931. OGPU prepared a thousand 'special settlements', each to receive up to 300 'kulak' families, in the north, the Urals and Kazakhstan. Two million people were exiled to these remote regions during 1930–31.

The destruction of the 'kulaks' was a catastrophe for the Soviet economy. It deprived the collective farms of the best and hardest-working peasants, because these are what the 'kulaks' actually were, ultimately leading to the terminal decline of the Soviet agricultural sector. But Stalin's war against the 'kulaks' had little to do with economic considerations—and everything to do with eliminating the defenders of the peasant way of life.

Large collective farms amalgamated land from several villages. Many of the smaller settlements and their churches were abandoned or destroyed. The peasants were turned into agricultural workers in kolkhoz brigades. They received a small cash payment once or twice a year, and they got a food ration, which they were expected to supplement by growing vegetables and keeping pigs and chickens on their private garden plots. Tied to the collective farm by an internal passport system, the peasants thought of collectivization as a 'second serfdom'.

The collective farms were a dismal failure. They never really worked. In the early years, few had tractors to replace the horses slaughtered by the peasantry (human draught was used). They were badly run by managers appointed for their loyalty to the state rather than their agricultural expertise. They were under constant pressure to minimize their running costs in order to fulfil their compulsory 'contracts' with the state. But Stalin's aims had been achieved: the independent peasantry had been eliminated as an obstacle to the revolution's progress; and the regime had got its hands on the agricultural surpluses to invest in industry.

The outcome of this wholesale seizure of the harvest—encouraged by exaggerated surplus estimates from local officials eager to win favour from Moscow—was widespread famine in 1932–3. The number of deaths is impossible to calculate accurately, but demographers suggest that up to 8.5 million people died of starvation or disease. The worst-affected areas were in Ukraine, where peasant resistance to collectivization was particularly strong and the grain levies were excessively high. This has prompted some historians to argue that the 'terror-famine' was a calculated policy of genocide against Ukrainians—a claim enshrined in law by the Ukrainian government and recognized in all but name by the United Nations and the European Parliament.

Stalin had a special distrust of the Ukrainian peasantry. He was more than capable of bearing grudges against entire nationalities, and of killing them in large numbers, as he would demonstrate during the

Great Terror and the war. The Kremlin was undoubtedly negligent towards the famine victims and did very little to help them. If it had stopped exporting food and released its grain reserves, it could have saved million of lives. Instead, the government prevented people fleeing from the famine area, officially to stop diseases spreading, but also to conceal the extent of the crisis from the outside world. Perhaps it used the famine as a punishment of 'enemies'. In the reported words of Lazar Kaganovich, who oversaw collectivization and grain procurements in Ukraine, the death of a 'few thousand kulaks' would teach the other peasants 'to work hard and understand the power of the government'.[9] But no hard evidence has so far come to light of the regime's intention to kill millions through famine, let alone of a genocide campaign against the Ukrainians. Many parts of Ukraine were ethnically mixed. There is no data to suggest that there was a policy of taking more grain from Ukrainian villages than from the Russians or other ethnic groups in the famine area. And Ukraine was not the only region to suffer terribly from the famine, which was almost as bad in Kazakhstan.

Millions of peasants ran away from the collective farms. By the early months of 1932, there was a whole people on the move, crowding railway stations, desperately trying to escape the famine areas. The cities could not cope with this human flood. Diseases spread. Pressure grew on housing, food and fuel supplies, encouraging the migrants to move from town to town in search of better conditions.

Peasants poured into the towns in search of work. Between 1928 and 1932 the urban population grew at the staggering rate of 50,000 people every week. Frightened that its industrial strongholds would be overrun by disgruntled peasants, the Politburo introduced a system of internal passports to control immigration to the cities. Passport checks were used by the police to purge the major towns of 'socially dangerous elements' ('kulaks', traders, disgruntled peasants) who might become a source of opposition to the Soviet regime. The mass influx did, however, provide Soviet industry with a plentiful and cheap supply of labour. During the first Five Year Plan the state invested heavily in big construction projects and mining where unskilled peasant labour could be used.

To meet the fantastic targets of the plan, industrial managers had to 'storm' production by working round the clock, paying workers piecerates dependent on their meeting output norms, and organizing shock brigades with the best workers on the highest rates. Brigades and factories competed with each other to fulfil their norms in 'socialist competitions' with league tables, medals and rewards for the highest productivity—a movement that would later become known as Stakhanovism (after the 'model' coalminer Aleksei Stakhanov, who broke all records in 1935 by mining fourteen times his quota, 102 tons of coal in less than six hours). The subject of a propaganda cult, Stakhanov and his emulators were rewarded with consumer goods, better housing, higher rates of pay, and often with promotion into management and official positions, which made them loyal Stalinists. But the system also led to friction between the shock-workers and their managers when problems at the workplace held back the brigades from meeting their production norms.

The 'storming' of production increased pressure on the factory managers to maintain supplies of fuel and raw materials. If production had to stop for want of these, workers could not meet their output norms and would suffer loss of pay. They were quick to accuse the managers of 'sabotage' or 'wrecking' when the real cause of the problem was the plan's unrealistic targets. The regime encouraged these accusations: it was the only way it could explain the chaos produced by its own planning. The Soviet press attacked the so-called 'bourgeois managers' (i.e. those who held their jobs before 1917), accusing them of industrial sabotage. Arrests began with the Shakhty Trial in 1928, when a group of fifty-three engineers in the North Caucasian mining town of Shakhty were tried for conspiring with the prerevolutionary owners of the mines to 'sabotage' the Soviet economy after a decline in production (five were shot and forty-four were imprisoned). This was the first of the show trials, and the start of the industrial terror when hundreds of 'bourgeois specialists' were sacked, shot or sent to labour camps.

In an unusually passionate speech to industrial managers on 4 February 1931, Stalin defended the ambitious targets of the Five Year Plan ('there are no fortresses the Bolsheviks cannot capture') and pointed to the failures of management as the only obstacle to their fulfilment. To slow down the tempo of industrial progress would expose the country to the danger of military defeat by hostile foreign powers, as had happened throughout Russia's history, he argued, and this would be a betrayal of Leninist principles. For the first time, Stalin invoked Russian nationalism in defence of the revolution—a theme he would repeat often after 1941:

> One feature of the history of old Russia was the continual beatings she suffered because of her backwardness. She was beaten by the Mongol khans. She was beaten by the Turkish beys. She was beaten by the Swedish feudal lords. She was beaten by the Polish and Lithuanian gentry. She was beaten by the British and French capitalists. She was beaten by the Japanese barons. All beat her—because of her backwardness . . .
>
> That is why we must no longer lag behind . . .
>
> Do you want our socialist fatherland to be beaten and to lose its independence? If you do not want this, you must put an end to its backwardness in the shortest possible time and develop a genuine Bolshevik tempo in building up its socialist economy. There is no other way. That is why Lenin said on the eve of the October Revolution: 'Either perish, or overtake and outstrip the capitalist countries.'
>
> We are 50–100 years behind the advanced countries. We must make up this distance in ten years. Either we do this, or they will crush us.[10]

Stalin's final warning turned out to be prophetic. Ten years later, in 1941, Germany invaded the Soviet Union.

The rates of growth that Stalin had demanded in the Five Year Plan could not have been achieved without the use of forced labour, particularly in the cold and remote regions of the far north and Siberia, where so many of the Soviet Union's precious economic resources (diamonds, gold, platinum and nickel, oil, coal and timber) were located but where nobody would freely go. The Gulag was the key to opening up these areas for Soviet industry. Sending millions of prisoners to dig mines and canals, build railways and chop down forests in Arctic zones made an incalculable contribution to the country's economic growth.

The word 'Gulag' is an acronym for the Main Administration of Corrective Labour Camps and Colonies. The Soviet prison system started as a means of isolating 'counter-revolutionary elements'. But with the beginning of the Five Year Plan it became a form of economic colonization—a cheap and rapid way of settling and exploiting the industrial resources of the far north and Siberia through an archipelago of labour camps and colonies, factories, canals, mines and railway-building sites—a slave economy that would spread its dark shadow over the entire Soviet Union.

Solzhenitsyn placed the Gulag at the heart of the Bolshevik experiment. Forced-labour camps had been set up in the Civil War, mainly as a means of punishing the revolution's enemies, but for economic projects too. In some ways the mentality that led to the Gulag had its origins in the Bolshevik view of human beings as raw material, a commodity to be expended by the state to reach the revolution's goals. Trotsky spoke of the labour armies he conscripted in the final stages of the Civil War as 'peasant raw material' (*muzhitskoe syr'ie*). Around the same time the Bolsheviks began to talk of the 'workforce' (*rabsila*) rather than the 'working class' (*rabochii klass*)—a symbolic shift that turned the workers from an active agent of the revolution into an object of the planned economy. Here were the intellectual origins of the Gulag—in the idea of dragooning long lines of half-starved and ragged slaves on to building sites. It was only later, to mask this slave economy, that the Bolsheviks developed the lofty rationale of *perekovka* (the 'reforging' of deviant human beings through corrective labour) as a philosophical justification for the Gulag labour camps.

The labour camps of the 1920s were basically prisons in which the inmates were made to work for their keep. The pattern was set at Solovki, the Solovetsky Camp of Special Significance (SLON), which had been established by OGPU in the former White Sea island monastery in 1923.

One of the prisoners at Solovki was Naftaly Frenkel, a businessman from Palestine arrested for smuggling contraband to Soviet Russia. Shocked by the prison's inefficiency, Frenkel wrote a letter setting out his ideas on how to run the camp, and put it in the 'suggestions box' (they had them even in prisons). Somehow the letter got to Genrikh Yagoda, the fast-rising OGPU boss. Frenkel was whisked off to Moscow, where he explained his Darwinian plans for the economic use of prison labour to Stalin. Prisoners, he said, should be organized by their physical abilities and given rations only if they met their work quota. The strong would survive and the weak would die, but that would improve efficiency and rations would not be wasted.

Frenkel was released in 1927 and placed in charge of turning SLON into a profit-making enterprise. The prison's population expanded rapidly, from 10,000 in 1927 to 71,000 in 1931, as SLON won contracts to fell timber and build roads, and took over factories in Karelia.

By 1929, the Soviet prison system could no longer cope with the mass arrests of 'kulaks', 'bourgeois specialists', 'wreckers', 'saboteurs' and other 'enemies' of Stalin's forced industrialization. The Politburo set up a commission, including Yagoda, to examine the possible use to which the prison population could be put. Stalin favoured Yagoda's proposal to develop the industrial resources of the far north and Siberia through a network of 'experimental' camps, each with 50,000 prisoners, controlled by OGPU. By concentrating larger numbers in the camps, Yagoda proposed, the costs of maintaining this slave labour force could be reduced through economies of scale from 250 to just 100 roubles per capita per year. In June 1929, the Politburo passed a resolution ('On the Use of Prison Labour') instructing OGPU to establish a network of 'correctional-labour camps' for the 'colonization of [remote] regions and the exploitation of their natural wealth through the work of prisoners'.

From this point, the political police became one of the main driving forces of Soviet industrialization. It controlled a rapidly expanding empire of corrective labour camps, whose population reached 1 million by 1934, when OGPU was replaced by the NKVD (People's Commissariat of Internal Affairs). The NKVD assumed control of the political police and through the Gulag ran the labour camps.

The first major Gulag project was the White Sea Canal (Belomorkanal), 227 kilometres of waterway between the Baltic and the White Sea, which employed 100,000 prisoners by 1932. It was a fantastically ambitious project, given that the planners intended to complete it without machines or even proper surveys of the land. Critics argued that the huge construction costs could not be justified given the little shipping on the White Sea. But Stalin was insistent that the canal could be built both cheaply and in record time—a symbol of the Party's will and power in the Five Year Plan—as long as OGPU supplied sufficient prison labour to dig it all by hand.

Frenkel was in charge of construction. The methods he had used in Solovki were re-employed on the canal, as were many of the prisoners. To save time and money, the depth of the canal was reduced from twenty-two feet to just twelve, rendering it virtually useless for all but shallow barges and passenger vessels. Prisoners were given primitive hand tools—crudely fashioned axes, saws and hammers—instead of dynamite and machinery. Worked to exhaustion in the freezing cold, an estimated 25,000 prisoners died during the first winter of 1931–2 alone. Their frozen corpses were thrown into the ditch.

In August 1933 the canal was opened by Stalin. A few weeks later it was toured by a 'brigade' of leading Soviet writers, who sang its praises in a volume commissioned by OGPU to celebrate its completion. Edited by Gorky, who had recently returned from exile to the Soviet Union, the book's chief theme was the redemptive power of physical labour. It was a propaganda victory. Western socialists were taken in (Sidney and Beatrice Webb called the canal 'a great engineering feat' and a 'triumph in human regeneration').[11] In the Soviet Union a new brand of cigarettes (Belomorkanal) was launched to mark this great breakthrough. Built on top of bones, the canal was a fitting symbol of the Stalinist regime, whose greatest propaganda successes were achieved with total disregard for the millions of lives they cost.

11

STALIN'S CRISIS

Stalin's wife committed suicide on 8 November 1932. They had been at a Kremlin dinner to celebrate the fifteenth anniversary of the October Revolution. Stalin had been flirting with the wife of a Red Army commander. He was cold and rude, as he often was, to Nadezhda. Their marriage was breaking down. Her determination to be more than a housewife by interesting herself in politics had annoyed him for some time. He knew that she was close to Bukharin, and that she was horrified by what she had learned about collectivization from her fellow-students at the Industrial Academy, where he had allowed her to study.

There was a lot of drinking at the dinner. Stalin had proposed a toast to the destruction of the 'enemies of the state'. Nadezhda did not raise her glass. Stalin goaded her, demanding to be told why she was not drinking. He threw orange peel and flicked cigarette butts at her across the table. Then she shouted at him to 'Shut up!', and stormed out. She went to her room and shot herself with a pistol.

Nadezhda had a history of depression with violent mood swings. Perhaps the humiliation of this scene had tipped her over the edge. But she left behind a note, which, according to their daughter Svetlana, was not only personal but political, 'full of reproach and accusations', in which she said she was opposed to everything that was going on. In her room there was a copy of the Riutin platform, a 194-page manifesto written by a senior Bolshevik and ally of Bukharin criticizing Stalin's policies and calling for the overthrow of his dictatorship. It had circulated widely among the Party's rank and file. After reading Nadezhda's suicide letter, 'it would have been possible for my father to think that my mother had been on his side only outwardly, but in her heart had been on the side of those who were in political opposition to him,' wrote Svetlana.[1]

Stalin was unhinged by Nadezhda's suicide. It humiliated him and reinforced his fear of enemies, even in his closest circles. The real cause of her death was concealed from the public, which was told instead that she had died of appendicitis. People wrote in their thousands to express their condolences to Stalin, whose cult ironically was boosted by this tragedy. But nothing could console him at the funeral, where 'tears ran down his cheeks' as he stood beside her open coffin, according to Molotov, his closest political ally, who had never seen him cry before. As they were about to close the lid, he bent down, lifted his wife's head, and began to kiss her ardently, weeping uncontrollably.[2]

Nadezhda's suicide was the last in a year of crises for Stalin. The bad run had begun that spring with a series of strikes in the Ivanovo and Volga industrial regions, Ukraine, Belorussia, the Urals and Siberia. Workers were refusing to operate machines, attacking officials, and looting stores.

Their living standards had been driven down by the Five Year Plan. In real terms workers' wages in 1932 were half their 1928 level. Pay rates were deflated by the mass influx of peasants into industry. Working hours were increased to meet the plan, and food rations were reduced to increase grain exports to pay for new machines and tools. 'There's no bread, no meat, no fats—nothing in the shops,' an OGPU official admitted to the British ambassador in an unguarded moment.[3]

In the Ivanovo region, 200 kilometres north-east of Moscow, 16,000 textile workers went on strike. The workers drew from their collective memory of labour protests during 1917. Older workers with families to feed were in the forefront of these strikes. They were angered by cuts in their rations and harsh new measures to enforce labour discipline.

Although their grievances were mainly economic, some of their leaders made political speeches denouncing the 'utopian' Five Year Plan and calling for the ending of the Bolshevik dictatorship. Quick to punish any protest as 'counter-revolutionary', OGPU arrested the strike leaders and the protests were subdued. But other signs of discontent—anti-Soviet graffiti, 'hooliganism', swearing at authority, thefts and absenteeism from work—were much harder to suppress.

People grumbled—sometimes openly—about the Soviet regime. They sang rhyming songs (*chastushki*) and told subversive jokes and anecdotes:

> A Bolshevik is explaining to an old woman what Communism will be like. 'There will be plenty of everything,' he said, 'food, clothing, every kind of merchandise. You will be able to travel abroad.'
>
> 'Oh,' she said, 'like under the Tsar!'

> 'Capitalism is the exploitation of man by man. Socialism is the opposite.'

> 'What nationality were Adam and Eve?'
>
> 'Soviet, of course. Who else would walk around barefoot and naked, have one apple to share between them, and think they were in Paradise?'[4]

The function of these jokes is not easy to interpret. For many they were just a way to have a laugh, to let off steam; for others an expression of freedom; but for some they were political, a challenge to the system, as George Orwell meant when he wrote in an essay about English humour that 'every joke is a tiny revolution'. That for sure is how they were regarded by the Soviet regime, because telling or listening to such jokes was deemed a crime against the state (Article 58-10 of the penal code: 'Anti-Soviet and counter-revolutionary propaganda and agitation') punishable by at least six months (and often many years) in the Gulag.

There was grumbling in the Party too. Stalin had brought the country to the brink of catastrophe by 1932. Crash collectivization and industrialization had created endless misery and chaos for which officials were made to take the blame. With famine stalking the countryside and people going hungry in the towns, it was they who had to deal with the consequences of Stalin's policies.

Stalin was a 'fallen idol'. That was the claim of a Moscow Party official in a letter to Trotsky's *Bulletin of the Opposition* in Paris written in the spring of 1932. Stalin's recent appearance at the Bolshoi Theatre had been 'greeted with cold silence' by the Party rank and file assembled there.[5] It was this groundswell of anti-Stalin opinion that made the emergence of opposition factions in the leadership so threatening to the General Secretary. Two factions came to his attention during 1932.

One was an informal group of Old Bolsheviks—the political élite of the revolution's first generational cycle—led by A. P. Smirnov, V. N. Tolmachev, the recently dismissed Interior Commissar, and N. B. Eismont, all three members of the Party's Central Committee. They held meetings in Eismont's apartment, and at one of these, on the fifteenth anniversary of the October Revolution, there was talk of removing Stalin from the leadership. Told about the meeting by someone who'd been there, Stalin had the Eismont group arrested by OGPU.

The other opposition faction was organized by Martemyan Riutin, an Old Bolshevik and follower of Bukharin, whose manifesto had been read by Stalin's wife. The manifesto of the Riutin Platform, 'Stalin and the Crisis of the Proletarian Dictatorship', was a blistering critique of Stalin's politics and personality, denouncing him as a mediocre theoretician, 'unscrupulous political intriguer' and the 'gravedigger of the revolution' by virtue of his catastrophic policies. Calling themselves 'The League of Marxist-Leninists', the group accused Stalin of 'breaking with Leninism', by which they meant not just the principles but the whole

Party culture of the generation that had carried out the October Revolution, and 'perpetrating violence against both the party and non-
party masses'. They demanded an end to collectivization, a slow-down
of industrialization, and the reinstatement of expelled Party members on the Right and Left (including Trotsky and his followers). In a
separate 'Appeal' to the Bolsheviks, Riutin called for the overthrow
of the Stalinist dictatorship.[6]

Betrayed by an informer, Riutin and his circle were arrested on 23
September. After a report by the Central Committee's Presidium, twenty-
four of them were expelled from the Party and exiled from Moscow as
'enemies of Communism and Soviet power, traitors to the Party and
working class, who have tried to form an underground bourgeois–kulak
organization under a fake "Marxist-Leninist" banner for the purpose of
restoring capitalism in the USSR'.[7] Several other Bolsheviks, including
Kamenev and Zinoviev, were expelled from the Party and exiled for
simply knowing of the group's existence and failing to report it to the
police.

There is a story that Stalin wanted the death penalty for Riutin and
his followers, but that he was blocked by a 'moderate' group of Politburo
members led by Sergei Kirov, the Party boss of Leningrad, who was
opposed to breaking Lenin's dictum against the spilling of Bolshevik
blood. If it's true, it would fit with what we know about Stalin's thirst for
vengeance against 'enemies' in the Party. Riutin was sentenced to ten
years in prison. But on Stalin's orders he was shot in 1937, five years into
his sentence.

The Riutin Affair set Stalin on his way to the Great Terror, the final
break with the revolution's Old Bolshevik phase. It left him with a para-
noid conviction that his 'enemies' were everywhere. He became obsessed
by the memory of the criticism he had faced in 1932 and by his desire
for vengeance not just against his critics but against those moderates in
the leadership who had prevented him from dealing them a mortal blow.
In the coming years he would refer frequently to the 'new situation'—by
which he meant a massive plot against the government—that had begun

in 1932. A large number of the Bolsheviks who fell victim to the Great Terror stood accused of having being been involved in the Riutin Affair.

Among the Politburo 'moderates' who tempered Stalin's policies was Ordzhonikidze, the Minister of Heavy Industry, who called for an end to the chaos and repression of the Five Year Plan and more stability in industry. And for a brief time there was a halt in the industrial terror. Economic managers enjoyed more security. 'Cadres decide everything!' became the slogan of the second Five Year Plan (1933–7).

The regime also gave the appearance of moving towards more legality. Under pressure from the moderates, a Soviet Procuracy was created, and OGPU was replaced by the NKVD, which did not have the power of its predecessor to impose the death sentence, nor to hand out 'administrative' punishments of more than five years in exile. Abuses by OGPU were investigated by a Politburo commission.

But Stalin never lost sight of his aim to tighten his control of the Party and police, using terror and extra-legal means to destroy his 'enemies'. In April 1933, he announced a general purge of the Party's ranks. The categories of people to be purged did not include groups opposed to Stalin's leadership. But these were clearly the main targets of the purge's stated mission to expel 'open and secret violators of the iron discipline of the Party . . . who cast doubt on and discredit its decisions and plans'.[8]

A staggering 18 per cent of the Party's 3.2 million members were expelled in the purge. Most were relatively new recruits, who had joined the Bolsheviks since 1929, when controls on enrolment were relaxed, resulting, it was feared, in the influx of 'careerists' whose loyalty could not be trusted. It is striking that the leadership remained so insecure more than fifteen years after coming to power. That insecurity was rooted in the problem—faced by many revolutionary movements—that once it found itself in power the Party could not trust its own members and needed constantly to test their loyalty. The problem was exacerbated by the speed with which the Party's membership had grown since 1917, with waves of mass enrolment from a population on which it could not rely to share the same commitment as the veterans of the underground or the early revolutionary years.

At purge meetings in Party and Soviet organizations, trade unions and institutes across the land, Bolsheviks were questioned about their political opinions. They were made to answer criticisms from comrades. These meetings could get very personal, as the eleven-year-old Elena Bonner discovered, when she observed a purge in the hostel of the Comintern (Communist International) in 1934:

> They asked about people's wives and sometimes about their children. It turned out that some people beat their wives and drank a lot of vodka ... Sometimes the one being purged said that he wouldn't beat his wife anymore or drink anymore. And a lot of them said about their work that they 'wouldn't do it anymore' and that 'they understood everything.' Then it resembled being called into the teacher's room: the teacher sits, you stand, he scolds you, the other teachers smile nastily, and you quickly say, 'I understand,' 'I won't,' 'of course, I was wrong,' but you don't mean it, or just want to get out of there to join the other kids at recess. But these people were more nervous than you were with the teacher. Some of them were practically crying. It was unpleasant watching them. Each purge took a long time; some evenings they did three people, sometimes only one.[9]

As well as purging the Party, Stalin promoted a new élite of workers from the factory floor (*vydvizhentsy*) who took jobs in management and the Soviet bureaucracy. The industrial revolution of the Five Year Plan created a huge demand for technicians, functionaries and managers in all branches of the economy. According to Gosplan (the state planning agency), 435,000 engineers and specialists were needed for the new demands of industry in 1930 alone. The old 'bourgeois specialists'— purged in their thousands during the industrial terror—also had to be replaced. Stalin's power was thus based on a social revolution, with loyal servitors from 'proletarian' origins given opportunities for promotion and the old managers and officials coming under pressure from below. Through this social revolution—which underpinned the terror of the 1930s—a new Stalinist élite emerged whose outlook shaped the character of the revolution's second generational cycle.

Education was the key to social mobility. Workers were encouraged to enrol in factory schools and technical institutes to train as engineers and managers. Between 1928 and 1932, 150,000 workers were given higher education on this affirmative-action programme; over a million left the factory for administrative jobs. They became the mainstay of the Stalinist regime. They believed in Stalin's vision of progress because they could see improvements in their lives from it. Through their loyalty to the leader they rose through the Party's ranks. Their ascent was quickened by the purges of the thirties, when bosses were removed, allowing those below to move into their jobs. By the end of Stalin's reign, the *vydvizhentsy* of the Five Year Plan would make up a large proportion of the Party leadership (fifty-seven of the top 115 ministers in the Soviet government of 1952, including Nikita Khrushchev, Leonid Brezhnev, Andrei Gromyko and Alexei Kosygin, had been promoted from the factory floor during 1928–32).

This new Stalinist élite was generally conformist and obedient to the leadership that had created it. Few had more than elementary schooling or much capacity for independent thinking about politics. Their knowledge of Marxist ideology was limited. They took their ideas from the statements of the Party leaders and parroted their Soviet-speak. Revering Stalin as the source of all wisdom, they were eager to promote their own careers by implementing his orders.

The values of this new élite were very different from those of the Old Bolsheviks whom they replaced. The Old Bolsheviks had generally lived in spartan conditions and denied themselves material rewards out of sacrifice for the revolutionary cause. During the 1920s there had even been a 'Party Maximum'—a cap on salaries for Bolsheviks. But the new Stalinist élites were rewarded for their loyalty with higher rates of pay, access to consumer goods in special shops for Party members, private apartments, Soviet titles and honours. In the competition for material and political rewards it did not take a lot for this type of functionary to turn against his rivals. This goes a long way to explain the ease with which the terror spread through Party ranks. An official wrote to Kalinin, the Soviet President, in December 1932:

> The trouble with Soviet power is that it gives rise to the vilest official—an official who carefully understands and carries out the general designs of the supreme authority, one that always heaps blame on the sinister machinations of the devil. This official never tells the truth because he doesn't want to distress the leadership. He gloats about famine and pestilence in the district controlled by his rival . . . All I see around me is loathsome politicizing, dirty tricks being played, and people being trapped for slips of the tongue. There's no end to the denunciations . . . Of course, the purge of your party is none of my business, but I think that as a result of it the more decent elements still remaining in your party will be cleaned out.[10]

In *The Revolution Betrayed* (1936), Trotsky wrote that Stalin's power rested on a vast 'administrative pyramid' of bureaucrats, which he numbered at 5 million or 6 million officials. This ruling caste was a 'new bourgeoisie'. Their interests centred on the comforts of the home, on the acquisition of material possessions, on 'cultivated' pursuits and manners.[11] They were socially reactionary, clinging to the customs of the patriarchal family, conservative in their cultural tastes, even if they believed in the Communist ideal. Their main aim was to defend the established Soviet order, from which they derived their material well-being and position in society.

Through the purging of opponents and the promotion of his supporters, Stalin thought he had reshaped the Party in his own image by the start of 1934. On 26 January, he told the 1,966 delegates at the opening session of the Seventeenth Party Congress, the first since 1930, that what he called the 'anti-Leninist' opposition groups within the Party (i.e. those who questioned Stalin's policies) had been defeated, although he also warned in threatening terms that 'remnants of their ideology still live in the minds of individual members of the Party'.[12] Bukharin, Rykov, Tomsky, Radek and other former critics of his policies publicly recanted their 'errors' and united behind Stalin's leadership. The correctness of Stalin and his Five Year Plan appeared indisputable.

The Congress coincided with the tenth anniversary of Lenin's death. Stalin gave his opening address exactly ten years after his 'Oath Speech', in which he had pledged to complete the revolution Lenin had begun (see page 132). The symbolic meaning of this carefully arranged coincidence was underlined by the orchestrators of the Stalin cult, which reached fever pitch in January 1934.

In the months leading up to the congress Stalin's image had started to appear alongside Lenin's in the press. On New Year's Day, *Pravda* published a long article, 'The Architect of Socialist Society', by Radek, the former Trotskyist, written as if it were a lecture in a series on 'The History of the Victory of Socialism' delivered on the fiftieth anniversary of the October Revolution. As if looking back from the perspective of 1967, Radek wrote of the decade between 1924 and 1934 as a 'world-historic victory of Leninism' brought about by Stalin. The General Secretary had proved to be 'Lenin's best pupil, the model of the Leninist Party', as 'far-sighted as Lenin', his equal as a thinker and revolutionary strategist, whose Five Year Plan had completed the building of a socialist society begun in October 1917. The fantasy concluded with a re-creation, in Socialist Realist style, of the scene in Red Square on May Day, 1934:

On Lenin's Mausoleum, surrounded by his closest comrades-in-arms—Molotov, Kaganovich, Voroshilov, Kalinin and Ordzhonikidze—stood Stalin in a grey soldier's greatcoat. His calm eyes gazed reflectively at the hundreds of thousands of proletarians marching past Lenin's tomb with the firm step of a shock troop of future conquerors of the capitalist world. He knew that he had *fulfilled the oath taken ten years earlier over Lenin's coffin*. And all the working people of the USSR and

the world revolutionary proletariat knew it too. And toward the com-
pact figure of our *vozhd'* [leader], calm as a promontory, flowed waves
of love and faith, waves of confidence that there, on Lenin's tomb, was
gathered the staff of the future victorious world revolution.[13]

Stalin was so pleased with this projected judgement of posterity that he
had Radek's article reissued as a pamphlet in a huge print-run of 225,000
copies.

On the opening day of the Party congress *Pravda* announced—as an
accomplished fact—socialism's triumph under Stalin's leadership. Its
headline dubbed it the 'Congress of Victors'.

In fact the congress marked the last revolt against Stalin from within
the Party's ranks. During the secret ballot to elect the Central Committee it was rumoured that Stalin had received at least 150 negative votes
(the custom in Party elections was to actively vote for or against each
candidate). But the ballot papers were destroyed. Only three votes were
recorded against him. There was, it seems, opposition brewing among
the regional Party secretaries, who were unhappy with Stalin's policies
and looking to replace him with the 'moderate' Kirov. Whether Kirov
knew of this alleged conspiracy remains unclear. It is unlikely that he
seriously considered joining it. Since the death of Stalin's wife, Kirov
had become extremely close to the leader; he was practically a member
of the family. But Stalin was angry. He saw treachery in everyone—a
paranoia amplified by the anonymous leadership ballot—and was afraid
of Kirov as a challenger.

On 1 December, Kirov was murdered in the Smolny Institute by a
disgruntled Party member known to be a danger but mysteriously
allowed by the NKVD to enter the building with a revolver and find
Kirov in his offices. Stalin's complicity in the assassination cannot be
established. But there is no doubt that he used it to eliminate his political enemies.

Within hours of the murder, Stalin took control of the investigation
and issued an emergency decree (approved by the Politburo two days
later) ordering summary trials and executions of suspected 'terrorists'

(6,500 people were arrested under the new law in December alone). Stalin blamed the 'Zinovievites' for the murder (Zinoviev was a former
Party boss of Leningrad) and demanded their arrest as 'German Fascist
White-Guard spies' (843 former associates of Zinoviev were arrested
in January–February 1935). The campaign of repression quickly spread
through Leningrad: 11,000 'former people' (members of the fallen aristocracy and bourgeoisie, tsarist bureaucrats, etc.) were arrested and sent to
camps or places of exile. It also went through the Party's ranks. In the
Party purge of 1935, a staggering 250,000 members were expelled, most
of them investigated by the NKVD and accused of being 'anti-Leninists'.
The close involvement of the NKVD in a Party purge was something
new. It set the pattern for the Great Terror.

Stalin was the driving force of this campaign. When Yagoda complained that his NKVD officials were uneasy about arresting so many
Party comrades, Stalin told him to be more vigilant, or else 'we will slap
you down'.[14] Yagoda's position was further undermined by the Kremlin
Affair, when Nikolai Yezhov, Stalin's main police assistant in the Party
purge, claimed to have uncovered a large network of 'foreign spies' and
'terrorists' in the Kremlin during the early months of 1935. Supposedly
organized by Trotsky and Zinoviev, the conspiracy had gone undetected
by the NKVD. On Stalin's orders, Yezhov began a purge of Kremlin
employees—cleaners, librarians and officials of the Central Executive
Committee, whose chairman, Abel Yenukidze, was expelled from the
Party for helping 'former oppositionists' find employment in the Kremlin.

Yenukidze was one of Stalin's oldest Georgian friends. He was Nadezhda's godfather and had danced with her at the Kremlin dinner on the
night she killed herself. Yenukidze's removal was the first blow felt by
Stalin's inner circle. It spelled the end of the collective leadership that
had emerged in support of Stalin's policies during the first Five Year
Plan.

Stalin's next attack was against Ordzhonikidze, his old comrade
from the Civil War. As Commissar of Heavy Industry, Ordzhonikidze
was a keen protector of 'his people' in the industrial bureaucracy. He
was the last effective defender of a collective leadership and the only

man who could put a brake on Stalin's purge of the Party. Stalin was determined to break his influence. He was angered by his patronage of V. V. Lominadze, who had dared to criticize his policies. In 1935, the NKVD began to fabricate a case against Lominadze, who committed suicide. Piatakov, Ordzhonikidze's deputy, was arrested for alleged links to Zinoviev and Kamenev in September 1936. Ordzhonikidze's older brother was arrested and tortured, a fact that Stalin let him know. Then, in November, a group of his executives was put on trial as 'Trotskyists' and 'wreckers' after an explosion in the Kemerovo coal mines in Siberia. Ordzhonikidze planned to criticize the arrests at the Central Committee plenum scheduled for the end of February. But on 18 February he died. His death was reported as a heart attack. But this was a lie. As with Stalin's wife, the truth was far too dangerous to reveal. In 1956 it was announced by Khrushchev that Ordzhonikidze had committed suicide, but rumours of his murder persisted. Who knows? Perhaps Stalin had him killed.

12

COMMUNISM IN RETREAT?

'Life has improved, comrades,' Stalin told a conference of Stakhanovites in November 1935. 'Life has become more joyous. And when life is joyous, work goes well.' After the grim and joyless years of the early 1930s, the Stalinist regime placed a new emphasis on material well-being and the pursuit of pleasure in the mid-decade as part of its consolidation of power. The goal of Communism was now said to be 'the organization of a rich and cultured life for all members of society'.

This was a far cry from the spartan culture of the early revolutionary years and the sacrifice demanded by the Five Year Plan. Since 1917 the Bolsheviks had tried to eradicate the 'petty bourgeois' wish for property. But now Stalin argued that this desire was a part of human nature which socialism could not change. At a congress for kolkhoz labourers in 1935 he defended the idea of letting workers keep three cows as personal property. 'A person is a person,' Stalin said. 'He wants to own something for himself.' There was 'nothing wrong in this', and it would 'take a long time to rework the psychology of the human being, to re-educate people to live collectively'.[1]

How should we explain this turnaround? Trotsky called it the 'Soviet Thermidor'—a reference to the Thermidorian Reaction against the Jacobins after 1794 when more conservative policies were introduced by the French revolutionaries—by which he meant that Stalin had retreated from the Communist ideals of October 1917. In *The Revolution Betrayed* Trotsky blamed this Thermidor on the triumph of the Stalinist bureaucracy, whose material aspirations were advanced by the regime in exchange for its loyalty.

From the other end of the political spectrum, the émigré professor of sociology Nicholas Timasheff would draw a similar conclusion in his influential book *The Great Retreat* (1946). He argued that the Bolsheviks had deliberately retreated from Communist initiatives, because these had clearly led to disaster and the loss of popular support. Faced with the growing military threat of Nazism, Timasheff maintained, the Soviet leadership had tried to strengthen national unity and rebuild state authority by appealing to the people's conservative interests—their desire for material improvement, the pursuit of happiness, traditional family values and nationalism in the arts. Communism was made national, and the national was recast in Soviet form. Whether one agrees with Timasheff or Trotsky, the consolidation of the Stalinist regime was surely based on its attempt to mobilize support on more solid and familiar principles than the revolution's earlier utopian dreams.

Stalinism was constructed on a social hierarchy structured by the granting of material rewards. For those at the top these rewards were immediately available for hard work and loyalty; for those lower down they were promised in the future, when Communism had been reached. In this way the regime was connected to an aspirational society. It sustained itself in power by permanently widening the range of winners in the Soviet system—state officials, the technical élites and intelligentsia, military and police officers, and the most industrious workers—and by rewarding them with better rates of pay, consumer goods and other benefits which only the government could give (private apartments, dachas, holidays in sanatoria, access to closed shops, etc.). At the heart of this social hierarchy was the idea of service to the state—not dissimilar to the way the tsarist system granted ranks and property to the nobility in exchange for its military and civil service before 1917.

After 1932 the government increased its investment in consumer industries, which had been starved of capital in the rush to build new factories and towns during the first Five Year Plan. By 1935, the supply of foodstuffs, clothes and household goods had markedly improved. Rationing was lifted, giving rise to an optimistic mood as shop windows filled with goods. Cameras, gramophones and radios were mass-produced for the aspiring 'middle class'. There was a steady rise in the production of luxury goods—perfumes, chocolate, cognac, caviar and 'Soviet champagne' (produced on Stalin's personal initiative)—whose prices were reduced on holidays.

The myth of the 'good life' that was just around the corner stood at the centre of Communist belief during the 1930s. It projected the illusion that luxury goods previously afforded only by the rich were being made accessible to the masses. Consumer magazines were published to inform the Soviet shopper about the growing availability of clothing, fashions and furnishings. Huge publicity was given to the opening of department stores and luxury food shops, like the former Eliseev store, renamed Grocery No. 1, which reopened on Moscow's Gorky Street in October 1934. Very few of these new luxuries were in practice available or affordable to ordinary people. Most were sold in model shops for prices well beyond the average citizen's earnings. But the publicizing of these consumer goods had an important impact on morale. Propaganda images of Soviet abundance created an incentive for people to work harder in the hope that one day they might afford these goods.

Despite its egalitarian ideals, the Soviet Union was in fact a highly stratified society. There were infinite gradations between employees—based on status in the workplace, skill level and experience—that defined their pay and access to rewards. Families of government workers received provisions which could be very hard to find in Soviet shops (meat, sausage, dairy products, sugar, caviar, cigarettes, soap, etc.). They could purchase clothes and shoes from special stores with coupons from the government. Below the Soviet élite nobody had much. Clothes and shoes were kept for years. Basic goods were often missing in the shops (a subject on which there was no shortage of Soviet jokes). Goods unavailable in the state stores were often sold at high black-market prices out of the back door. To cope with the problems of supply an 'economy of favours' operated through informal networks (a system known as '*blat*'). It was possible to obtain almost anything through contacts.

The 1930s saw a marked increase in wage differentials between the highest- and lowest-paid workers. This was a retreat from the earlier Soviet policy of wage equalization—one of the main goals of the workers' revolution in 1917.

Housing too reflected growing inequalities. While new blocks of private flats were built for the élite, 80 per cent of the urban population lived in overcrowded communal apartments in the 1930s—a way of living that remained the norm for urban residents throughout the Stalin period. The mass influx of peasants into the cities put enormous pressure on the urban housing stock. In Moscow the average person had just 5.5 square metres of living space in 1930, falling to only 4 square metres in 1940. In the new industrial towns, like Magnitogorsk, where house-building lagged far behind the growth of the population, the situation was far worse. Most of the workers lived in factory barracks or dormitories where families were broken up and a curtain around their plank-beds provided privacy.

The communal apartment was a microcosm of the Communist society. Its inhabitants knew almost everything about their neighbours: the timetable of their normal day; their personal habits; their visitors and friends; what they bought and ate; what they said on the telephone (normally located in the corridor); even what they said in their own room, for the partition walls were very thin. Eavesdropping, spying and informing were all rampant in the *kommunalka* of the 1930s, when people were encouraged to be vigilant. There were frequent arguments over personal property—foodstuffs that went missing from the shared kitchen, thefts from rooms, noise or music played at night—and it did not take a lot for these squabbles to develop into denunciations to the authorities.

Remembering the 1930s, many people later talked about the sense they had then that they were living for the future rather than for the present. This feeling was particularly strong in the generation that grew up after 1917—young people who were totally immersed in the values and ideals of the Soviet system. For them the Communist Utopia was not a distant dream but a tangible reality, which would soon arrive. We can see this in the writings of schoolchildren in the 1920s and 1930s. These depicted Communism as a world where all their hopes and dreams were realized; but they imagined it as a transformation of their own immediate reality (cows full of milk, busy factories) rather than in far-off science-fiction terms.

This was how the 'radiant future' was portrayed by Socialist Realist art. Its monumental images of happy factory and kolkhoz workers were not meant to represent Soviet life as it actually was in the present but as it would become (and was becoming) in the Communist future. In its formulation by the Writers' Union in 1934, Socialist Realism meant the 'truthful, historically concrete representation of reality in its revolutionary development'. The idea was not to let the people dream about the future but to help them see the signs of its becoming in the Soviet reality around themselves. The acceptance of this vision was the basis of Communist belief.

In *Ideology and Utopia* (1929) Karl Mannheim wrote about the tendency of Marxist revolutionaries to see time as a 'series of strategic points' along a path to their revolution's end in a future paradise. Because this future is an active element of the present and defines the course of history, it gives meaning to everyday realities. This sense of time structured the Soviet idea of progress through the Five Year Plans. The goal of the Plan and its 'storming' of production was to speed up the arrival of the Communist future by increasing the whole tempo of the industrial economy. 'The Five Year Plan in Four!'

The speed of change in the USSR in the early 1930s was intoxicating. New factories, dams, canals, railways, even entire cities were built at a fantastic rate. With the capitalist world in crisis as a consequence of the Great Depression, these signs of progress led huge numbers of people (including many Western intellectuals) to invest unbounded faith in the Communist Utopia. To accept this vision of the future entailed adopting certain attitudes that smoothed the way to collusion with the Stalinist regime. It meant accepting that the Party line was right, that its Revolutionary Truth was more important than the observed truth of existing reality, and that the human cost in this 'march to Communism' was both unavoidable and acceptable.

Moscow was a symbol of this better life to come. Under Stalin's personal supervision it was transformed in a few years from a run-down provincial city of churches into an imperial capital in the monumental architectural style. There was a new route for parades through the centre to the Lenin Mausoleum, the sacred altar of the revolution on Red Square, from which the Kremlin ruled its Communist empire. Moscow's claim to global dominance was confirmed symbolically in October 1935, when the first red stars were installed on the Kremlin's towers to replace the Romanov double-headed eagles, which strangely had not been removed after 1917. The five points of the stars symbolized the continents which would soon share in the Communist dream.

The Moscow Metro was a tangible symbol of Communist progress. When the first line opened, in 1935, it was hailed by Kaganovich, the Commissar of Transport, as a palace of the proletariat: 'When our worker takes the Metro, he should be cheerful and joyous. He should think of himself in a palace shining with the light of the advancing, all-victorious Socialism.'[2] The stations were like palaces, with spacious halls, chandeliers, stained-glass panels, brass and chrome fittings, walls of marble, porphyry, malachite. Mayakovsky Station (1938) matched the beauty of a church, with its oval ceiling cupolas, mosaic designs, marble-patterned floors and stainless-steel arches. The splendour of these public spaces, which stood in such stark contrast to the people's squalid 'living space', played an important moral role, not unlike the part played by the church in earlier eras. By inspiring civic pride and reverence, the Metro helped to foster mass belief in the public goals and values of the Soviet order.

The most ambitious architectural icon of the Communist future in Moscow was the Palace of the Soviets, intended for the site of the Cathedral of Christ the Saviour, demolished in 1931. The Palace was supposed to be the tallest building in the world (at 416 metres it was to be eight metres taller than the Empire State Building, which had opened in New York in 1931) with a colossal statue of Lenin (three times the size of the Statue of Liberty) at its summit. The skyscraper was never built. But pictures of it continued to appear on matchboxes, and the local Metro stop (today's Kropotkin Station) continued to be called the Palace of the Soviets until 1957. The site was later turned into a swimming pool.

From the middle of the 1930s there was a new emphasis on jolly entertainments, sport and gymnastics to keep the Soviet population fit and occupied. Following the example of Hollywood, the Soviet cinema churned out happy musicals, romantic comedies and war adventures like *Chapaev* (1934), said to be Stalin's favourite film, which revived the cult of the Civil War hero for a new generation of Soviet youth. After the industrial stories which had dominated Soviet cinema during the first Five Year Plan, these entertainments were a light relief, allowing people to forget their worries after work. The people did not have much bread, but they had a lot of circuses.

Dancing, which had been seen by the early Bolsheviks as a frivolous pursuit, was officially encouraged during the 1930s. It became the rage, with dance schools opening everywhere. Jazz bands thrived. Classical composers such as Shostakovich incorporated jazz themes in their works. They were supposed to compose light and simple music, easily accessible to the masses, with happy optimistic tunes.

There were carnivals in parks and huge parades to celebrate the Soviet holidays. In contrast to the military style of parades during the first Five Year Plan, those of the later 1930s were joyous occasions.

The May Day parade through Red Square in 1935 had 5,000 people dressed in folk costumes. New Year's Eve was promoted as a national children's holiday to take the place of Christmas, with the decorating of fir trees (topped by a red star instead of an angel) officially permitted in 1935 for the first time since the revolution. Grandfather Frost (the Russian Santa Claus), an old folklore hero previously denounced as an 'ally of the kulak and the priest', was revived in the same year. The Soviet press associated him with the paternal figure of Stalin.

Under Stalin's leadership, the Bolsheviks retreated from their earlier revolutionary policies towards the family. Instead of undermining it, as they had tried to do in the 1920s, they now tried to restore it. As Trotsky wrote, it was an admission by the Soviet regime that its attempt to 'take the old family by storm'—to replace its 'bourgeois' customs with collective forms of living—had been impossibly utopian.

From the mid-1930s a series of decrees aimed to strengthen the Soviet family: the divorce laws were tightened; fees for divorce were raised substantially; child support was raised; homosexuality and abortion were outlawed. Marriage was made glamorous. Registration offices were smartened up. Marriage certificates were issued on high-quality paper instead of on the wrapping paper used before. Wedding rings, which had been banned as Christian relics in 1928, were sold again in Soviet shops from 1936. There was also a return to conventional and even prudish sexual attitudes among the political élites, who had been more experimental in their lifestyles in the early revolutionary years. The good Stalinist was supposed to be monogamous, devoted to his family, as Stalin was himself, according to his cult. Bolshevik wives, like Stalin's, were expected to return to the traditional role of raising children at home.

This dramatic policy reversal was partly a reaction to the demographic and social disaster of 1928–32: millions had died in the famine; the birthrate had dropped, posing a threat to the country's military strength; divorce had increased; and child abandonment had become a mass phenomenon, as families fragmented, leaving the authorities to cope with the consequences—homeless orphans, prostitution and teenage criminality. The Soviet regime needed stable families to sustain the rates of population growth its military needed to compete with the other totalitarian regimes, which heavily supported the patriarchal family in their 'battles for births'.

But the Soviet turnaround was also a response to the 'bourgeois' aspirations of Stalin's new industrial and political élites, most of whom had risen only recently from the peasantry or the working class. They did not share the contempt for bourgeois values or the same commitment to women's liberation which had been such a vital part of the Old Bolshevik intelligentsia world-view characteristic of the revolution's earlier generational cycle. According to Trotsky, who wrote a great deal about the Soviet family, the Stalinist regime had betrayed the revolution's commitment to sexual equality:

> One of the very dramatic chapters in the great book of the Soviets will be the tale of the disintegration and breaking up of those Soviet families where the husband as a party member, trade unionist, military commander or administrator, grew and developed and acquired new tastes in life, and the wife, crushed by the family, remained on the old level. The road of the two generations of the Soviet bureaucracy is sown thick with the tragedies of wives rejected and left behind. The same phenomenon is now to be observed in the new generation. The greatest of all crudities and cruelties are to be met perhaps in the very heights of the bureaucracy, where a very large percentage are parvenus of little culture, who consider that everything is permitted to them. Archives and memoirs will some day expose downright crimes in relation to wives, and to women in general, on the part of those evangelists of family morals and the compulsory 'joys of motherhood,' who are, owing to their position, immune from prosecution.[3]

Trotsky's assertion is supported by statistics, which reveal how household tasks were split within working-class families. In 1923–34, working women were spending three times longer than their men on household chores, but by 1936 they were spending five times longer. For women nothing changed—they worked long hours at a factory and then did a second shift at home, cooking, cleaning, caring for the children, on average for five hours every night—whereas men were liberated from most of their traditional duties in the home (chopping wood, carrying water, preparing the stove) by the provision of running water, gas and electricity, leaving them more time for cultural pursuits and politics.

The restoration of the patriarchal family was closely tied to its promotion as the basic unit of the state. 'The family is the primary cell of our society,' wrote one educationalist in 1935, 'and its duties in child-rearing derive from its obligations to cultivate good citizens.' The role of the parent was supported as a figure of authority enforcing Soviet rule at home. 'Young people should respect their elders, especially their parents,' declared *Komsomolskaya Pravda* in 1935. 'They must respect and love their parents, even if they are old-fashioned and don't like the Komsomol.'[4]

This represented a dramatic change from the moral lessons which had been drawn in the early 1930s from the cult of Pavlik Morozov—a fifteen-year-old boy from a Urals village who had denounced his father as a 'kulak' to the Soviet police. In the first stages of his propaganda cult, Pavlik was promoted as a model Pioneer because he had placed his loyalty to the revolution higher than his family. Soviet children were encouraged to denounce their elders, teachers, even parents, if they appeared anti-Soviet. But as the regime strengthened parent power, the cult was reinterpreted to place less emphasis on Pavlik's denunciation of his father and more on his hard work and obedience at school.

From the middle of the 1930s the Stalinist regime portrayed itself through metaphors and symbols of the family—a value-system familiar to the population at a time when millions of people found themselves in a new and alien environment. There was nothing new in this association between state and family. The cult of Stalin presented him in paternal terms, as the 'father of the people', just as Nicholas II had been their 'father-tsar' before 1917. Stalin was depicted as the protector and ultimate authority in the household. In many homes his portrait hung in the 'red corner', a place of honour, or above the doorway, where the icon was traditionally displayed. He was often photographed among children, and posed as their 'friend'. In one famous image he was seen embracing a young girl called Gelia Markizova, who had presented him with a bunch of flowers at a Kremlin reception in 1936. The girl's father, the Commissar for Agriculture in Buryat-Mongolia, was later shot as a 'Japanese spy'. Her mother was arrested and sent to Kazakhstan, where she committed suicide.

There was also a retreat from the permissive cultural policies that had allowed the avant-garde to flourish after 1917. The clampdown had begun in 1929, when institutions such as the RAPP (Russian Association of Proletarian Writers) started a 'class war' against the 'bourgeois enemies' of Soviet literature which it claimed were hidden in the left-wing avant-garde. The great poet of the revolution, Mayakovsky, was driven to his death (suicide or murder, it is not entirely clear) by the attacks of the RAPP.

By the beginning of the 1930s, any writer with an individual voice was deemed politically suspicious. The Five Year Plan was not just a programme of industrialization. It was a cultural revolution in which all the arts were called up by the state to build a new society. According to the plan, the duty of the Soviet artist was to raise the workers' consciousness, to enlist them in the 'battle' for 'socialist construction' by producing art with a social content which they could understand and relate to as positive ideals. In this way the artist was to create a new type of human being. 'The production of souls is more important than the production of tanks,' Stalin told a meeting of writers and officials at Gorky's house in 1932. 'And so I raise my glass to you, writers, the engineers of the human soul.'

It was at this meeting that the doctrine of Socialist Realism was formulated, although at the time it was not clear to Gorky, whose writings were its model, that it would become a regimented orthodoxy for all

Soviet artists. Gorky's understanding was that Socialist Realism would unite the critical realist traditions of nineteenth-century literature with the revolutionary romanticism of the Bolshevik tradition. It would combine the depiction of everyday reality with a vision of the revolution's heroic promise. This formulation left a lot of freedom to the writer. But in Stalin's version of the doctrine, as policed by the regime's cultural institutions after 1934, it imposed a deadening conformity on artists and writers, who were now expected to be uniformly optimistic about Soviet life and easily accessible to the masses. They were meant to be the chroniclers of a master narrative—the progress of humanity towards the Communist Utopia—defined for them by the state.

From 1934, the regime launched a concerted press campaign against the artistic avant-garde. The attack reached fever pitch in January 1936, when *Pravda* published a diatribe ('Chaos Instead of Music') against Shostakovich's opera *Lady Macbeth of Mtsensk*, which had been a great success with hundreds of performances since its première in 1934. The unsigned article accused the composer of 'Formalism' and 'Leftist distortions' because his music was too dissonant for the masses to enjoy. It was evidently written with the support of Stalin, who, just a few days before it appeared, had seen the opera and clearly hated it. This was not just an attack on Shostakovich, who was lucky to avoid arrest. It was a clear warning of the regime's intention to force all Soviet artists to conform to Socialist Realist conventions. The theatre director Vsevolod Meyerhold, who spoke out in defence of Shostakovich, was subjected to denunciations of a feverish intensity (he was later arrested, brutally tortured by the NKVD, and then shot; his wife was stabbed to death by unidentified assassins who broke into their Moscow apartment).

The assault against the avant-garde was a counter-revolution in cultural politics. The regime abandoned its commitment to the revolutionary project of creating a new 'proletarian' form of universal culture, divorced from the 'bourgeois' culture of before 1917, and promoted a return to the nationalist traditions of the nineteenth century which it reinvented in its own distorted forms as Socialist Realism. This reassertion of the 'Russian classics' was an important aspect of the Stalinist programme, which used cultural nationalism to counteract the 'foreign' avant-garde and create the popular illusion of stability in the age of mass upheaval over which it reigned. In its use of nationalism, at least, the Stalinist system was similar to the totalitarian regimes in Italy and Germany.

The nineteenth-century classics were held up as a model for the Soviet arts. The complete works of Pushkin and Tolstoy were issued in their millions. Landscape painting, which had been a dying art in the 1920s, was suddenly restored as the favoured medium of Socialist Realist art, particularly scenes which displayed the mastery of nature by Soviet industry. In music, too, the regime put the clock back to the nineteenth century: Glinka and Tchaikovsky became favourites in the concert repertory and were held up as the standard for Soviet music.

Part of this return to national traditions was the promotion of folklore. It was a sick irony that, after the destruction of the village and its culture by collectivization, the Stalinist regime should put on show its fairy-tale official version of peasant arts and crafts through museums of folklore, state folk choirs and dancing troupes. Made up of professional musicians and dancers, these groups performed a type of song and dance that bore little relation to the authentic forms of 'national culture' they were supposed to represent.

This reinvention of folklore was connected to a turnaround in Soviet nationality policies. During the 1920s the Party had encouraged the development of national cultures within the Soviet Union. It believed that history involved an evolution from clans and tribes to ethnic groups and nationalities, ending in the victory of socialism, when all nations would conjoin in one international culture. Nation-building was thus seen as socially progressive, as long as national sentiments were expressed within a Soviet framework ('National in form, Socialist in content' was the idea). Under the policy of *korenizatsiia* (affirmative action for the indigenous population), every nationality was to have its own territorial autonomy with its own national culture, education and administration in its own language.

From the 1930s, the Stalinist regime began to reverse its progressive policies towards the national minorities. The change was not immediately obvious. Stalin continued to pay lip-service to the 'brotherhood of socialist nations', and to claim that the tsarist legacy of Russian chauvinism had been overcome by the Soviet Union. His regime trumpeted the cultural achievements of the national minorities. It crowned a people's poet for each nationality (Taras Shevchenko for Ukraine, Shota Rustaveli for Georgia, Ianka Kupala for Belorussia) and allowed each nation to promote its 'folk culture'. But republican leaders were purged as 'bourgeois nationalists' if they deviated from the Moscow line, which meant subordinating these 'folk cultures' into higher forms of art on Russian lines (Russian composers, for instance, were sent to Central Asia and the Caucasus to establish 'national operas' and symphonic traditions where there had been none before). In the Soviet 'family of nations' the Russians were assigned the leading role. From 1938, learning Russian became compulsory in Soviet schools. It was the only language of the Red Army. Here was the start of a major shift in the revolution's ideology—from Soviet internationalism to Russian nationalism—which would gain momentum in the Second World War.

13

THE GREAT TERROR

It was late at night on 11 October 1937 when the NKVD came for Vladimir Antonov-Ovseenko, the man who had led the storming of the Winter Palace almost exactly twenty years before. Like most victims of the Great Terror, he had not expected his arrest. The accusations against him—belonging to a 'Trotskyist organization of terrorists and spies'—were far-fetched. He had been close to Trotsky in the 1920s, but he had since more than proved his loyalty to the leadership, first as the Chief Prosecutor of the Russian Republic and then as the Soviet Consul-General in Barcelona, where, despite his sympathies for the Trotskyist and Anarchist militias defending Catalonia in the Spanish Civil War, he had overseen their persecution by Communist forces loyal to Stalin and the Comintern. He believed in the Great Purge. On the day of his arrest, shortly after his recall to Moscow, he had written to his wife Sofya in Sukhumi:

> Have you read in *Izvestiia* today about the intrigues of Fascist agents among Soviet wives? I come across these little provocations everywhere. We need to be more alert and vigilant to expose them, to root them out and destroy them.[1]

Held in the notorious Butyrka prison, Antonov-Ovseenko entertained his cell-mates with stories of his part in the October seizure of power. After three months of interrogation with little food or sleep, he was sentenced to ten years but in fact was shot on 8 February 1938. When he was taken from his cell to the execution yard, he took off his overcoat, his jacket and his shoes, gave them to the other prisoners, and told them: 'I beg anyone who gets to freedom to tell the people that Antonov-Ovseenko was a Bolshevik and remained a Bolshevik till his last day.'[2]

His execution was symbolic but not unusual. The Old Bolsheviks were nearly all wiped out by the Great Terror of 1937–8. They knew too much, they were too independent in their thinking, and, since his crisis year of 1932, Stalin suspected most of them of holding opposition views. The Party that had rallied behind Stalin at the Seventeenth Party Congress in 1934 was virtually destroyed: of the 139 Central Committee members, 102 were shot in the purges, while only one third of the delegates survived to attend the Eighteenth Party Congress in 1939. The 'Congress of Victors' was in fact the 'Congress of Victims'.

But the Great Terror was more than a bloodletting among Bolsheviks. It was a complex series of repressions involving many different groups. The striking thing about it, compared to other waves of Soviet terror, is that such a high proportion of the victims were murdered. Of the 1.5 million people arrested by the secret police (and we do not have the figures for arrests by the regular police), 1.3 million were sentenced, and more than half of these (681,692 people) were executed by a firing squad for 'counter-revolutionary activities'. At the height of the Great Terror, between August 1937 and November 1938, on average 1,500 people were shot each day. The population of the Gulag labour camps meanwhile grew from 1.2 to 1.9 million, a figure which conceals at least 140,000 deaths within the camps themselves.

The sheer scale of the Great Terror makes it all the harder to explain. The types of people caught in it were so diverse. Some historians have maintained that it is best understood as a number of related but separate waves of terror, each one capable of being explained on its own but not as part of a single phenomenon. There was certainly a complex amalgam of different elements that made up the Great Terror: the

purging of the Party, the great 'show trials', the mass arrests in the cities, the 'kulak operation' and 'national operations' against minorities.
But while it may be helpful to analyse these various components separately, the fact remains that they all began and ended simultaneously,
which does suggest that they were part of a unified campaign that needs
to be explained. To begin to understand it, we must look at the Great
Terror, not, as some have argued, as an uncontrolled or accidental happening, a product of the chaos and infighting of the Stalinist regime,
nor as something driven by social pressures from below, as argued by
'revisionist' historians, but as an operation, which we now know from
studying the archives was masterminded and controlled by Stalin
directly in response to the circumstances he perceived in 1937.

There were many waves of terror in the Stalin period—the arrests of
'bourgeois specialists', 'wreckers', and 'saboteurs' during the industrial
terror, the mass repressions of the 'kulaks' and their families, the trials of
'bourgeois nationalists', 'Rightists', 'Zinovievites' and 'Trotskyists' in Stalin's battles with the Bolsheviks, and large-scale arrests of 'former people'
and 'socially alien elements' in 1934-5—but the Great Terror was excep-
tional. It was not just a routine wave of mass arrests, isolating 'enemies' by
sending them to camps, but a calculated policy of mass killing.

Stalin's thinking in this social holocaust is made clear in the steno-
graphic record of the Central Committee Plenum of February–March
1937. He was afraid of an approaching war: the military aggression of
Nazi Germany and the occupation of Manchuria by the Japanese had
convinced him that the Soviet Union was threatened on two fronts, and
he wanted to eliminate any 'anti-Soviet elements' that could become a
'fifth column'. He was acutely conscious of the revolutionary dangers in
a war. As a Bolshevik—a party that had come to power by exploiting
Russia's military weaknesses—he had learned that lesson from 1917.

Stalin did not place much hope in any Soviet alliance with the Western powers to contain the Axis threat. The Western states had failed to
intervene in Spain. They were appeasing Nazi Germany. It seemed to be

their aim to divert Hitler's forces to the East rather than confront them in the West. By 1937, Stalin was convinced that war was imminent. The Soviet press whipped up fears of the country being threatened on all sides by hostile powers. It claimed there were fascist infiltrators—'spies' and 'hidden enemies'—in every corner of society.

The Spanish Civil War strengthened Stalin's conviction that a purge of unreliables was needed to prepare the country's defences. He took a close interest in the Spanish conflict, seeing it as a 'valid scenario for a future European war' between Communism and fascism. He believed that the factional infighting between the Spanish Communists, Anarchists and other left-wing groups was principally to blame for the military failures of the Republicans, and from this concluded that political repression was required in the Soviet Union to crush all potential opposition before the outbreak of a war with the fascists.

This rationale was justified by Molotov several decades later:

> Nineteen thirty-seven was necessary. If you consider that after the revolution we were slashing left and right, and we were victorious, but enemies of different sorts remained, and in the face of impending danger of fascist aggression they might unite. We owe the fact that we did not have a fifth column during the war to '37. After all, even among Bolsheviks there were the sorts who were fine and loyal when everything was going well. . . . But if something started, they would falter and switch sides.[3]

Kaganovich similarly justified the Great Terror in later years. But these were not just post-war rationalizations. In a speech to Party workers in June 1938 Kaganovich said that the mass repressions were necessitated by the threat of war. He was probably repeating ideas that had circulated in the leadership.

Stalin's fear of a fifth column is confirmed by his heavy underlining of a section in the draft of Molotov's speech to the February–March Plenum where Molotov had claimed the Trotskyists would 'save their strength for a more important moment—for the beginning of the war' (in August 1940, on Stalin's orders, Trotsky was assassinated in his home in Mexico). In his own speech to the Plenum Stalin added this idea: 'to win a battle in wartime several corps of soldiers are needed. And to subvert this victory on the front, all that is needed are a few spies somewhere in army headquarters.'[4]

On this reasoning, Stalin was prepared to arrest thousands of innocent people to catch just one spy. As he calculated, if only 5 per cent of those arrested turned out to be truly enemies, 'that would be a good result'. According to Khrushchev, who was then the Moscow Party boss, Stalin 'used to say that if a report [denunciation] was ten per cent true, we should regard the entire report as fact'. Everybody in the NKVD knew that holding back from their quota of arrests would get them into trouble for lack of vigilance. 'Better too far than not far enough,' Yezhov warned his operatives. If 'an extra thousand people will be shot, that is not such a big deal'.[5]

In the Soviet Union the mass arrests were known as the *Yezhovshchina* ('the rule of Yezhov'), and in many people's minds it was the NKVD boss and not Stalin who had been responsible for them. People wrote to the Soviet leader asking for his help to get arrested relatives released. The Russians had traditionally written to the Tsar as the highest source of justice in the land. 'The Tsar is good, but the boyars are bad' was an old myth. In fact, Yezhov was Stalin's loyal executioner. More than any other police chief, he was prepared to indulge Stalin's paranoiac fantasies by fabricating evidence of 'counter-revolutionary conspiracies' and 'spy rings' everywhere.

For some time, Yezhov had promoted the outlandish theory that, on Trotsky's orders from abroad, Zinoviev and Kamenev had organized a terrorist conspiracy to murder Stalin and other members of the Party leadership. The two Bolsheviks had already been tried in secret in 1935. But Stalin wanted a show trial to 'prove' the existence of a Trotsky–Zinoviev Centre. Not trusting Yagoda, who had expressed his doubts about this conspiracy, Stalin placed Yezhov in charge of 'building up the case'. Arrested suspects were tortured until they made the necessary confessions and agreed to speak the lines prepared for them in the courtroom. In August 1936, Zinoviev, Kamenev and fourteen other Party leaders were put on trial. All of them were sentenced to death, along with 160 other people arrested for their connections to the convicted. For his part in the preparation of the trial, Yezhov was promoted by Stalin to take the place of Yagoda as the NKVD chief in September.

The 'trial of the Sixteen' was the first of the 'show trials', whose mission was to expose and eliminate a coordinated ring of 'spies' and 'terrorists' organized by former oppositionists. It was not enough to convict and punish the accused: that could be done in secret. The whole aim of the show trials was to prove the existence of these 'conspiracies' by having the accused confess their guilt, according to a prepared script, before the Party and the world. In Bolshevik circles the confession was regarded as the highest form of proof because it exposed the hidden truth about a person's real beliefs. In any case, there was no better evidence against the accused.

A second show trial, in January 1937, witnessed the conviction of Piatakov, Radek and fifteen other former supporters of Trotsky for industrial sabotage and espionage. Then, in May–June, eight of the country's senior military commanders, including Marshal Tukhachevsky (Deputy Commissar of Defence), General Uborevich (Commander of the Belorussian Military District) and General Yakir (Commander of the Kiev Military District) were arrested, tortured brutally until they agreed to false confessions, and tried in secret in a military tribunal of the Soviet Supreme Court, where they were convicted of belonging to a 'Trotskyist-Rightist anti-Soviet conspiracy' and of espionage on behalf of Nazi Germany. Within hours of their conviction all eight of them were shot. The army had been the one institution capable of standing up to Stalin in his quest for complete power (which is why the Trial of the Generals had been in secret). Now its leadership was virtually destroyed: of the 767 members of the high command, 512 were shot, 29 died in prison, 3 committed suicide and 59 remained in jail.

Stalin played the directing role in all these carefully managed trials. Nothing could be left to chance in the courtroom. The accused were broken to the point where they were sure to speak the words scripted for them by their torturers. Their guilt was taken as a proven fact—their sentences decided by Stalin—before the trial began.

In the last and biggest of the show trials, in March 1938, Bukharin, Yagoda and Rykov, along with thirteen other Bolsheviks, were sentenced to be shot for conspiring with the 'Trotsky–Zinoviev terrorist organization' to assassinate the Soviet leaders, sabotage the economy and spy at the behest of the fascist states. Bukharin had been implicated in the conspiracy by Yezhov, who cited testimony from various former oppositionists at the Central Committee Plenum of December 1936. Bukharin had not helped his cause by trying to defend himself. It had infuriated the other leaders, who accused him of acting like a 'bourgeois lawyer' by arguing against the details of the prosecution case, when, in their eyes, his guilt had been proved already, and it was his duty as a Bolshevik to submit to the judgement of the Party.

Imprisoned in the NKVD headquarters in the Lubianka, Bukharin was broken down by 'methods of physical influence' and threats against his young wife and infant son until he signed a confession of general responsibility for his crimes but not going into the particulars. From his cell, he wrote to Stalin with a strange appeal for mercy in which he declared that there was 'something great and bold about the political idea of a general purge' and agreed to play the guilty part in a show trial, yet continued to protest his innocence of the charges against him. At his trial Bukharin continued with this line, pleading guilty to the general charges of belonging to a 'counter-revolutionary organization' but underlining that he did so 'irrespective of whether or not I knew of, whether or not I took part in, any particular act'.[6] Was he trying to subvert the trial, to let his prosecutors know that he could demolish their whole case? Or perhaps to send a signal to posterity? We shall never know.

The first show trial sent a signal through the Party ranks: suspected oppositionists, or anyone associated with them in the past, needed to be reported to the NKVD. Failure to do so would invite suspicion of 'lack of vigilance', widening the circle of police investigations and arrests.

When a leader was arrested, everybody in his social orbit came under suspicion. The Soviet provincial town was ruled by a clique of senior officials—the district Party boss, the police chief, the heads of local factories, collective farms and prisons, the local Soviet leader— who all had their own client networks in the institutions they controlled. These officials protected one another as long as their power circle was maintained. But the arrest of one official would inevitably lead to the arrest of all the other members of the ruling clique, as well as their hangers-on, once the NKVD got to work revealing the connections between them.

In 1937, the NKVD arrested the Party Secretary of Nikopol, in the eastern Ukraine. According to Viktor Kravchenko, a local Soviet official, it also arrested his

> assistants, his friends, the men and women whom he had put into jobs anywhere in Nikopol. The Commandant of the Nikopol Garrison went into the hunters' bag, then the local Prosecutor and all his legal staff, finally the chairman of the Nikopol Soviet . . . The local bank, the newspaper, all commercial institutions were 'cleaned' . . . the manager of the Communal Administration, the chief of the Fire Brigade, the head of the Savings Institution . . . Crowds of women and children swarmed around the NKVD building in Nikopol at all hours despite the bitter cold.[7]

The terror thus spread down through the Party ranks, Soviet institutions and society itself, as colleagues, friends and relatives came under suspicion too. The more senior a Party member was, the more likely he was to be arrested. Juniors in the ranks were often ready to denounce superiors to help themselves and perhaps replace them in their posts. They were encouraged to report on them.

A popular perception of the Great Terror was that it affected mainly Party circles and the intelligentsia. That is certainly the impression given by Khrushchev's speech at the Twentieth Party Congress and by intelligentsia memoirs written after 1956. But the vast majority of the terror's victims were ordinary citizens. For every Bolshevik there were ten others arrested in the mass operations of 1937–8.

The 'kulak operation' (Order 00447) accounts for half of all arrests (669,929) and more than half the executions (376,202) in these years. The targeted groups ('former kulaks, criminals and other anti-Soviet elements') were divided into two: those to be shot and those to be sent to labour camps for 8–10 years. Each district was given quotas for arrests but these could be increased by local officials. The district NKVDs would compile lists, arrests were made, interrogations carried out, and new names added to the lists from the 'testimonies' obtained by torture.

Most of the victims were former 'kulaks' and their families who had recently returned from special settlements and Gulag labour camps. They had completed five- or eight-year sentences for 'counter-revolutionary agitation' imposed during the collectivization of agri-culture. Stalin was afraid that the country would be swamped by disgruntled and embittered 'kulaks' who might pose a threat in time of war. In his eyes an enemy was an enemy for life. The operation was par-ticularly brutal in border regions and in areas such as Ukraine where the regime feared the population most.

There were also 'national operations', wholesale deportations of minorities who were deemed potential 'spies' in the event of war: Soviet Poles, Germans, Finns, Latvians, Armenians and Greeks, Koreans, Chi-nese, even Harbin Russians, who had returned to the Soviet Union from Manchuria following the sale in 1935 of the Eastern China Rail-way to the Japanese puppet state of Manchukuo. In all, around 350,000 people were arrested and two thirds of these were shot. Stalin's distrust of the Poles was particularly strong. It dated from the Civil War, when he had made some tactical mistakes as a commissar in the disastrous Soviet invasion of Poland. Stalin saw the Soviet Poles (as well as Belorus-sians and some Ukrainians) as a fifth column of the 'fascist' Polish state, which he feared would unite with Nazi Germany to attack the Soviet

Union. As a result of Directive 00485, 140,000 Poles were arrested, of whom 111,000 were executed. The rest were sent to the Gulag.

Informers were everywhere—in factories and offices, in public places and communal apartments. By the height of the Great Terror, millions of people were reporting on their colleagues, neighbours, friends. The level of surveillance varied widely between cities. In Moscow, which was heavily policed, there was at least one informer for every six or seven families, according to a former NKVD official. In Kuibyshev the police claimed to have about 1,000 informers in a population of 400,000 people. These figures do not include the paid 'reliables' (factory and office workers, student activists, watchmen, caretakers, etc.) who acted as the eyes and ears of the police in every nook and cranny of society. Nor do they account for the everyday reporting and denunciation—unsolicited by the NKVD—which made the police state so powerful.

There were two broad categories: voluntary informers, who were often motivated by material rewards, political beliefs, or malice towards their victims; and involuntary informers, who were entrapped by the police through threats or promises to save arrested relatives. It is difficult to judge the second category. Many acted out of fear for their own lives. How might we have acted in their place?

People often wrote denunciations in the sincere conviction that they were performing their duty as citizens. They believed the propaganda about 'spies' and 'enemies', and set out to expose them among their bosses, colleagues, friends. Above all, they were frightened of getting into trouble if someone in their circle was arrested and they had failed to denounce them. It was a crime to conceal one's contacts with 'enemies'. People rushed to denounce others before they were denounced by them. This mad scramble of denunciations does not explain the colossal number of arrests—the mass operations were done with prepared lists of names—but it does explain why so many people were sucked into the police system as willing informers. Hysterical citizens would appear at the NKVD and Party offices with the names of friends and even relatives who might be 'enemies of the people'. One old woman wrote to the Party office of her factory to inform them that her sister had once worked as a temporary cleaner in the Kremlin and had cleaned the office of a man who was later arrested.

Many denunciations were motivated by malice. The easiest way to remove a rival was to denounce him to the police. Sexual and romantic jealousies often played a part: husbands, lovers, wives could rid themselves of unwanted partners by reporting them. Lower-class resentments of the Bolshevik élite fuelled the Great Terror. Workers denounced managers, kolkhoz workers chairmen, if they were unpopular, a practice that has led some revisionist historians to conclude that the Great Terror was 'empowering' for the masses. It was certainly a chance for ambitious workers and Stakhanovites to move into the jobs of the bosses they denounced.

How much fear did ordinary people feel? The terror did not affect all social classes equally and there were many families, especially among Russian workers, who were not touched by it at all. Fear could be felt to varying degrees at different times. At the height of the mass arrests people lay awake at night in fearful expectation of the Black Maria pulling up outside and the sound of footsteps in the corridor before the knock on the door. Some kept a packed bag underneath their bed to be ready. But in the day they went about their business and found distractions to forget their fear. And over time they learned to live with fear. They might not even be conscious of it, this constant background of anxiety, although it was bound to influence their thinking and behaviour in the longer term. Yet we must not underestimate the impact of a million and half arrests. If not every family was affected, almost everyone would know a family that lost someone.

People were confused by the arrests. There was no rationale to explain them. Heroes of the revolution such as Antonov-Ovseenko were suddenly exposed as 'enemies of the people'? The pattern of arrests was so random that nobody was safe. It seemed that anyone could be arrested for almost anything—a loose word, a joke, a mistake in their past, a relative with the wrong occupation or social origins. The revolution had happened so fast—there had been so many changes in the twenty years since 1917—that no one had a clean record.

Sofya Antonov-Ovseenko was arrested three days after Vladimir. Brought back to Moscow, she wrote to her husband, without realizing that he was in prison too.

> My darling. I do not know if you will receive this, but somehow I sense that I am writing to you for the last time. Do you recall how we always said that if someone in our country was arrested then it must be for good reason, for some crime—that is for something? No doubt there is something in my case as well, but what it is I do not know . . . For the past three days I have been thinking through my life, preparing for death. I cannot think of anything (apart from the usual shortcomings that differentiate a human being from an 'angel') that could be considered criminal, either in relation to other human beings or in relation to our state and government . . . I thought exactly as you thought—and is there anybody more dedicated than you are to our Party and country? You know what is in my heart, you know the truth of my actions, of my thoughts and words. But the fact that I am here must mean that I have committed some wrong—what I do not know . . . I cannot bear the thought that you might not believe me . . . One more thing: it is time for Valichka [Sofya's daughter from her first marriage] to join the Komsomol. This will no doubt prevent her. My heart is full of sorrow at the thought that she is living in the belief that her mother is a scoundrel. The full horror of my situation is that people do not believe me, I cannot live like that . . . I beg forgiveness from everyone I love for bringing them such misfortune . . . [8]

The Great Terror undermined the trust that holds together families. Wives doubted husbands; husbands doubted wives. People did not know what to believe when a relative was arrested. Their instincts told them that there must be a mistake. How could they believe that the person they loved was an 'enemy'? But how could they question the authorities when there were, it seemed, so many 'enemies'? For Sofya, as for every person who was unjustly arrested as a 'traitor' to the state, the worst torture was the thought that their family would stop believing them.

Families were put under pressure to renounce arrested relatives. If a husband was arrested, his wife might lose her job, or the family be evicted from their home. Children were excluded from the Komsomol, from university and from certain jobs. The stigma of arrest affected families for many years. When both parents were arrested, children were taken in by other relatives, or, like Sofya's fifteen-year-old daughter, they were sent to an orphanage, where they were encouraged to create a new identity and were sometimes given a new name. There were millions of orphans in these children's homes in the 1930s and '40s. The moral system of the orphanage—with its Soviet indoctrination and strong collective and weak familial ties—made it one of the main recruiting grounds for the NKVD and the Red Army.

People were afraid of making contact with the families of 'enemies of the people'. They crossed the street to avoid them. Colleagues, neighbours, friends became strangers. In this way the terror atomized society. It broke up the collective unities—the solidarities of profession, neighbourhood, friendship and so on—that might have led to more resistance against the repression of individuals. People did not dare to question the arrests. They suspended their conscience, tried not to think about what was happening in society, suppressed their doubts, or found ways of rationalizing them to preserve the basic structures of their belief in the system. They told themselves that their own loved ones had been arrested by mistake (the police were bound to make mistakes if there were so many enemies, as the newspapers said, and so well concealed) whereas others had been guilty of something ('no smoke without fire'). On this reasoning the 'enemy' was always someone else—the husbands of the other women in the queue to hand in parcels at the prison gates—never one's own relatives.

At the rate the arrests were going on, it would not be long before doubts spread. How many 'enemies of the people' could there be? By 1938 it was becoming clear that unless the arrests came to an end the terror system would be undermined. The terror was getting out of control. In January Stalin warned the NKVD not to carry on arresting people solely on the basis of denunciations without first checking their veracity. He spoke against 'false vigilance' and careerists who made denunciations to promote themselves. Yezhov's power was gradually reduced. In November he was replaced by his deputy, Lavrenty Beria, who immediately announced a full review of the arrests in Yezhov's reign. By 1940, 1.5 million cases were reviewed; 450,000 convictions were quashed, 128,000 cases closed, 30,000 people released from jail, and 327,000 people let out of the Gulag's labour camps and colonies.

These releases restored many people's faith in Soviet justice. They allowed those with doubts to explain the 'Yezhov terror' as a temporary aberration rather than as a product of the system. Their reasoning went like this: the mass arrests had all been Yezhov's doing, but Stalin had corrected his mistakes, and uncovered Yezhov as an 'enemy of the people' (he was shot in 1940), who had tried to undermine the Soviet government by arresting so many innocent people and thus spreading discontent. People now accepted that anybody not released by Beria, and everyone arrested under him, must be guilty of the crimes for which they stood accused. The belief system had been stabilized, allowing rule by terror to go on.

14

REVOLUTION FOR EXPORT

On the twentieth anniversary of the October Revolution, the last of five red stars, each with a hammer and sickle in the middle, was placed on top of the Kremlin's five towers. The first had been placed there two years earlier, in 1935. The red star had been the emblem of the Red Army since 1918. Worn on the front of the soldiers' caps, it was associated in folklore with the goddess *Pravda*, whose red star on her forehead symbolized her fight for light and justice in the world against the dark forces of *Krivda*. In Bolshevik ideology, as it was told to the soldiers, the star's five points stood for the five continents, which their revolutionary struggle would one day liberate from exploiters. 'The Red Star of the Red Army is the star of *Pravda*,' it was explained in one leaflet. 'And the Red Army servicemen are the brave lads who are fighting *Krivda* and her evil supporters so that truth should rule the world.'[1]

The revolution's global reach was a dominant theme of its early iconography. One of the most famous Civil War posters ('Lenin Cleans the Earth of Filth') showed the Bolshevik leader with a worker's cap and broom standing on top of the globe and sweeping off the surface of the world an emperor, a king, a capitalist and a priest. At least one design of the Lenin Mausoleum put at the centre of its ensemble a globe supported by four Soviet toilers with a red star on the top.

Lenin never lost sight of the revolution's international scale. As he saw it, socialism was unsustainable in a backward peasant country such as Russia without the revolution spreading to the more advanced industrial states. Moreover, the globalization of the capitalist system made class struggle no respecter of national boundaries, and as the first socialist society Soviet Russia had a mission to emancipate humanity by spreading revolution through the world.

The Bolsheviks conceived their revolution as only the beginning of an international civil war between socialism and capitalism. Recognizing the World War as a revolutionary catalyst, they aimed to turn it into a series of civil wars in which the workers of the warring nations would follow Russia's example and overthrow their imperialist rulers. From day one of Soviet power, they waited with impatience for this struggle to begin, receiving every report of a strike or protest as 'the start'.

Germany was the focus of their highest hopes. It was the home of the Marxist movement and had the most advanced labour movement in Europe. The November 1918 Revolution was greeted with joy by the Bolsheviks. Its workers' and soldiers' councils seemed to suggest that Germany was moving on the Soviet path. But there was no German 'October'. The German socialists (SPD), the largest left-wing party, put their weight behind a democratic republic by entering government and crushing the uprising by the Communists in January 1919.

Even so, the prospects of socialist revolution in Europe looked favourable that spring. The Austro-Hungarian Empire had collapsed, and in Hungary a Soviet Republic had been established by the Communists, a party led by Béla Kun with 40,000 members, including many soldiers, who looked to Moscow for support. Following the lead of the Hungarian revolution, Communists had also seized power and installed Soviet republics in Bavaria and Slovakia. There were smaller but no less active Communist movements in Serbia, Romania, Greece and Austria, all of them inspired by the October Revolution.

The Bolsheviks were keen to control these new parties by organizing them through the Comintern (Communist International) and keeping them apart from the Social Democrats of the Second International (1889–1916). They were scornful of the European socialists who had backed their national governments in the First World War. It was to set themselves apart from them that the Bolsheviks had in 1918 decided to describe themselves as Communists rather than as Social Democrats.

The Comintern was an international organization of Communist parties united by their common aim to overthrow the capitalist system and establish Soviet republics modelled on the October Revolution. Moscow's control of the Comintern was set firmly from the start. At its founding congress in the Kremlin, in March 1919, the Bolsheviks insisted on structuring the Comintern as a centralized bureaucracy in their own image. At the second congress, in July–August 1920, all the parties of the Comintern were made to sign the '21 Conditions', which meant breaking off relations with the socialists in their countries and accepting the decisions of its Russian-dominated Executive Committee.

The Russocentrism of the Comintern was rooted in the messianic mission of the Russian Revolution to liberate the world. Because Soviet Russia was the only socialist society, the prime duty of the Comintern was to follow its example and protect it from attack by the capitalist powers. It was the height of the Russian Civil War and the Allied Intervention in Russia. For the embattled Bolsheviks, the Comintern provided them with their best means of military defence: to go on the political offensive against the Western states.

While the Second Comintern Congress was in session the Red Army was advancing on Warsaw in the final act of the Soviet–Polish war which had begun with the Polish invasion of Ukraine in 1919. Following the Soviet forces was a Provisional Polish Revolutionary Committee led by Dzerzhinsky, the Cheka boss, with instructions to install the Communists in power once it had arrived in the Polish capital. The Bolsheviks believed that the Sovietization of Poland would act as a catalyst to socialist revolutions in Europe. But the uprisings they were counting on did not materialize. The Red Army was pushed back from Warsaw by Polish soldiers and workers, whose patriotism and hatred of the Russians proved more powerful than the class divisions on which a Soviet revolution would depend.

Since this would not be the last time the Red Army moved across the

Russian border into Europe (it would do so again in 1939 and 1944–45) it is important to work out the Bolsheviks' motives. If the Reds had captured Warsaw, would they have pushed on to Berlin in a revolutionary war against the West, as some historians have claimed?

There is no doubt that the Bolsheviks had wanted their offensive to be the start of a revolutionary war. If it had sparked Communist uprisings in the West, they would have been keen to exploit them, perhaps by advancing their forces in support. But Lenin was a pragmatist. Brest-Litovsk had demonstrated that. He was not prepared to overstretch and run the risk of military defeat for the Soviet regime. In a speech to the Ninth Party Conference, in September 1920, in the aftermath of the Red Army's retreat from Warsaw, Lenin claimed that it had only been their aim to 'give a shake' to the Versailles system, imposed by the Allies at the end of the war, which rested on the West's support for Poland as a buffer against Germany and Soviet Russia. No doubt Lenin was playing down the campaign's ambitions to boost the Party's morale in the wake of its defeat; but, even so, this does suggest that the Bolsheviks were pushing into Europe hopefully but cautiously with a 'wait-and-see' approach towards the possibility of using Poland as a bridgehead for a broader revolutionary war.

Forced to recognize defeat against the Poles, the Bolsheviks negotiated over the contested borders with Poland and, anxious to secure peace at a time of unrest at home, signed the Treaty of Riga in March 1921. It was the start of a new era of peaceful co-existence between Russia and the West.

Defeat in Poland was the first of several setbacks that made Lenin think again about exporting revolution to Europe. In March a large strike action planned by the German Communists in the Halle and Mansfeld industrial regions of Saxony failed to develop into a revolt, as the Comintern and its agents in Germany had hoped. After this defeat, the Third Congress of the Comintern steered a course away from revolutionary adventurism towards more patient propaganda and trade union work. 'Only now do we see and feel that we are not immediately close to our final aim, to the conquest of power on the world scale,' Trotsky told the delegates in June 1921. 'We told ourselves back in 1919 that it was a question of months, but now we say that it is perhaps a question of several years.'[2]

Conceding that the export of the Revolution was no longer an immediate option, the Bolsheviks divided their foreign policy into two parallel strategies: the long-term preparation of revolutionary initiatives by the Comintern and short-term practical diplomacy by the Commissariat of Foreign Affairs. It was not just a dual policy; it was duplicitous— the Commissariat seeking to improve relations and develop trade with the capitalist countries, while the Comintern continued to subvert these states by fostering the Communist movements. Through the Profintern (the Red International of Trade Unions) it developed links to the labour movement in the West. In the British General Strike of 1926 Moscow sent financial aid to the strikers, resulting in a worsening of Anglo-Soviet relations and the 'war scare' of 1927 which Stalin used to justify his crash programme of industrialization.

The Five Year Plan was introduced in the belief that the Soviet Union was entering a new and final stage of international struggle with capitalism. At its Sixth Congress, in 1928, the Comintern adopted the theory that capitalism was entering a 'third period' of economic crisis and revolutionary upheaval following the 'first' (characterized by proletarian disturbances) during the period of the Russian Civil War and the 'second' (capitalist consolidation) during the NEP. The Wall Street Crash and the Great Depression underpinned this conviction. New revolutionary opportunities were created as workers in the West moved to the Left to fight for jobs and looked towards the Soviet Union as an alternative to the capitalist system.

Predicting a fresh wave of labour protests more violent than those of the 'first period', the Comintern concluded that the time was ripe to turn them into socialist revolutions through more militant and subversive policies than it had pursued in the NEP period. In this class war Communists were ordered to mobilize the unemployed and to cut all links with the socialists, denounced as 'social fascists', who were to be opposed as vehemently as the liberals and the Right because of their moderate parliamentary policies.

The Comintern's new policy had fateful consequences in Germany, where the refusal of the Communists to cooperate with the SPD was a major factor in Hitler's rise to power. Stalin was particularly mistrustful of the SPD because of its firm commitment to the post-war Versailles settlement and the Western orientation of its policies in government during the 1920s. He thought the Social Democrats had to be crushed before a Communist revolution could succeed in Germany—just as the Mensheviks (with whom he compared them) had been destroyed by the Bolsheviks in 1917. On Stalin's instructions, the German Communists issued a new Party programme in which they promised to annul the Versailles Treaty and denounced the SPD as lackeys of the West. On Moscow's orders in 1931, the Communists in Prussia even allied with the Nazis in a plebiscite against the SPD state government.

It is debatable whether a united front of German Communists and socialists could have prevented Hitler from coming to power. But there is no question that the Communists aided him to do so by their actions. In 1932, the SPD leaders asked the Soviet embassy in Berlin for help to resist the Nazi threat. Explaining the Soviet refusal, an attaché told the German socialists: 'Moscow is convinced that the road to a Soviet Germany leads through Hitler.'[3]

In Stalin's way of thinking there was no moral distinction between Nazism and democracy (socialist or liberal): they were equally the products of the 'capitalist system' and could both be used—or played off against each other—to advance Moscow's revolutionary goals. Stalin was counting on a lasting conflict between the West and Nazi Germany to give the Soviet Union the breathing spell it needed to build up its industrial economy and arm itself against both sides.

Like Lenin before him, Stalin saw the revolutionary potential of a long war between the capitalist states. By staying out of the conflict for as long as possible, the Bolsheviks could exploit the social crises that were likely to result from the military exhaustion of both sides, only entering the war in the final stages to revolutionize the countries liberated by the

Red Army. Stalin was planning for this scenario from as early as 1925 and his revolutionary vision of the coming war remained remarkably consistent through the 1930s and '40s:

> Conflicts and wars among our enemies are . . . our great ally . . . they are the biggest help to our government and our revolution . . . If a war breaks out, we will not sit by with folded arms—we will have to take to the field, but we will be *last* to do so, and only then to throw the decisive load onto the scales.[4]

Hitler may have had a place in Stalin's revolutionary plans, but the Nazi domination of Europe certainly did not. Stalin was sufficiently alarmed by German military aggression to join the Western states in building collective security. Within two years of Hitler's coming to power, the Soviet Union had joined the League of Nations (a creation of the Versailles Treaty previously reviled as a tool of Anglo-French imperialism in Soviet thinking) while the Comintern had made a complete turnaround from its policy of non-cooperation with the socialists to support a United Front with Western socialist and democratic parties to resist the spread of fascism.

France was the key to the United Front. It was at the heart of non-fascist Europe geographically, and it had in the Parti Communiste Français (PCF) the largest Communist party (outside the Soviet Union itself) after Hitler's crushing of the German Communists in 1933. France also had a powerful grassroots anti-fascist movement, which came on to the streets in the general strike of February 1934. Organized by the PCF and French socialists to defend the Third Republic against fascist riots, the strike was joined by over 1 million workers in Paris alone. It polarized society between Left and Right and stirred the republican middle class to unite behind the anti-fascist movement, eventually leading to the election of the Popular Front government in May 1936.

French actions impressed Georgi Dmitrov, the Bulgarian Communist and refugee from Nazi Germany, who became the General Secretary of the Comintern Executive in Moscow in June 1934. In the light of the events in France, Dmitrov championed a United Front. The Comintern instructed Communist parties to unite with socialists against the fascist threat. It even allowed them to join Popular Front coalitions with 'bourgeois' parties (e.g. liberals and peasant-based popular parties) where this could stop the fascists. The new policy was a radical departure from the Leninist position, which since 1917 had violently rejected any compromise with parties outside the socialist camp. It made sense only because Stalin's goal was not to make a revolution but to block a fascist one by reinforcing parliamentary democracy and, if necessary, mobilizing workers to defend it on the streets.

The immediate upshot of the United Front was a bilateral pact of mutual assistance between the Soviet Union and France in May 1935. The French Communists were now instructed to end their opposition to the government of Pierre Laval and support its military budget, including its proposal to extend compulsory military service from one to two years, a policy the Communists had bitterly opposed. Stalin's thinking was to strengthen France's fighting potential so that it would not be overrun by Nazi Germany in the event of war.

With its anti-fascist front the Soviet Union presented a friendly face towards the West. Maxim Litvinov, an educated European-oriented Jew, was the perfect instrument of Stalin's foreign policy in this respect. As the People's Commissar of Foreign Affairs in the 1930s, Litvinov worked hard to strengthen collective security by forging closer links between the Soviet Union and the Western states. It was through Litvinov's initiative that the United States recognized the Soviet Union in 1933; and his doing that the USSR joined the League of Nations the next year.

Through the United Front the Soviet Union won over many sympathizers in the West. Soviet propaganda portrayed the USSR as the leader of 'progressive humanity', as the world's only socialist state, and as its main hope against the fascist threat. Western intellectuals were taken in. In June 1935, a Moscow-financed International Writers' Congress for the Defence of Culture was held in Paris at which famous writers such as André Gide, André Malraux, E. M. Forster and Aldous Huxley declared their solidarity with their Soviet comrades (including Boris Pasternak and Ilya Ehrenburg, who attended as guests) in the struggle against fascism. This was a time when Western intellectuals (the so-called 'fellow-travellers') allowed their left-wing sympathies and fears of fascism to cloud their judgement of Soviet political realities. They saw progress in the Soviet Union but were blind to the famine and terror. Many were impressed by the Soviet Constitution of 1936, a bogus declaration which promised social rights and religious and political freedoms unknown by the Soviet people in reality. Not a few believed that the show trials were genuine and necessary. The British socialist Beatrice Webb believed that Stalin had 'cut out the dead wood'.[5] Others turned a blind eye to the trials, or suppressed their doubts, refusing to criticize the Russian revolution, which in their eyes was the great defender of humanity against fascism.

The Communist parties of Western Europe grew dramatically, partly in reaction to the fascist threat and partly from a sense of solidarity with the Soviet Union. In France the PCF increased from 87,000 members in 1935 to 325,000 in 1937, making it the largest French party. In Spain the Communist Party grew from 40,000 to 250,000 members during these same years. The movement's growing international strength fuelled the Kremlin's ambitions. From the vantage point of Moscow, it seemed as if the whole world were engulfed in the struggle against fascism, and that Communism should emerge triumphant from the fight.

By 1938 Stalin was becoming increasingly sceptical about the commitment of the Western powers to stand up to the military aggression of the Axis powers, Germany, Japan and Italy, which were united by their opposition to the Comintern. The British and the French appeared set upon a course of appeasement. They had failed to act against the German occupation of the Rhineland, Hitler's annexation of Austria and the subsequent attack on Czechoslovakia; while the Soviet Union had been the only power to support the anti-fascist cause in Spain.

Collective security was something for the Western states to talk about, but it meant nothing if they were not prepared for military sanctions to enforce it. Nothing was done by the League of Nations to stop the Italian conquest of Ethiopia, although both were member nations of the League; nor to oppose the Japanese invasion of China, prompting Moscow, alarmed at the prospect of Japan attacking through Manchuria against Siberia, to send guns and planes to the Chinese.

Stalin was afraid of what seemed like the growing likelihood of the Soviet Union having to fight a two-front war against the Germans and the Japanese. It seemed to him that the real aim of the Western powers and the policy of appeasement was to turn the Nazis' military aggression east, towards the Soviet Union, hoping that the fascist and Communist regimes would wipe each other out. Stalin's aim was the opposite: to keep the 'two factions of the capitalist system'—the liberal and the fascist—engaged in a long war in the West to allow the USSR to rebuild its military strength and join the war at the decisive moment to turn it to its revolutionary advantage. In October 1938 he talked of leading a 'crusade' against the capitalist powers to 'help the proletariat of those countries to liberate themselves from the bourgeoisie'.[6]

As the danger of a two-front war increased, along with German and Japanese aggression, Stalin lost any belief in the alliance with the British and the French as a means of guaranteeing collective security. He began sending signals to the Germans with a view to offering a deal of Soviet neutrality in the event of a European war. The first sign came in his speech to the Eighteenth Party Congress in March 1939 in which he underlined that the Soviet Union would not get involved in conflicts between the capitalist states. Then, in May, Litvinov was replaced as Foreign Minister by Molotov, who in July gave a speech in which he clearly signalled Soviet disenchantment with the British and the French. He called them 'crooks and cheats' for delaying talks with the Soviet Union over a tripartite military alliance, the only guarantee the Soviets would accept to join the Western powers against Germany.

By this time Hitler was preparing the invasion of Poland. In case this resulted in a declaration of war by Britain or France, he needed Soviet neutrality to avoid a two-front war. Stalin also needed peace with

Germany. His forces were involved in a border war with the Japanese in Mongolia and Manchuria, and would not overcome their stiff resistance along the Khakhin Gol River until September. Aware that it would raise their price to the Germans, the Soviets continued to negotiate with the British and the French. But the Western powers were not serious about a military alliance with the Soviets. They came to Moscow without even a detailed plan for joint operations with the Soviet Union. They suspected Stalin of harbouring aggressive intentions towards Finland and the Baltic states, which they feared would be pushed into the German camp. In any case, the Poles would not agree to Soviet forces on their soil. So the talks broke down.

On 23 August 1939, the Soviet Union signed a Non-Aggression Treaty with Nazi Germany, leading directly to the start of the Second World War. There was a secret protocol, revealed only after 1945, granting the Soviet Union a sphere of influence in the Baltic states, Finland, eastern Poland and Bessarabia. The Soviet Union would effectively reclaim the western territories the Russian Empire lost in 1917.

For Communists around the world the Nazi–Soviet pact was a tremendous shock. It seemed like a betrayal of their most fundamental ideological principles. The leading role of the Soviet Union in the struggle against fascism was one of the many myths by which they had lived and held on to their beliefs. Later they would try to justify the pact in tactical terms, arguing that the Soviet Union needed more time to prepare for war. Stalin also used this argument, claiming that his tactics had been Leninist in so far as Lenin too had signed a peace with Germany to gain a necessary 'breathing spell' for the revolution. But in fact at the time Stalin meant to stay out of the war simply for as long as possible. On 7 September, he told his inner circle that they would wait for the Western Allies and Nazi Germany to exhaust themselves in a long war that would undermine the capitalist system before they stepped in to 'tip the scales' and emerge as the victors. 'We have no objection to their having a good fight, weakening each other,' he said on the outbreak of the war.[7] On Stalin's orders the Comintern instructed Communists to use the war to organize unrest inside their countries, as the Bolsheviks had done in 1917. War and revolution would go hand in hand.

Assured of Soviet neutrality, Germany invaded Poland from the west on 1 September; two days later Britain and France declared war on Germany; and shortly afterwards the Red Army entered Poland from the east.

Stalin saw the invasion as a chance to renew the revolutionary crusade that had been stopped by the Poles at the gates of Warsaw in August 1920. The invading Soviet troops were accompanied by NKVD units to carry out arrests and executions ('cleansing operations') of those deemed 'enemies'. They built their revolution by playing on the local ethnic hatreds between west Ukrainians, Belorussians and the dominant Polish majority. In the eighteen months of Soviet occupation they deported around 300,000 Poles and arrested about 120,000 others (mostly landowners, businessmen, intellectuals and those involved in the police and administration), of whom half were executed or died in captivity. On Stalin's orders they also executed 15,000 Polish POWs and 7,000 other 'bourgeois' prisoners in the Katyn Forest near Smolensk—a massacre the Soviet government denied for as long as it was in power.

Next the Soviets occupied the Baltic states. They imposed Soviet rule through rigged elections and began arresting 'anti-Soviet elements' in a 'cleansing operation' that deported or killed 140,000 Latvians, Estonians and Lithuanians during the twelve months of occupation by the Red Army.

But Finland proved more difficult than Stalin had expected when he launched his invasion on 30 November 1939. Soviet troops were unprepared for winter fighting, and could not breach the solid Finnish defences. In March 1940 Molotov admitted that 52,000 Red Army soldiers had been killed among the quarter of a million casualties. But Stalin told his inner circle that they were still on course for the 'world revolution' which the offensive had begun. Eventually Soviet reinforcements were able to break through the Finnish lines, and the Finns sued for peace. But it was a costly victory, and Soviet weaknesses had been exposed.

Hitler had always wanted to invade the Soviet Union. In *Mein Kampf* (1925) he had claimed that it was Germany's destiny to 'turn east' for '*Lebensraum*' ('living space'). In his racist ideology the Soviet people were 'sub-human' Slavs ruled by 'Jewish Bolsheviks' whom it was his mission to destroy. The ease of his early victories over Poland and the Western Allies—combined with the weaknesses of the Red Army exposed by the Finnish war—encouraged Hitler to believe that an easy victory was possible against the Soviet Union. With Soviet food and fuel the Germans would be too strong for the British.

Stalin persisted with his revolutionary strategy, providing Germany with the economic resources it needed for a long war with the Western powers in the belief that he could trust Hitler not to turn his armies east against the Soviet Union. Under the trade agreements signed as part of the Nazi–Soviet pact, the USSR agreed to send to Germany millions of tons of war matériel—foodstuffs, fuel, cotton, minerals—in an unequal exchange for German manufactured goods. In 1940, more than half of all Soviet exports went to Germany (there were few other customers). Convinced that Hitler would not attack the Soviet Union until he had beaten the British, Stalin thought he could buy time to build up his forces and use the Nazis in his revolutionary plans by supplying them with economic resources. The Soviets continued shipping goods to the Germans right up until they began their invasion of the Soviet Union in June 1941.

Stalin ignored intelligence reports of German preparations for their offensive, discounting the last, which were quite specific about the place and date of the attack, as a British ploy to lure the Soviet Union into war. The Red Army's generals knew exactly where the Germans were preparing to attack but did nothing about it. No one dared to question Stalin's judgement or authority. The Great Terror had paralysed the army's leadership, depriving it of all initiative, and in this sense the catastrophe of 1941 was also a result of the revolution's tragic course since 1917.

15

WAR AND REVOLUTION

The Germans launched their offensive, Operation Barbarossa, on a warm and sunny early summer morning, Sunday, 22 June 1941. Nineteen Panzer tank divisions and fifteen motorized divisions, supported by a huge fleet of Luftwaffe planes, opened up the way for 3 million troops, the largest invasion force in history, to advance along a 2,900-kilometre front. The German assault was so powerful and swift that it left Soviet forces in total chaos. Because of Stalin's negligence, Soviet defences were in disarray. Red Army units were rushed to the front to plug the gaps, only to be smashed by the German tanks and planes, which had control of the sky. By 28 June, German forces had advanced in a huge pincer movement to capture Minsk, 300 kilometres into Soviet territory, and were on the road to Moscow, while further north they cut through Lithuania and Latvia to threaten Leningrad.

Stalin was shaken by the fall of Minsk. 'Everything's lost,' he was heard to say that day. 'I give up. Lenin founded our state and we've fucked it up.'[1] Stalin must have realized that he was to blame for the disaster. Ignoring the intelligence reports of the German military build-up, he had failed to prepare for war, while his terror had seriously weakened the army. Over 80,000 Red Army officers were executed between 1937 and June 1941—including more than half the regiment commanders—so that inexperienced juniors had been thrust into positions of command.

Confused and despondent, Stalin retreated to his dacha, suffering a sudden loss of confidence for the next few days. It was not until 1 July that he returned to the Kremlin and, only two days later, that he made his first war speech to the country. Pausing frequently, he addressed the people, not as 'comrades', but as 'brothers and sisters, friends', calling on them to unite in this 'war of the entire Soviet people'.[2]

The invasion was the gravest crisis of the revolution. Hitler's aim was to destroy the 'Jewish Bolshevik' regime, to colonize and exploit the resources of the Soviet Union for the Third Reich. By exporting food to Germany, the Nazis planned to starve to death some 30 million Soviet people during the winter of 1941–2. The Jews would be eliminated, and the remaining population used as slave labour, deported, murdered, or, if they were strong and survived the war, assimilated to the Aryan colonists. This was where the revolution became clearly linked to the nation's survival.

Millions of people volunteered at once to go off to the front. People's Militias were formed in towns and factories. But not everyone responded equally to Stalin's call for national unity. Many criticized the Soviet leadership for its lack of preparation for the war. Workers were bitter at the flight of factory and Party bosses to the rear. They went on strike against ration cuts and stringent labour discipline. The industrial cities returned to the revolutionary atmosphere of 1917. In a strike in Ivanovo, when the Party bosses tried to calm the crowds, the strike leaders shouted to the workers: 'Don't listen to them! They know nothing! They've been deceiving us for twenty-three years!'[3] According to police reports, many workers welcomed the invasion because they hoped that it would sweep away the Soviet regime. It was said that only Jews and Communists had anything to fear from the Germans.

On 20 July, Stalin took control of the military command. Like the Tsar in the First World War, he was gambling all his power on his ability to save the country from catastrophe. Stalin ordered a counter-offensive on the Moscow front. For a while the German advance slowed.

Part of the invading force was diverted to the south to seize the land, industries and coal mines of Ukraine, which Hitler thought would make the Third Reich invincible. The Germans advanced south-east in a huge pincer movement and encircled Kiev, which they took after heavy fighting on 19 September.

Meanwhile, further north, they reached the shores of Lake Ladoga, effectively surrounding Leningrad by 8 September. Wanting to preserve his northern troops for the battle of Moscow, Hitler decided to lay siege to the city and starve its population out of existence rather than try to conquer it.

In strictly military terms the fate of Leningrad was not crucial to the outcome of the war, which would be decided on the Moscow and Ukrainian fronts. But as the birthplace of the revolution, Leningrad had a symbolic importance, making it impossible to abandon. Stalin sent his top commander, General Zhukov, to try to save the besieged city. Propaganda urged its 3 million people not to leave. The authorities were slow to evacuate them anyway (a mere 400,000 left before the Germans closed the exit routes). Many people chose to stay from patriotic motives or because they were afraid of being separated from their homes. But staying could have far worse consequences: one third of the population died from cold, starvation and disease before the siege was lifted in January 1944.

The conquest of Moscow was more important for Hitler's war against the Bolsheviks, and in the autumn of 1941 he concentrated his forces on that. He vowed that Moscow would be totally destroyed, its ruins flooded by an artificial lake created from the Moscow–Volga Canal. The Soviet troops defending Moscow were falling back in chaos on the Western Front when Zhukov arrived from Leningrad to take control of the capital's defence on 10 October. Five days later, Stalin ordered the evacuation of the government to Kuibyshev on the Volga. Panic spread as the bombing of the city became more intense. Huge queues formed at the food shops, and looting was not stopped by mass arrests.

Stalin made a radio broadcast pledging to defend the city to the end. More than Leningrad, Moscow's defence was essential to the survival of the revolution and Russia. If the Germans captured it, the whole country would be split in two; they would control the railway system, whose web of lines was centred on the capital; while the Soviet people would think the revolution had ended, so their willingness to go on fighting for it might well collapse.

Moscow's population rallied to the defence of the Soviet capital. How far they were motivated by their feelings for the city and how far by revolutionary loyalty is difficult to tell. A quarter of a million Muscovites dug defences on the city's edge, carted supplies to the front (only thirty kilometres from the Kremlin at the height of the fighting), and cared for injured soldiers in their homes. Thousands volunteered for the People's Militia to fight alongside military units, scratched together from the shattered armies that had fallen back from the Western Front and reinforcements from Siberia.

This new spirit of determination was symbolized by Stalin's bold decision to hold the Revolution Day Red Square parade as usual. Against the advice of his air commanders, who were afraid of German bombing, Stalin insisted that the symbolic importance of the parade at this decisive moment outweighed any military risks. In his speech from the Lenin Mausoleum (which was empty because Lenin's body had been secretly evacuated to Tyumen) Stalin called on the assembled troops to emulate the Red Army's spirit in the Civil War:

> Recall the year 1918, when we celebrated the first anniversary of the October Revolution. At that time three quarters of our country was in the hands of foreign interventionists . . . We had no allies, we had no Red Army—we had only just begun to create it—and we experienced a shortage of bread, a shortage of arms, a shortage of equipment. At that time fourteen states were arrayed against our country, but we did not become despondent or downhearted.[4]

From Red Square the troops marched straight to the front.

By mid-November, the German forces had become bogged down in mud and snow. They were unprepared to survive a Russian winter and exhausted after marching for five months without a break. For the first time, they were taking heavy casualties. The Soviets launched a counter-offensive, and by April had pushed the Germans back towards Smolensk. The relief of the capital was a huge uplift for Soviet morale. People started to believe in victory. The country was still in a terrible position. It had lost 3 million troops, more than half the number that had begun the war; much of Soviet industry had been destroyed; and 90 million citizens, nearly half the pre-war Soviet population, lived in territories occupied by the Germans; but Moscow's survival was a turning-point for the whole war.

No one can deny the extraordinary courage and sacrifice of the Soviet people in the war. But who can explain it? Why did so many Soviet soldiers fight with so much fierce determination and at times, it seems, without regard for their own lives? Was it something in the 'Russian character', as some have claimed, or in the revolutionary tradition?

Terror and coercion provide part of the answer. The practices of the pre-war terror system were reimposed to keep the soldiers fighting in the war. At the height of the Soviet collapse, on 28 July 1942, as the Germans threatened Stalingrad, Stalin issued Order No. 227 ('Not One Step Backwards!'), not publicly acknowledged until 1988, calling on the troops to defend each metre of Soviet territory 'to the last drop of blood', and threatening the death penalty for 'panickers' and 'cowards' who shirked their duty. Special 'blocking units' (*zagradotriady*) were set up to bolster the existing NKVD units. They swept behind the Soviet front and shot soldiers who lagged behind or tried to run from the fighting. During the course of the war 158,000 Soviet troops were shot by these units; 436,000 were imprisoned; while 422,000 were made to 'atone with their blood' for their crimes before the Motherland by serving in the special penal battalions used for the most dangerous military tasks.

The impact of the terror system should not be exaggerated, however. Order 227 was used at desperate moments, like the battle for Stalingrad, when an estimated 13,500 Soviet troops were executed in the space of a few weeks. But otherwise it was ignored by commanders, who learned from experience that military unity and effectiveness were not served by such drastic punishments.

Appeals to patriotism were more successful. The majority of Soviet soldiers were peasant sons: they were fighting not for Stalin or the Party, which had brought ruin to the countryside, but for their homes and families, for their own vision of the 'motherland' (*rodina*), a term in Russian (not unlike the German word *Heimat*) that can mean a kinship group, village, nation or homeland.

Soviet propaganda increasingly jettisoned revolutionary symbols in favour of older nationalist ideas of 'Mother Russia' that carried greater weight among the troops. Stalin's image became less conspicuous. The 'Internationale' was replaced by a new national anthem. Military heroes from Russian history appeared on Soviet medals. The Russian Ortho-dox Church was granted a new lease on life, as the state lifted many of its pre-war political controls on religious activities in exchange for the Church's moral support in the war campaign.

Propaganda also played on nationalist emotions of hatred and revenge. The Germans had committed so many atrocities on Soviet soil that it was not difficult to fan the Soviet people's rage to fighting pitch. According to a study of the Red Army's rank and file, it was hatred of the Germans, more than anything, that made the soldiers go into battle. The poem 'Kill Him!' (1942) by Konstantin Simonov—calling on the soldiers to kill 'every German' in revenge for the fascist rapes of Russian mothers and in remembrance of the sacrifice of their fathers in the First World War—was often read to soldiers by their officers before they went to fight.

The cult of sacrifice was a crucial aspect of the Soviet campaign, and constituted its single biggest advantage over capitalist societies where individual interests were more developed and the imperative of personal sacrifice for the collective good was harder to impose. In the Soviet Union the idea of sacrifice had been indoctrinated into the younger

generation since the Civil War. It was fundamental to the Five Year
Plans that hardships had to be endured. By 1941, the Soviet people were
prepared for the privations of the war—the sharp decline in living standards, the breaking up of families, the disruption of ordinary life—
because they had been through all of these and more during the 1930s.

In the first year of the war, the spirit of self-sacrifice was essential to
the Soviet Union's survival, as it struggled to recover from the catastrophic summer of 1941. The actions of ordinary soldiers and civilians,
who sacrificed themselves in huge numbers, made up for the failures of
the military command and the paralysis of nearly all authority. This
ethos was particularly intense in the 'generation of 1941' (people born
in the 1910s and early 1920s) who had been brought up on legendary
tales of Soviet heroes: record-breaking pilots and Stakhanovites; Arctic
explorers; soldiers of the Civil War; Communists who went to fight in
Spain. It was in emulation of their actions that so many youthful volunteers rushed headlong into the war.

The call to arms connected them to the heroic tradition of the Civil
War and the first Five Year Plan—the two great romantic episodes in
Soviet history when 'great achievements' were accomplished by collective enterprise and sacrifice. In the words of the poet David Samoilov
(who was twenty-one when he joined the army in 1941): 'the Civil War—
that was our fathers. The Five Year Plan—that was our older brothers.
But the Patriotic War of '41—that is us.'[5]

Reflecting on her own determination to fight against the Germans,
Rita Kogan speaks for that part of the 'generation of 1941' who joined
the army straight out of school:

I was just eighteen in 1941 . . . I saw the world in terms of the ideals of
my Soviet heroes, the selfless pioneers who did great things for the
motherland, whose feats I had read about in books. It was all so
romantic! I had no idea what war was really like, but I wanted to take
part in it, because that was what a hero did . . . I did not think of it as
'patriotism'—I saw it as my duty . . . I could have simply worked in the
munitions factory and sat out the war there, but I always wanted to be

an activist: it was the way I had been brought up by the Pioneers and the Komsomol.[6]

This generation fought with heroic bravery and recklessness, from the first day of the war. It bore the greatest human cost: only 3 per cent of the Soviet soldiers who were Rita's age would be still alive in 1945.

Fighting for a city—Moscow, Leningrad or Stalingrad—was also important. Local patriotism was a powerful motive. Soldiers and civilians were more prepared to fight when they identified the Soviet cause with the defence of a particular community, a real network of human ties, than when they were called upon to fight for some abstract notion of a 'soviet motherland'.

In Leningrad, as in Moscow, there was a complicated mix of motives behind the people's decision to stay and fight during the blockade. Some, like Petr Kapitsa, a sailor in the Baltic Fleet, were fighting for the birthplace of the October Revolution; they understood their cause as a continuation of this heroic tradition. 'It is clear,' he wrote in his diary on 22 March 1942:

> that the character of Piter's [Leningrad's] workers and intelligentsia—
> their revolutionary character, solidarity and determination—was
> formed by fighting tsarism and the White Guards and that in those
> years a specific type of people was created. There is a direct link between
> the unity of those who stormed the Winter Palace and the brother-
> hood of those united by the struggle of the siege.[7]

Others felt that they were holding out, not so much for Leningrad, but more for St Petersburg, the spiritual centre of Russia's European civilization and the old imperial capital; or for their beloved city to which they were attached by personal and collective memories as well as by the power of its cultural and revolutionary myths.

Comradeship was also crucial to military cohesion and effectiveness.

Soldiers tend to give their best in battle if they feel loyalty to a small unit of comrades. The rates of loss were so high in the first year of the war that small groups seldom lasted long. But after 1942 military units began to stabilize and the comradeship which men found within them became a crucial factor in getting them to fight. Veterans recall these friendships with nostalgia, often claiming that people in the war had 'bigger hearts' and 'acted from the soul', as if they had found in these small collective units a purer sphere of ethical relationships and principles than was possible to find in the Communist system, with all its compromises and contingencies.

By January 1943, the Red Army had forced the Germans back from Stalingrad. The spearhead of the German army was cut off. Battling as much against the cold and hunger as against the Soviets, the Germans kept up an intense resistance before finally surrendering on 2 February. The victory was a huge boost to Soviet morale.

From Stalingrad, the Soviet army pushed on towards Kursk, where it concentrated 40 per cent of its entire infantry and three quarters of its armoured forces to defeat the bulk of the German army in July. Kursk ended German hopes of victory on Soviet soil. The Red Army drove the Germans back to Kiev, reaching the outskirts of the Ukrainian capital by September and finally recapturing it on 6 November, just in time for the Revolution Day parade in Moscow the next day.

There were many reasons for the turnaround. First, unlike Hitler, Stalin realized that his commanders were best left to get on with the military campaign on their own. The running of the war was gradually transferred from the Military Council, dominated by political officers, to the General Staff, which took the lead in planning operations and merely kept the Party leadership informed. The power of the commissars in the units was also drastically reduced. Released from the Party's tight control, the officers developed a new confidence, and a stable corps of professionals emerged, whose expertise was crucial to the victories of 1943–5.

To reinforce this professional ethos, the government restored the epaulettes that had been worn by tsarist officers—a hated symbol of the old regime destroyed in 1917—and brought back the title 'officer' to replace the egalitarian 'comrade'. Medals also played a vital role. Eleven million medals were given out to Soviet servicemen—eight times more than awarded by the United States—between 1941 and 1945.

Soldiers who had distinguished themselves in battle were also encouraged to join the Party as requirements for entry from the army's ranks were lowered. By 1945, over half the Party's 6 million members were serving in the armed forces, and two thirds of them had joined it in the war. The Party lost much of its pre-war revolutionary character as a result of this influx. The outlook of the new members was more pragmatic, not so ideological, less inclined to view the world in terms of class, and more impatient with bureaucracy, compared to the Bolsheviks of the 1930s who were imbued with the Stalinist spirit of the Five Year Plan. The new mood was summarized by *Pravda* when it argued in 1944 that the 'personal qualities of every Party member should be judged by his practical contribution to the war effort'.[8] The test of a good Bolshevik was his conduct in the war.

The Soviet military revival was also the result of a transformation in the industrial economy. After the catastrophe of 1941, when the Red Army was poorly equipped compared to its adversary, there was a dramatic improvement in the production of tanks, planes, cars, radars, radios, artillery, guns and ammunition, allowing the formation of new tank and mechanized divisions which fought far more effectively. The rapid reorganization of Soviet industry was where the planned economy really came into its own, where the revolution won the war.

Without state compulsion, none of these industrial changes could have been achieved in so little time. Thousands of factories and their workers were evacuated east; virtually all industrial production was geared towards the needs of the military; railways were built or redirected to connect the new industrial bases of the Urals with the military fronts; and factories were placed under martial law to tighten labour discipline and productivity. Under the new work regime there were severe punishments for negligence, absenteeism or simply being late for work. Seventy-hour weeks became the norm, with many workers taking all their meals and sleeping in their factories, for fear of being late in the morning. Comprehensive rationing was introduced to reduce costs and keep people at their place of work, where they received their ration.

Gulag labour also played an important part in the wartime economy, producing perhaps 15 per cent of all Soviet ammunition, a large proportion of the army's uniforms, and desperately needed coal and oil, precious metals and raw materials, much of them from remote Arctic regions like Noril'sk and Vorkuta, which were only opened up by Gulag labour during the war. One of the advantages of the Gulag in a system built for war was that prisoners could be worked harder—and fed less—until they died. The death rate in the labour camps in 1942 was a staggering 25 per cent. But the supply of slave labour could always be replenished by making more arrests and taking prisoners of war as the Red Army conquered territories from the Germans and rounded up 'collaborators' with the enemy, Ukrainian or Baltic 'nationalists', and partisans opposed to the Soviet regime.

The same rationale applied to the Red Army: there was almost no limit to the number of lives that the Stalinist regime was willing to expend to achieve its strategic goals. That was the logic of a system built on revolutionary imperatives: the individual counted for nothing. In Western armies strategic decisions were generally reached by calculating the gains to be made by a manoeuvre against the likely cost in casualties. In the Red Army no such calculation was ever really made. Military objectives were set regardless of the cannon fodder they consumed. This was particularly true in the final stages of the war when Stalin pressed his generals to do all they could to reach Berlin before the Allies. Only by considering this criminally wasteful rationale can we explain the extraordinary losses of the Red Army during the Great Patriotic War—8.6 million in uniform alone between 1941 and 1945—a daily rate of losses twice as high as all the Allied casualties on D-Day.

For all that, many Soviet people would recall the war, despite its horrors, as a period of relative freedom, certainly compared to the years before. Forced to act on their own initiative, without thinking of the risks, they felt more independent, more useful and connected to the nation, and from this activity a new sense of the public good emerged. The historian Mikhail Gefter, then an army doctor, described the war as a period of 'spontaneous de-Stalinization'.

The American writer Hedrick Smith recalls a conversation he heard in the house of a Soviet scientist in the 1970s. The scientist had said that the war was 'the best time of our lives' and explained to his surprised friends: 'Because at that time we all felt closer to our government than at any other time in our lives. It was not their country then, but our country. It was not they who wanted this or that to be done, but we who wanted to do it. It was not their war, but our war. It was our country we were defending, our war effort.'[9] And that collective effort seemed to hold out hope of change for the better once the war was won.

The war was transformative in another way as well. It allowed bonds of comradeship to grow among the soldiers and encouraged them to exchange political ideas in ways that would have risked arrest during the 1930s. These small groups of trusted friends were a relatively safe environment in which to discuss what they were fighting for. As they entered Europe and saw a better way of life, they began to question the Soviet system. Most were peasant sons who had come into the army with a propaganda image of the capitalist world. But now they could see it with their own eyes. Many talked about the need to abolish the collective farms, open churches, increase democracy, or end the Party system root and branch. Officers were in the forefront of this army movement for reform.

The Soviet leadership was anxious about what would happen when these men came back from war. It was aware of the historical parallel with the aftermath of the Napoleonic Wars, when officers returned to tsarist Russia with the Western ideas of liberal reform which went on to inspire the Decembrist uprising of 1825. The regime dealt with this threat through a mixture of brutal repression and concessions. On their return to the Soviet Union, Soviet servicemen were interrogated by the NKVD in 'filtration' camps, where those with potentially subversive views and 'collaborators' with the enemy were weeded out and sent to the Gulag. But those who had a good war record and had proved their loyalty were given special access to higher education and rapid promotion to élite jobs.

Exposure to the West also fuelled a growing expectation of reform at home. The alliance with Britain and the USA had opened up Soviet society to Western influence. After years of isolation, the USSR was flooded with Hollywood films, Western books and goods imported by the Lend-Lease agreement with America since 1941. Millions of people began to understand what life in the West was like—not the ideal of Hollywood perhaps but a long way from the gloomy images of Soviet propaganda during the 1930s. Restaurants and commercial shops reappeared on Moscow's streets, giving rise to hopes that something like the NEP might be restored after the war. People thought that Soviet life should become easier, more permissive and open to the West, once they had achieved the longed-for victory.

But their hopes were dashed. There was no reform in 1945. The ending of the war meant a return to the autarky and austerity of the Five Year Plan to rebuild the devastated Soviet economy. Ideologically the Stalinist regime tightened its control to arm the country for the struggle with the West in the Cold War.

Stalin presented the military victory as a triumph for the Soviet system rather than the people's achievement. At a banquet for his senior commanders on 24 May, he made a famous toast to the 'tens of millions' of 'simple, ordinary, modest people . . . who are the little screws [vintiki] in the great mechanism of the state'.[10] With these words the popular conception of the Great Patriotic War as a 'people's war'—which had taken root as a potential challenge to the Soviet dictatorship—was officially dismissed. From now on the victory would be invoked as the justifying myth of Soviet power and everything it had accomplished after 1917. Indeed in many ways the Great Patriotic War replaced the Great October Socialist Revolution as the main foundation myth of the Soviet state.

16

REVOLUTION AND COLD WAR

As the Red Army advanced into Eastern Europe, Stalin thought about its revolutionary role. The victories of 1944–5 had opened up the possibility of imposing Soviet-style regimes on the liberated territories. He had been planning for this since before the war began. He had realized that the war would break down states and national boundaries, giving him the chance to export the revolution by liberating European lands. If the First World War had allowed the Bolsheviks to carry out the first stage of their revolution, in Russia, a second would 'allow us to take power in the whole of Europe', Molotov explained to the Lithuanian Foreign Ministry in 1940.[1]

Stalin was careful to conceal his ambitions from the Allies, instructing foreign Communists who followed in the footsteps of the Soviet troops to join other anti-fascist groups in united or 'national fronts' in order to disguise their revolutionary intentions. In May 1943 he dissolved the Comintern and gave an interview to *The New York Times* in which he disclaimed any intention of subverting other states—a claim that fooled American intelligence. Yet all the time Moscow was preparing Communists who would be installed in power by the Red Army in Poland, eastern Germany, Hungary, Yugoslavia and Bulgaria. At the Tehran Conference, in November 1943, Stalin pushed the British and Americans to agree to major territorial gains for the USSR, including eastern Poland up to the Curzon Line (the 1919 border) and the Baltic states, in effect reclaiming the lands he had won and Sovietized as Hitler's ally in 1939–41.

Stalin's first goal was to control Poland as a buffer zone to protect the Soviet Union against the threat of any post-war German revival. In July 1944, the Red Army crossed the River Bug and entered territory which Moscow was prepared to recognize as part of a future Polish state. Without consulting anyone it installed in power in Lublin the Polish Committee of National Liberation, a cover for the Communist Party, which Stalin henceforth treated as Poland's legitimate government. He would have no truck with the Polish government in exile in London, dismissing it as an agent of imperialism, and allowed the Nazis to destroy the Polish Home Army by holding back his forces on the Vistula when it launched the Warsaw uprising. Once the uprising had been crushed by the Germans, the Red Army entered Warsaw without any resistance from the Poles. By the end of January 1945, the Lublin Communists had formed a Provisional Government in the rubble of the Polish capital.

With the Red Army racing to Berlin and Soviet help required for the war against Japan, Roosevelt and Churchill had no real option but to appease Stalin in the early months of 1945. By the time the Big Three met at Yalta on 4 February, the Red Army had crossed the River Oder into Germany, while the Western Allies had not yet reached the Rhine. The Americans and British agreed to Stalin's plans to move the Soviet Union's borders westward to the Curzon Line, compensating Poland with land in eastern Germany, and to his proposals for a Polish government friendly to the Russians, insisting only on a vague undertaking by the Soviets to reorganize the Provisional Government 'on a broader democratic basis' to include the London Poles. When Molotov advised Stalin that the wording of the agreement might block their plans to Sovietize Poland, Stalin responded: 'Never mind. We'll do it our own way later.'[2] By April, the NKVD-trained security police in Poland had arrested 40,000 Poles deemed to be opponents of a Communist regime. They were held with German POWs in Auschwitz and other concentration camps.

Stalin thought of Poland as part of the Soviet 'sphere of influence'. At his meeting with Churchill in Moscow the previous October, the two leaders had carved up Eastern Europe into Soviet and Western zones (the Percentages Agreement). But where the British and Americans took these spheres of influence to mean traditional protectorates (without interference in domestic politics by the occupation force), Stalin saw them as a licence for the Sovietization of the liberated countries. 'Whoever occupies a territory,' he told the Yugoslav Communist Milovan Djilas, 'also imposes on it his own social system. Everyone imposes his own system as far as his army can reach. It cannot be otherwise.'[3]

By the early summer of 1945, Stalin was counting on a sphere of influence to include Finland, Sweden, Poland, Latvia, Estonia, Lithuania, Hungary, Czechoslovakia, Yugoslavia, Romania, Bulgaria and Turkey, including Soviet control of the Dardanelles. The Red Army's conquest of Berlin hardened his ambitions. Wherever Soviet troops were in control they carried out arrests and executions of anyone suspected of potentially opposing Russian domination—civil servants, businessmen, landowners, 'kulaks', nationalist partisans and collaborators with the Nazis. Conquest bred imperial attitudes. The Russians lorded it over the countries they had conquered. Zhukov, for example, filled his home with looted paintings and treasures from the Soviet zone in Germany. In the Baltic lands and west Ukraine there were mass deportations of the population—the start of a broad campaign of what today would be called ethnic cleansing—to make room for mainly Russian but also east Ukrainian immigrants.

Stalin arrived in Berlin for the Potsdam Conference in July like a conquering emperor. He set about imposing his conditions for the dismemberment of Germany, for the Polish–German border, and for reparations to the USSR in exchange for Soviet involvement in the planned invasion of Japan—at that point imagined as being potentially as brutal and protracted as the invasion of Germany had been. But then Truman, the new US President, surprised Stalin by announcing that the Americans had developed the atom bomb and would use it against the Japanese. The bomb altered everything.

So far Stalin had been relatively cautious in his strategy for the Sovietization of the countries occupied by the Red Army. In addition to telling the Communists to join the national fronts, in effect returning to the anti-fascist stance of the Comintern in the 1930s, rather than to push for revolutions of their own, he also held back from supporting the Communists in Greece, which was in the Western sphere of influence. In the Soviet zone of Germany he told the Communists not to go beyond the 'minimum programme' of land reforms and nationalizations, hoping that would broaden their appeal to the Western half of the country. In Stalin's view Eastern Europe was ready for a bourgeois-democratic revolution, a February 1917, but not yet for an 'October'. The Communists were small minorities, and nationalism was too strong. He supported the idea that each society should advance at its own pace on 'separate paths to Communism'.

All that changed with the dropping of the bomb. Stalin saw Hiroshima as a warning to the Soviet Union. It strengthened his conviction that to counteract that threat he needed to be tougher in his dealings with the West. He would use the offensive potential of his troops in Eastern Europe as a defence against the US bomb. 'The atomic blows against Japan forced us to re-evaluate the significance for the USSR of the entire East European bridgehead,' recalled Andrei Gromyko, the Soviet ambassador in Washington.[4]

A sign of that new toughness was the rigging of elections and intimidation of the opposition parties in Eastern Europe from the autumn of 1945. In Hungary, for example, the conservative Smallholders Party won a clear majority in the November elections. But Marshal Voroshilov, Stalin's 'pro-consul', imposed a coalition government with Communists controlling the Interior Ministry and the police, which enabled them to push opponents out of office by investigating and arresting them for their 'fascist' connections. One after another, by these 'salami tactics', the Smallholders Party was destroyed.

Aggressive posturing towards the West was also part of Stalin's tougher line. In his first major speech of the post-war era, in the Bolshoi Theatre on 9 February 1946, he called for renewed discipline and sacrifices by the Soviet people in another Five Year Plan, not just to recover from the damage of the war, but to prepare the country for the coming global conflict with its capitalist enemies, which, he said, was bound to come about 'as long as capitalism exists'. The speech was taken in the West to mean alarmingly that the Soviets were actually willing to engage in war. It was soon followed by a toughening of the US position towards the Soviet Union.

That new policy of 'containment' had its origins in the 'Long Telegram' sent by George Kennan, the deputy head of the US Mission in Moscow, to James Byrnes, the Secretary of State. Kennan was opposed to cooperation with the Soviet Union, which he argued was incapable of peaceful co-existence with the capitalist world. The historic fears and insecurities of Russia's leaders—'unable to stand comparison or contact with political systems of Western countries'—had been reinforced since 1917 by the Leninist idea that conflict between socialism and capitalism was both permanent and unavoidable. The revolution's ideology served to give a rational explanation for Stalin's fear of 'capitalist encirclement' and thus justified the Soviet dictatorship's determination to isolate and protect the country from a hostile world. The USSR would defend itself by threatening its capitalist enemies, because in Soviet thinking 'offense and defense [were] inextricably confused'.[5]

To contain the Soviet threat Kennan argued that US policy should aim to strengthen democratic institutions in the West and exert counter-pressure against the USSR 'at a series of constantly shifting geographical and political points'. The key to this strategy would be the combination of US atomic power and the British Empire's military bases around the globe. Recalled to Washington, Kennan helped to shape the Truman Doctrine of providing military and economic aid to countries (beginning with Greece and Turkey in 1947) to prevent them falling to the Communists.

The Marshall Plan was part of this containment policy. Developed in the State Department under Kennan's influence and named after

George Marshall, the Secretary of State, the plan aimed to rebuild the war-devastated economies of Europe through huge grants, credits and free trade (which would help the US recovery), linked to the building of democracy. Marshall offered aid to the Soviet Union and its allies. The strength of left-wing feeling in France and Italy—two countries deemed essential for the plan—made this politically necessary. But Stalin was suspicious. Although he welcomed the possibility of US credits to rebuild the Soviet economy, he rightly suspected that the real aim of the Plan was to drive a wedge between the USSR and the countries in its sphere of influence. At the Paris conference to discuss Marshall's proposals in June 1947 the Soviets took a cautious line. Stalin was hoping that the post-war economic slump might turn France and Italy against the Americans, strengthening his revolutionary hand. But once it looked as if the Czechoslovaks and the Poles might sign up for the Marshall Plan, he pulled out of the talks and forced East European governments to do the same. The Czechoslovak Foreign Minister was summoned to Moscow for a dressing down by Stalin. Under pressure from the Kremlin the Czechoslovaks and Poles, followed by the rest of the nations in the Soviet zone, withdrew from the Paris conference.

Cominform (the Communist Information Bureau) was the Soviet response to the Marshall Plan. Established in September 1947, its aim was to facilitate direct Soviet control over the Communist parties and, through them, interference in the politics of the East European satellites by coordinating policies. Its foundation was a turning-point in the Kremlin's plans for the Sovietization of the Eastern bloc. Whereas Moscow had previously accepted that each society would follow its own separate revolutionary path, it now insisted on ideological conformity ('Cominformity') within the Soviet zone. Moscow would no longer tolerate any deviation from its international policies by governments within its sphere of influence. This meant the end of the national fronts, as Stalin pushed the Communists to seize power in 'Octobers' of their own.

The methods they employed varied in each country but almost everywhere the results were the same. In Czechoslovakia, where the

Communists were expected to do badly in the spring 1948 elections, they came to power through a pre-emptive coup in February—first by purging oppositionists from the police to provoke the resignation of the opposition parties from the government, and then by intimidating President Beneš to concede to their demand for a Communist-dominated government through mass workers' demonstrations and seizures of the ministries by Action Committees modelled on the Red Guards of 1917. In Hungary the Communists combined their 'salami tactics' with the rigging of elections and threats of intervention by Moscow to force the opposition leaders out of the country and absorb the Social Democrats into their own ranks, effectively creating a one-party state. In both cases the Communists had learned their ruthless tactics from the Bolsheviks.

It was only in Yugoslavia that the Communists resisted the Cominform's prescriptions. Tito's partisans had won the war in Yugoslavia without much help from the Red Army. Their revolution was united by a strong sense of national independence. Stalin was angered by Tito's disobedience. His relations with the West were complicated by the Yugoslav conquest of Istria, an Italian territory, and by Tito's support of the Communists in the Greek Civil War. Tito's plans to incorporate Albania and Bulgaria in an enlarged Yugoslav Federation also irritated the Kremlin, which feared the rise of Yugoslavia as a rival Communist centre of power in Europe. Accused of breaking with the Leninist tradition, Yugoslavia was expelled from the Cominform in June 1948. Throughout the Soviet bloc there were purges and arrests of 'Titoists'— Communists in favour of a nationalist road to socialism independent of Moscow, although the term 'Titoist' was used interchangeably with 'Trotskyist' and 'counter-revolutionary'. One way or another, Stalin was determined to prevent Tito's mutiny from spreading.

In all the Cominform countries Five Year Plans modelled on the Stalinist prototype of 1928–32 were imposed. Smallholding farmers were forced to join collective farms—almost everywhere with the same disastrous economic consequences and mass arrests of 'kulaks' as in the Soviet Union. Huge industrial targets were handed down by the Party leadership. Heroes of Labour were promoted—versions of the Stakhanov cult. Portraits of Stalin were displayed everywhere, alongside the portraits of the 'Little Stalins' who ruled his Soviet satellites. New industrial cities—concrete urban grids with factories, tower blocks and Soviet names like Sztálinváros (in Hungary) and Stalinstadt (in East Germany)—were constructed in the High Stalin architectural style. There were no churches in these 'socialist cities'.

Throughout Eastern Europe Stalinization meant Russification—a major source of irritation and resentment for East European citizens, especially for intellectuals who thought of Russia as an alien place beyond the pale of civilization. Every schoolchild was made to learn Russian; knowing the language was a requirement for almost any job where higher education was called for. Russian books and films, Russian music and folk dance, Russian history, Russian food and drink were held up as superior to anything these Europeans could produce.

Pride in the military victory of 1945 had given rise to a type of cultural imperialism. The Soviet Union (for which read Russia) portrayed itself as the saviour of Europe and the world. In a speech on Revolution Day in 1946, Stalin's chief of ideology, Andrei Zhdanov, claimed in messianic mode that Russian literature, 'because it reflects a system far superior to any bourgeois democratic order, a culture many times higher than any bourgeois culture, has the right to teach other peoples a new, universal, morality'.[6]

The Cominform countries were all made to bow down and acknowledge the moral leadership of the Soviet Union, to worship at the cult of the October Revolution as the Liberator of Humanity. Even China, whose Maoist revolution brought a quarter of humanity into the Communist orbit, was kept in a position of subservience to the USSR, upon which it depended for military and technical support. After the victory of his revolution in 1949, Mao made several requests to meet Stalin. But he was rebuffed. Stalin was suspicious of the Chinese revolution because it was not based on working-class support (a peasant revolution could not be taken seriously). He feared that Mao might become a rival to his leadership of the Communist world. Eventually, the Chinese leader was invited to Moscow for Stalin's official seventieth-birthday celebrations in December of that year. But instead of being treated as an honoured guest, Mao was given a brief meeting with Stalin and then packed off to a dacha outside Moscow, where he was made to wait for several weeks for a formal audience with the man he called the Main Master.

In the Soviet Union the Cold War meant an end to the wartime relaxation in the cultural sphere. The Stalinist regime prepared the country for the international struggle by tightening its ideological grip on the intelligentsia and sealing off the country from Western influence.

Stalin was quick to clamp down on the ideas of reform that had surfaced in the war. In his Bolshoi Theatre speech he argued that the military victory had proved the superiority of the Soviet system, vindicating everything that had been done by his leadership before the war. Ruling out political reform, he ordered his subordinates to deliver 'a strong blow' against any talk of democracy. Censorship was reinforced. The NKVD was strengthened and reorganized as two separate bureaucracies: the MVD was henceforth to control domestic security and the Gulag system; while the MGB (the forerunner of the KGB) was placed in charge of counter-intelligence and espionage (although in a world where the regime's enemies were by definition 'foreign spies', their mandate spilled over into the surveillance of the domestic scene as well). The post-war years saw no return to the terror levels of the 1930s. But every year tens of thousands of people were arrested and convicted by the courts for 'counter-revolutionary' activities.

Stalin launched a new purge of the army and the Party leadership, where rival power centres, formed by groups perceived as 'liberal' reformers, were seen by him as a potential challenge to his personal authority. His first priority was to cut down the top army leaders, who enjoyed popular authority as a result of victory in 1945 and, in the case of Marshal Zhukov, had become the focus of the people's reform hopes. On Stalin's orders, Zhukov was demoted to commander of the Odessa Military District, and later sent to an obscure posting in the Urals. Zhukov's name vanished from the press. He was written out of war accounts, in which Stalin now appeared as the sole architect of victory.

Stalin also turned against the Party leadership of Leningrad, a city with a strong sense of independence from Moscow (strengthened further by the solidarity of the Leningraders in the siege) and a vibrant literary culture rooted in the European values of the nineteenth century. Leningrad's Party leaders were neither liberals nor democrats: they were technocrats who believed in the rationalization of the Soviet system. During the war, a number of them had risen to senior positions in Moscow, largely due to the patronage of Zhdanov, the former Party boss of Leningrad. In 1949, several leading Leningrad officials were arrested, including the Director of Gosplan and Politburo member Nikolai Voznesensky, who had been the mastermind behind the planning of the Soviet war economy and had since developed ideas of economic reform based on the NEP. These were the first in a series of arrests and fabricated cases (known as the 'Leningrad Affair') through which Stalin destroyed leaders he perceived as threats to his personal rule.

The post-war political clampdown was matched by a return to the austerity of the planned economy. A new Five Year Plan was introduced to rebuild Soviet industries after the destruction of the war and rearm the country for the new conflict with the West. Huge building projects were drawn up for the restoration of the country's war-torn infrastructure and housing. The war on Soviet soil had destroyed 1,710 towns, 70,000 villages, 6 million buildings, and 31,580 factories—all in all about a quarter of the country's pre-war physical assets; it had left 20 million people homeless and an even greater number in housing without heating, running water or electricity.

Forced labour played an increasingly important role in the post-war Soviet economy. The Gulag population rose by at least 1 million in the five years after 1945, and there was an army of unpaid labour in the 2 million German POWs, who were mostly used for timber-felling, mining and construction, including many of the showcase building projects which came to symbolize the post-war confidence and achievements of the Soviet system—the Volga–Don Canal, the Kuibyshev hydro-electric station, the Baikal–Amur and Arctic railways, the extensions to the Moscow Metro, and the Moscow University ensemble on the Lenin Hills, one of seven wedding-cake-like structures ('Stalin's cathedrals') in the ostentatious 'Soviet empire' style which shot up around the capital in these years.

To reduce consumer spending and inflationary pressures there was a currency reform (exchanging old roubles for new ones at a rate of ten to one) in 1947. Taxes on collective farms increased by one third between 1946 and 1948. Grain exports rose to pay for industrial and military spending. But there was famine in the countryside, following a poor harvest in 1946, which left around 100 million people hungry and took the lives of at least 1 million people through starvation and disease. Despite the promise of a better life to come after the war, for most people it seemed that nothing much had changed since the 1930s, the years of austerity and sacrifice.

In the cultural sphere the ideological struggle against the West was intensified through Zhdanov's policies. It is by his name (the *Zhdanovshchina*) that the official clampdown against Western ('anti-Soviet') tendencies in all the arts and sciences became known.

The *Zhdanovshchina* had its origins in the victory of 1945, which gave rise to a xenophobic Russian nationalism promoted by the Soviet leadership. Absurd claims were made for the achievements of Soviet science. The aeroplane, the steam engine, the radio, the incandescent bulb—there was scarcely an invention the Soviets did not claim. Stalin's intervention in the sciences led to the promotion of frauds and cranks like Timofei Lysenko, who claimed to have developed a new strain of wheat that would grow in the Arctic.

With the onset of the Cold War, Stalin called for iron discipline to purge all Western elements in cultural affairs. The starting-point of this campaign was Leningrad. The clampdown began on 14 August 1946, when the Central Committee published a decree censoring the journals

Zvezda and *Leningrad* for publishing the work of two great Leningrad writers, Mikhail Zoshchenko and Anna Akhmatova. In singling out these writers for attack the Kremlin aimed to underline the subordination of the Leningrad intelligentsia to the Moscow-based regime. Akhmatova had acquired tremendous moral influence during the war. Although her poetry had been rarely published in the Soviet Union since 1925, she remained a symbol of the spirit of endurance that had enabled Leningrad to survive the siege.

Zoshchenko was equally a thorn in Stalin's side. He was the last of the Soviet satirists—Mayakovsky, Zamyatin and Mikhail Bulgakov had all perished—a literary tradition dictators cannot tolerate. Stalin had long been irritated by Zoshchenko's stories. He recognized himself in the figure of the sentry in 'Lenin and the Guard' (1939), in which Zoshchenko portrayed a rude and impatient 'southern type' with a moustache, whom Lenin treats like a little boy.

The attacks against Akhmatova and Zoshchenko were followed by a series of repressive measures against 'anti-Soviet elements' in all the arts and sciences. The State Museum of Modern Western Art was closed down. A campaign against 'Formalism' and other 'decadent Western influences' in Soviet music led to the blacklisting of several composers (including Shostakovich, Khachaturian and Prokofiev) charged with writing music that was 'alien to the Soviet people and its artistic taste'. In January 1947, the Politburo issued a decree against *A History of European Philosophy* (1946) by G. F. Alexandrov, the head of Agitprop (the Central Committee's Department of Agitation and Propaganda), accusing him of having undervalued the Russian contribution to the Western philosophical tradition.

In July, the Central Committee published an ominous letter censuring the scientists Nina Kliueva and her husband, Grigorii Roskin, for 'obeisances and servility before foreign and reactionary bourgeois Western culture unworthy of our people'. The scientists were accused of giving information about their cancer research to the Americans during a US tour in 1946. They were dragged before an 'honour court', a new institution to examine acts of an anti-patriotic nature in the Soviet establishment, and were made to answer hostile questions before 800 spectators.

As the Cold War and official xenophobia intensified, Soviet society was gripped by fear of foreigners. People did not need long memories to recall the Great Terror. The American journalist Harrison Salisbury remembers returning to Moscow as a correspondent in 1949: none of the Russians he had known from his previous stay in 1944 would now acknowledge him. The briefest contact with a foreigner was enough to warrant a person's arrest. The Soviet jails were filled with Soviet citizens who had been on trips abroad. In February 1947, a law was passed to outlaw marriages to foreigners. Hotels, restaurants and embassies were watched by the police for Soviet girls who met foreign men.

Much of this xenophobia was directed against the 2 million Soviet Jews. Their fortunes were connected to the foundation of Israel and its position during the Cold War. Despite his anti-Semitism, Stalin had been an early supporter of a Jewish state in Palestine. He had hoped to turn it into a Soviet satellite in the Middle East. When Israel turned out to be pro-American, he became afraid of pro-Israeli feeling among the Soviet Jews, suspecting them as a potential fifth column. His fears were reinforced by Golda Meir's arrival in Moscow as the first Israeli ambassador to the USSR in the autumn of 1948. Everywhere she went she was cheered by crowds of Soviet Jews.

In 1948, Solomon Mikhoels, the director of the Jewish Theatre in Moscow, was killed in a car accident arranged by the MVD. In 1949, the Jewish wives of Politburo members Molotov and Kalinin were arrested. The same year saw the start of a vicious campaign against 'cosmopolitans' (i.e. Jews) and other 'anti-patriotic groups' in the cultural sphere, with sackings and expulsions from the Party, the Writers' Union, universities and research institutes.

The campaign reached fever pitch with the 'Doctors' Plot' in 1952. The plot had its origins in 1948, when Lidya Timashuk, a doctor in the Kremlin Hospital who also worked for the MGB, wrote to Stalin two days before Zhdanov's death, claiming that his medical staff had failed to recognize the gravity of his condition. The letter was ignored and filed away, but three years later it was used by Stalin to accuse the Kremlin doctors of belonging to a 'Zionist conspiracy' to murder Zhdanov and the rest of the Soviet leadership. Hundreds of doctors and officials were arrested and tortured into making confessions, as Stalin concocted a huge international conspiracy that linked Soviet Jews in the medical profession, the Leningrad Party organization, the MGB and the Red Army to Israel and the USA. The country seemed to be returning to the atmosphere of 1937 with the Jews in the role of the 'enemies of the people'.

In December 1952, Stalin told a meeting of the Central Committee that 'every Jew is a potential spy for the United States', thus making the entire Jewish people the target of his terror. Thousands of Jews were arrested, expelled from jobs and homes, and deported as 'rootless parasites' from the major cities to remote regions of the Soviet Union. Stalin ordered the construction of a vast network of new labour camps in the Far East where all Jews would be sent. Rumours spread of Jewish doctors killing babies in their wards. Pregnant mothers stayed away from hospitals. People wrote to newspapers calling on the Soviet authorities to 'clear out' the 'parasites', to 'exile them from the big cities, where there are so many of these swine'.[7]

And then, at the height of this hysteria, Stalin died.

17

THE BEGINNING OF THE END

Stalin had collapsed from a stroke and lay unconscious for five days before he died on 5 March 1953. He might have been saved if medical assistance had been called in early enough. But in the panic of the Doctors' Plot none of Stalin's inner circle dared take the initiative. It is a fitting irony that Stalin's death was caused by his own politics.

The news was announced to the public on 6 March. Huge crowds came to the Hall of Columns near Red Square, where his body lay in state. Moscow was mobbed by mourners, who had travelled to the capital from all corners of the Soviet Union. Hundreds were killed in the crush.

For nearly thirty years the Soviet people had lived in Stalin's shadow. He was their moral reference point, their teacher, guide, national leader and saviour against the enemy, their guarantor of justice and order. The grief they showed on Stalin's death—when even the dictator's victims mourned—was a natural response to the confusion they were bound to feel. The tears were born of a strange tension and hysteria. There was no release from fear. On the contrary, people did not know what would happen next—there might be mass arrests in retaliation for his death—and so old fears resurfaced. The only place where Stalin's death was welcomed with undisguised rejoicing was in the Gulag's camps and colonies. In the Viatka labour camp Vera Bronstein and her fellow-prisoners set down their tools and began to sing and dance when they heard the news: 'We are going home! We are going home!'[1] Among the prisoners it was commonly assumed that they would be released on Stalin's death. Hopes and expectations were extremely high.

A collective leadership assumed control on 5 March. It signalled a return to the Leninist idea of government, but also showed that the Politburo (known then as the Presidium) was divided—not least over whether to continue with Stalin's policies or introduce reforms. These differences were complicated by personal rivalries. Beria was the dominant figure. With his power base in the MVD and MGB, he ran the government with Georgii Malenkov and Voroshilov, who were Chairman of the Council of Ministers and of the Supreme Soviet Presidium respectively. But Khrushchev, now the General Secretary of the Central Committee, campaigned against him with the Defence Minister, Nikolai Bulganin.

Senior Party and military leaders were suspicious of Beria's programme, which involved the dismantling of the Gulag and a relaxation of Soviet policies in the newly annexed territories of western Ukraine, the Baltic region and East Germany.

In the spring of 1953, Beria imposed a series of reforms on the East German leadership. The Communist hardliners in the GDR dragged their heels over implementing them, resulting in mass demonstrations on the streets of East Berlin in mid-June. Back in Moscow, Beria was blamed for the uprising by Khrushchev, Molotov and even Malenkov. On 26 June, he was arrested in a Kremlin coup organized by Khrushchev with senior army personnel. Tried in secret, he was later shot. There was no legal basis for the coup. There was nothing he had done without the agreement of the collective leadership. The verdict was announced before his trial was held. But none of the leaders opposed the coup. They were a docile group of functionaries, quick to bend their principles when they sensed a shift of power at the top. Khrushchev emerged from the coup with new authority and confidence.

A flamboyant and tempestuous character, derided by his opponents as boorish, overbearing, and inclined to make blunders, Khrushchev was born in 1894 to a poor peasant family and had only four years of schooling. He worked in mines and factories before joining the Red Army and the Party in the Civil War. His was a typical career path of so many Bolsheviks who hitched themselves to Stalin during the 1920s. Khrushchev rose through the Party ranks as a loyal executor of Stalin's policies. He was deeply implicated in the mass repressions of the 1930s, first as the Moscow Party boss, and then in Ukraine, where he was responsible for the arrest of a quarter of a million citizens.

Khrushchev took a leaf from Stalin's book in his use of policies to defeat his rivals for the leadership after 1953. Having opposed Beria, he stole his programme for his own, pushing through reforms to undermine his next main rival, Malenkov. Like Stalin, Khrushchev built up his support among the regional Party secretaries. He liberated them from police supervision and gave them more autonomy from the Moscow ministries, where Malenkov had his power base. He also spoke of reinforcing 'socialist legality', a term used throughout the Soviet period but never taken very seriously, and ordered a review of all 'counter-revolutionary crimes' since 1921. He took a particular interest in the Leningrad Affair, in which his rival Malenkov had served as Stalin's main henchman. Several MGB officials linked to Malenkov were arrested. In 1955, Malenkov himself was accused of 'moral responsibility' for the Leningrad Affair and removed as the head of the government. He was instead put in charge of electricity. It was a sign of how far things had changed that Malenkov was merely demoted. Under Stalin he would have been shot.

'Now those who were arrested will return, and two Russias will look each other in the eye: the one that sent these people to the camps and the one that came back.'[2] With these words Akhmatova anticipated the drama that unfolded as prisoners released from the Gulag confronted the colleagues, neighbours, friends who had put them there. Their return provoked a wide range of emotions—fear, shame, resentment and malice—in those who had remained on the right side of the Soviet authorities. They never thought their victims would be seen again.

The first to leave the camps were about a million prisoners, mainly criminals on shorter sentences, who were released by an amnesty on Stalin's death, just as prisoners had been amnestied when the Tsars died. Political prisoners were excluded from the amnesty. Their cases needed to be reviewed by the Soviet Procuracy, a long and complex process obstructed by authorities reluctant to acknowledge their mistakes. By 1955, the Procuracy had reviewed a quarter of a million appeals from political prisoners, but only 4 per cent resulted in release.

Two million 'politicals' returned from Gulag camps and colonies— and an equal number from the special settlements—between 1953 and 1960. Around three quarters of a million former prisoners were rehabilitated, many of them posthumously, during the same period. Rehabilitation was meaningful to those who had dedicated themselves to the revolution's goals. It restored some meaning to their lives. But the process of obtaining it was not restorative. It involved standing in long queues in offices, completing endless forms, and battling with officials who were often hostile to their cause. When rehabilitation was eventually granted, it came with no apology for the suffering, or for the wasted years, and in the eyes of most authorities did not eliminate a person's guilt. As one ex-prisoner was told by an official: 'Rehabilitation does not mean that you were innocent, only that your crimes were not all that serious. But there's always a bit left over!'[3]

Millions of people never returned from the camps. For their families, the years after 1953 were a long and agonizing wait for their return, or for news about their fate. In many cases it was not until the 1980s, when glasnost or 'openness' became the watchword of the Soviet government, and sometimes not until the 1990s, that they discovered what had happened to their missing relatives. There are families today that still don't know.

With so many prisoners returning from the camps, the regime needed to say something to explain what had gone on. But how much of the truth could be revealed? All the leaders were afraid of what might happen if the full extent of the terror was exposed. Would they be held accountable for it? Wouldn't people ask why they had failed to stop the mass arrests?

The decision to expose and denounce Stalin's terror was made by the collective leadership after it had heard the findings of a special commission instructed by the Central Committee to find out how it had been possible for Stalin to repress so many Party members between 1935 and 1940. Headed by Petr Pospelov, the former editor of *Pravda*, the commission reported to the Presidium of the Central Committee on 9 February 1956. The Politburo was shocked by its findings—both by the huge scale of arrests and executions and by the fabrication of the evidence on which they had been based—and decided to report them to the Twentieth Party Congress, the first since Stalin's death, whose 1,430 delegates assembled in the Kremlin on 14 February in the expectation that their leaders would explain the official status of the dead leader.

The Politburo was bitterly divided about how much to reveal from the commission's findings. Khrushchev wanted full disclosure to restore the people's faith in the Party. But Molotov and Kaganovich (now First Deputy Chairman of the Council of Ministers) were afraid that this would undermine the leadership's authority, as questions would be asked about their role in Stalin's policies. They settled on the compromise solution of a secret speech in which only half the truth would be revealed. The text was prepared collectively and Khrushchev took responsibility for its delivery on 25 February.

Given its momentous impact on the revolution's later history, Khrushchev's speech seems relatively tame. He gave details of the unjust repression of Party members in the later 1930s and of Stalin's blunders in the war, attributing them both to the dictator's deviation from Leninist principles (Lenin, he argued, would never have allowed the killing of other Bolsheviks, even if they had made ideological errors) and to the un-Marxist 'cult of the personality' (in stark contrast to Lenin's modesty) which had ruled out resistance to Stalin's policies. By emphasizing that the current leadership had found out about these details only recently, Khrushchev tried to absolve it and shift the guilt on to Stalin. There was no question of blaming the Party. Khrushchev presented the

Party as a victim—indeed the only victim of the Stalinist terror in so far as he failed to mention the mass arrests of ordinary citizens (or any mass repressions before 1935, when the current leadership had gone along with Stalin's policies). The whole purpose of the speech was to restore belief in the Party and return Leninism to power by presenting Stalinism as an aberration from October's socialist ideals. 'Our Party fought for the implementation of Lenin's plans for the construction of socialism,' Khrushchev told the delegates.

> This was an ideological fight. Had Leninist principles been observed during the course of this fight, had the Party's devotion to principles been skilfully combined with a keen and solicitous concern for people, had they not been repelled and wasted but rather drawn to our side, we certainly would not have had such a brutal violation of revolutionary legality and many thousands of people would not have fallen victim to the methods of terror. Extraordinary methods would then have been resorted to only against those people who had in fact committed criminal acts against the Soviet system.[4]

Like all the Party leaders, Khrushchev was afraid that, if they did not speak of Stalin's crimes, there would be more radical debate in intelligentsia circles. 'The thaw might unleash a flood, which we wouldn't be able to control and which could drown us all,' Khrushchev wrote in his memoirs. The veteran Politburo member Mikoyan was later asked why all the show trials could not simply have been declared illegal. 'No, they can't,' Mikoyan replied. 'If they were, it would be clear that the country was not being run by a legal government, but by a group of gangsters.' He thought for a moment and then added: 'Which, in point of fact, we were.'[5]

But there was more to Khrushchev's motives than the preservation of the status quo. If we are to believe his memoirs, he was plagued by his moral conscience and wanted to repent. He genuinely thought that truth was the only way to restore Party faith and unity—and thus save the Party from a fatal loss of self-belief. This was how he justified the speech to Party meetings afterwards. Like Gorbachev with glasnost,

Khrushchev saw this openness in the Leninist tradition of self-criticism, and believed it was the key to the Party's revolutionary strength. As Lenin had once said:

> All revolutionary parties that have perished until now, perished because they became self-satisfied. They could no longer see the sources of their strength and were afraid to talk about their weaknesses. But we will not perish, because we are not afraid to talk about our weaknesses and we will learn how to overcome them.[6]

The truth also helped Khrushchev to undermine his rivals for the leadership by building up support in those sectors of the Party and society that embraced his ideas of reform and Leninist renewal, returning to the ideals of October 1917.

Khrushchev ended his speech with a plea for secrecy: 'This subject must not go beyond the borders of the party . . . we must not provide ammunition for our enemies, we mustn't bare our injuries to them.'[7] His speech, however, did not remain secret very long. A transcript was sent to Party organizations across the Soviet Union with instructions for it to be read to Communists in workplaces. It was heard by 25 million members of the CPSU and the Komsomol in factories and offices, institutes and universities. It was also sent to the Communist governments of Eastern Europe. Walter Ulbricht, the East German leader, tried to conceal it from the population of the GDR, but the Polish leaders published it, and a copy reached *The New York Times*, which ran it on its front page on 4 June. From the West, the text of Khrushchev's speech filtered back to the GDR, Hungary and the Soviet Union.

The speech threw the Party into confusion. It came as a huge shock to the rank and file, whose world of certainties was suddenly destroyed. There were heated arguments about what to make of the revelations, with some Party members blaming leaders who had failed to speak out earlier, and others criticizing Khrushchev for raising all these questions at an awkward time. Many were sceptical about the leaders' claims that they had not known of Stalin's crimes; they asked why they had failed to prevent them. By June, the leadership was so concerned by these voices of dissent that it sent out a secret circular to local executives urging them to purge and arrest Party members who overstepped accepted boundaries of discussion. It published articles as a guide for the 'right' interpretation of the speech.

Outside the Party, some took Khrushchev's speech as a signal to discuss and question everything. The intelligentsia was the first to speak. 'The congress put an end to our lonely questioning of the Soviet system,' recalls Liudmilla Alexeyeva, later a well-known dissident but at that time a Moscow University student.

> Young men and women began to lose their fear of sharing views, information, beliefs, questions. Every night we gathered in cramped apartments to recite poetry, read 'unofficial' prose and swap stories that, taken together, yielded a realistic picture of what was going on in our country.[8]

At public meetings to discuss the speech there were angry condemnations of Stalin as an 'enemy of the people'. Statues and portraits of the leader were destroyed. From attacking Stalin it was a short step to questioning the Soviet system as a whole. Meetings called for multi-party elections and real rights and freedoms to prevent the terror from happening again.

Yet such questioning was generally confined to the intelligentsia. Ordinary people were too cowed by the Stalinist regime to speak openly or critically. From the long years of terror they had learned to remain silent, not to question the authorities. They were frightened to step out of line. Many people still revered Stalin. They took pride in Soviet achievements under Stalin's leadership—industrialization and victory in the war—that gave meaning to their lives. They were confused by Khrushchev's speech, which now cast doubt on all of this. Stalin loyalists were vocal in their opposition to the speech—nowhere more so than in Stalin's native Georgia, where public anger at the attack on him exploded in violent nationalist demonstrations in Tbilisi from 4 to 10 March.

Khrushchev's 'secret speech' marks the beginning of the revolution's third and final phase. The generation that came after it was fundamentally different—as a result of the revelations it contained—from the one that came before. The speech changed everything. It was the moment when the Party lost authority, unity and self-belief. It was the beginning of the end.

The Soviet system never really recovered from the crisis of confidence created by the speech. How could people continue to believe in a revolution that had killed so many in the people's name? In leaders who had told so many lies? For the first time the Party was admitting that it had been wrong—not wrong in a minor way but catastrophically. How could it rebuild its credibility?

Khrushchev believed it could by appealing once again to the Leninist ideas of October 1917. If people could accept that Stalin's policies had been an aberration in the Bolshevik tradition, they might re-embrace the revolution's founding principles—the one-party state as the embodiment of the Dictatorship of the Proletariat, state ownership of the means of production, the hegemony of collective over individual interests, etc. There were many in the Party and intelligentsia who found hope and inspiration in this idea of Leninist renewal. They formed a generation, 'the people of the sixties' (shestidesiatniki), whose world-view had been shaped by the Twentieth Party Congress and the Khrushchev Thaw. They were mostly children of Old Bolsheviks, or, like Gorbachev, from pro-Soviet families that had been repressed by Stalin during the 1930s. Khrushchev gave them the belief that they could reconnect with the revolutionary ideals of their parents' generation and carry on the work that they had left undone. But as well as giving many people hope his speech gave rise to widespread scepticism and disbelief. Its revelations invited questions not just about Stalin but about the system as a whole; and once they started questioning the system, they thought about alternatives to it.

Khrushchev's speech had an immediate impact in Poland, where workers seized on it to challenge the authority of the Communist system which Stalin had imposed. At the end of June the industrial city of

Poznań was engulfed by strikes and mass protests against the Communists and their Soviet-styled command economy. On Moscow's orders, Polish troops dispersed the crowds, killing dozens, wounding several hundred and arresting many more. But the Polish Communists also made concessions, appointing a new leader, Władysław Gomułka, who had been accused of 'nationalist tendencies' during Moscow's struggle with the 'Titoists'. Reassuring the Kremlin that Poland would remain inside the Soviet bloc, Gomułka began a series of reforms and talked about a 'Polish road to socialism' to appeal to nationalist sentiment.

News of these concessions encouraged the Hungarians. On 23 October, 20,000 mainly student protestors gathered at the statue of General Bem, a Polish-born hero of the Hungarian Revolution in 1848, and, in emulation of those earlier revolutionaries, sang the outlawed 'National Song' in which they vowed 'not to be slaves'. Huge crowds assembled in Budapest. A nine-metre statue of Stalin was toppled. The Soviet hammer and sickle was cut out of the national flag. Protestors fought with the police. The uprising spread to other towns.

The Hungarian leadership called for Soviet troops. Tanks entered Budapest within hours. They were resisted by civilians who organized militias, erected barricades and threw home-made bottle bombs (Molotov cocktails) at the Soviet tanks. The Communist reformist Imre Nagy took control of the situation, managing to bring the fighting to a halt by declaring a new national government committed to negotiating a withdrawal of Soviet troops from Hungary. On 1 November, he announced Hungary's exit from the Warsaw Pact.

This was enough to make up Khrushchev's mind to intervene again. If Hungary left the Warsaw Pact, the whole Soviet empire in Eastern Europe might unravel. On 4 November, Soviet tanks rolled in again. It took them a week to crush the uprising, at the cost of over 20,000 killed and wounded Hungarian civilians, and many more arrested later on. Denounced by Moscow as a 'counter-revolutionary', Nagy was arrested, tried in secret, and later executed 'as a lesson to all the other leaders in Socialist countries'.[9]

Distracted by the contemporaneous Suez Crisis, the West's reaction was subdued. But the Soviet action led to an international crisis in the Communist movement, with many of its leading figures resigning from the Party in protest. Not since the crushing of the Kronstadt Uprising had a Soviet action done so much to discredit the Russian Revolution among those who followed it abroad.

The Soviet population reacted little to events in Hungary. There were minor protests at Moscow University but that was about all. The press portrayed the Hungarian uprising as a 'fascist counter-revolution' which the West had organized. But more and more people did not believe this. The thaw had made it easier to access information from abroad. Illegally copied Western journals were passed from hand to hand, and people listened on short-wave radios to foreign radio stations for real news.

The thaw had begun in literature, a surrogate of politics throughout Russian history. Once the hand of Stalinist conformity had been removed, writers strived to portray Soviet life with more sincerity and honesty. Ehrenburg's *The Thaw* (1954)—which gave its name to this period—tells the story of a woman oppressed by her husband, a despotic factory boss and one of the 'little Stalins' found in every sphere of Soviet life. With the spring thaw she finds the courage to leave him.

Even more explosive was Vladimir Dudintsev's *Not by Bread Alone* (1956), the saga of a Soviet engineer whose inventiveness is stifled by the narrow-mindedness of the industrial bureaucracy. The book was hailed by supporters of the thaw as a battering ram against the Soviet establishment. It was an inspiration to young professionals looking for an outlet for their own creative ambitions and frustrated by the conservatism of their seniors, promoted under Stalin, who said no to anything that was not specifically allowed by the authorities. Dudintsev later said it had been his aim to unmask as the real 'enemies of the people' those Soviet officials whose careerist interests had sapped the revolution's energies.

The high point of the thaw came in November 1962 with the publication of *One Day in the Life of Ivan Denisovich*, the first novel to explore the theme of Stalin's labour camps, in the journal *Novyi Mir*. One million copies of Solzhenitsyn's novel were sold in the first six months, and each copy was read by many readers, who passed it from hand to hand. But if the literary exploration of the camps was cautiously allowed, the October Revolution could not be criticized by Soviet writers. In 1956, *Novyi Mir* refused to publish Pasternak's *Doctor Zhivago*, an epic human drama set against the backdrop of the Revolution and the Civil War, on the grounds that it was anti-Soviet. Simonov, the journal's editor, took the view that in posing the central question of his novel—whether the Russian intelligentsia had made the right decision to accept the October Revolution—Pasternak had set things up so that it could only be answered in the negative: that by deciding to go along with the Bolsheviks, the intelligentsia had betrayed their duty to the Russian people, to Russian culture and humanity. Smuggled to the West, *Doctor Zhivago* became an international bestseller. Pasternak was nominated for the Nobel Prize in 1958. But under severe pressure from the Soviet government he turned it down. The novel soon began to circulate in *samizdat* (illegally printed copies). When its author died of lung cancer in 1960, thousands turned out for the funeral, which threatened to become a political demonstration when one of his banned poems was read out. In no other country did literature attain as much authority—as the voice and conscience of the people—as it did in Soviet Russia.

Part of the thaw was the opening of Soviet society to the West. For the first time since 1917, foreigners arrived in large numbers in Moscow and Leningrad as the Khrushchev government started to see international tourism as a way of earning dollars and demonstrating Soviet achievements to the world.

In 1957, Moscow hosted the World Festival of Youth—the largest in the history of the left-wing student movement with 34,000 delegates from 131 countries. The Kremlin's aim was to win over the young people of the capitalist countries to the Soviet way of life. But the outcome was the opposite. With their jeans and easy-going manner the visitors converted Soviet youth to the Western way of life. Rock and roll and its attendant fashions captured the imagination of a generation of Soviet students who were too educated and sophisticated to be satisfied by the boring and conformist culture of the Komsomol. On their short-wave radios, they listened to the Voice of America and Radio Free Europe, where rock and jazz were the draw for news and information about the freedoms of the West. In the *stiliagi* they had their own versions of the Teddy Boys—mostly children of the Soviet élite who dressed in colourful American fashions, greased their hair, wore make-up, and spoke a slang to set themselves apart from the grey mass of Soviet society. They formed their picture of the West through Hollywood, whose films had a massive influence on Soviet youth, particularly *The Magnificent Seven*, *Some Like It Hot* and the *Tarzan* movies, for some time banned by the Soviet authorities on the grounds that they promoted juvenile delinquency. According to the poet Joseph Brodsky, whose tongue was only half in cheek, the *Tarzan* films 'did more for de-Stalinization than all Khrushchev's speeches at the Twentieth Party Congress and after'.[10]

From Khrushchev to Gorbachev, one of the revolution's biggest challenges was how to engage this young generation in its system of values and beliefs. The October Revolution was becoming old, an ever more remote historical event, to which a declining proportion of the Soviet people could relate at all. By the end of the 1950s, only 10 per cent of the population were aged over sixty years, old enough to remember the October Revolution as adults, and only 35 per cent were between thirty and sixty years of age, a generation shaped by the revolution but reduced in number by the war, but 55 per cent, a huge proportion, were under thirty years of age. There was a serious generation gap. The country had a declining population of pensionable age, for whom the revolution was the meaning of their lives, and a growing number of young people, for whom it meant very little, if anything at all. According to a survey by the Institute of Public Opinion in 1961, the majority of Soviet youth was disenchanted and even cynical about the ideals of the October Revolution, which they considered distant and abstract; they were mainly motivated by material interests. The revolution's survival would depend on satisfying them.

With the renunciation of terror, the regime had to find new ways of popular control and mobilization. It could no longer count on fear. Seeking to return to the Leninist idea of collective action, Khrushchev attached greater weight to mass participation in policy campaigns and grassroots organizations designed to reawaken the enthusiasm of the Revolution's early years. Among these initiatives were street patrols, which employed millions of volunteers; house and work committees, which were given legal powers to combat 'idlers and social parasites'; and public courts with citizen jurors. But the most ambitious was the 'Virgin Lands' campaign, in which hundreds of thousands of young men and women volunteered to work and settle on the steppelands of Kazakhstan.

Khrushchev promoted the campaign as a 'Leninist' response to the crisis of collectivized agriculture. The collective farms were too inefficient to feed the Soviet population. In 1953, Malenkov proposed to solve the problem by raising procurement prices, lowering taxes on the collective farms, and enlarging the kolkhoz workers' private plots, the small gardens where they kept pigs and chickens and grew vegetables to sell in the peasant markets found in every town. Khrushchev attacked Malenkov's proposals as a retreat from the collective principle, and presented the Virgin Lands campaign as an ideologically pure alternative. Kazakh leaders warned that it would fail to yield results in the long term: the lands were not just virgin but infertile. They were opposed to the settlement of traditional Kazakh pastoral lands by Russians and Ukrainians. But the campaign went ahead.

Propaganda trumpeted the achievements of the settlers on the Virgin Lands. Invoking Lenin's idea of the NEP, that the international class struggle would be fought out in the economic sphere, Khrushchev stressed the campaign's importance as a visible example of 'the advantages of the socialist over the capitalist system'. But its results were mixed: 40 million hectares of new land were brought into production in the decade after 1954, and grain output rose, but harvest yields were variable, and steadily declined from 1958, largely as a result of shortages of fertilizer to compensate for the poor soil. The Kazakh leaders had been right.

Agrarian societies throughout the Third World, however, saw a model of development in the Virgin Lands campaign and the Soviet 'economic miracle'. There was a growing perception that the Soviet Union was catching up with the United States, offering societies emerging from colonial exploitation a real alternative to the capitalist system. The Soviet economy grew by almost 10 per cent a year—three times faster than the American—between 1955 and 1960. The launching of the Sputnik programme in 1957—culminating in the first manned space-flight by Yury Gagarin in 1961—gave the USSR huge prestige in the developing world.

China's Great Leap Forward was inspired by the Soviet model, in particular by Khrushchev's speech to Communist leaders in Moscow on the fortieth anniversary of the October Revolution, in 1957, in which he boasted that in fifteen years the Soviet Union would not only catch up with but overtake the United States in industrial output. Mao responded to the speech by boasting that China would surpass Britain as an industrial power within the same period. His campaign of forced collectivization and industrialization led to an estimated 42 million deaths by 1961—surpassing even Stalin's Five Year Plan of 1928–32 in the human suffering it inflicted.

From this point China and the Soviet Union competed for influence in the Third World. Each claimed to have the correct revolutionary ideology—China's based on Mao's conception of peasant revolution and the Soviet Union's on the Leninist idea of a vanguard party of the urban working class. Khrushchev's Third World strategy signalled a return to the Leninist idea of separate national revolutionary paths. He supported anti-colonial nationalist movements—neglected by Stalin as part of the capitalist world—on the assumption that they might in time develop into socialist revolutions with vanguard Marxist parties of their own. This was gambling at long odds, since it was hardly likely that left-wing nationalist leaders in the Third World would be able to resist the pressures of the global capitalist market and persuade their people that their interests lay in the Soviet sphere of influence. None of the leaders backed by Khrushchev (Nasser in Egypt and Syria, Nkrumah in Ghana, Sukarno in Indonesia) proved reliable clients, despite receiving huge transfers of military aid, industrial investment and technical advisers from the Soviet Union.

Only Cuba was a winning bet, although Moscow had not staked a lot on Castro's revolutionary movement before its overthrow of the Batista government in January 1959. A limited amount of Soviet arms had been channelled secretly to Castro's rebels from the end of 1958. But the Kremlin held out little hope for the new revolutionary government, assuming that it would not go beyond the bourgeois-democratic phase (a Cuban 'February'). Moscow's attitudes began to change from the autumn of 1959, as the Cuban revolution became more Communist in its policies and requested Soviet support. Risking its relations with the United States, the Soviet leadership voted to send Warsaw Pact weapons to Cuba at the end of September. Soviet intelligence officers began to arrive in Havana. 'You Americans must realize what Cuba means to us old Bolsheviks,' Mikoyan told Dean Rusk, the US Secretary of State, after signing a trade treaty with the Castro government in February 1960. 'We have been waiting all our lives for a country to go communist without the Red Army. It has happened in Cuba, and it makes us feel like boys again.'[11]

Washington was alarmed by the Soviet involvement in Cuba. Khrushchev might have been more cautious in his policy so as not to jeopardize the promise of détente following his visit to the United States in 1959. He needed cuts in military spending to invest more in the Soviet economy. But he was being pressured by the Chinese to prove his revolutionary credentials, and he was provoked by the Americans, whose U-2 spy-planes were exposed when one of them was shot down in Soviet airspace on 1 May 1960. After the Americans attempted to overthrow the Castro government in the Bay of Pigs invasion in April 1961, Khrushchev, who had pledged to defend Castro's revolution with Soviet missiles, began to deploy those atomic warheads to Cuba, within easy striking distance of the United States. He had overplayed his hand. The missiles were discovered by the CIA spy-planes, and for thirteen days the world stood on the brink of a nuclear war, until Khrushchev climbed down and agreed to withdraw the missiles from Cuba in October 1962. The humiliation sealed his downfall and the end of his reforms.

18

MATURE SOCIALISM

Khrushchev had never been secure in power. His programme of de-Stalinization was opposed from the start by senior Party leaders whose careers had been built as Stalin's loyal servitors. In June 1957, Khrushchev had defeated a coup attempt led by three of them in the Politburo—Kaganovich, Molotov and Malenkov—by mobilizing his supporters in the Central Committee. But by 1964 that support was wearing thin. His political reforms had weakened the positions of the regional Party secretaries by dividing their responsibilities for economic management and by requiring that at least one quarter of the Central Committee, where they exercised their influence and patronage, be renewed at every election. Khrushchev's erratic leadership, his tendency to act on intuition and then attack his critics, his meddling in affairs where he lacked expertise, and his dangerous adventurism in Cuba lost him the support of Party colleagues who wanted a more stable and collective style of government.

Khrushchev was removed from power suddenly in October 1964. He had gone on vacation to Georgia and was phoned by the leader of the coup, Leonid Brezhnev, who summoned him to an emergency meeting of the Politburo. Voted out of office, Khrushchev was allowed to retire 'from ill health' to preserve his popularity abroad. Knowing he was beaten, he went quietly. Later he remarked sarcastically that the mode of his departure was his greatest achievement: 'Stalin would have had them arrested.'[1]

Brezhnev emerged as *primus inter pares* of the colourless regime that replaced Khrushchev. Politburo decisions were reached collectively and names were listed alphabetically to restore the appearance of collective leadership. Yet slowly Brezhnev became dominant. He was a creature of the system, a grey and mediocre functionary rather than a revolutionary, although once in power he developed a colourful taste for luxury cars, natty suits, hunting parties and a lifestyle more appropriate for the playboys of the Western world. Like so many apparatchiks suddenly promoted to the higher Party ranks during Stalin's purges and the war, he had more practical than intellectual capacities. He was good at building political alliances and patron–client networks of mutual support. He had extensive patronage among the regional Party leaders, many of them comrades from the 1930s when he had risen from the factory floor to the First Party Secretary in Dnepropetrovsk. No other Politburo member had such influence. But all the major players—Alexei Kosygin (Chairman of the Council of Ministers), Mikhail Suslov (the Party's ideologist), Alexander Shelepin (sometime head of the KGB and leading Stalinist) and Ivan Kapitonov (in the Moscow apparatus)—had their clientèle networks in the lower Party organizations. The Brezhnev system was a coalition of Politburo oligarchs.

What united them was the preservation of the status quo. They wanted to prevent the shake-up of the Party that Khrushchev had begun, to restore a stable system of administration that would keep them at the top. They were from an older generation than the Party reformers inspired by the Twentieth Party Congress and the Khrushchev Thaw. As long as Brezhnev was in power, the Party's leaders were allowed to grow old in their posts. The average age of the Politburo rose from sixty in 1964 to over seventy in 1982. This was a gerontocracy whose only ideology was to make things stay the same. Brezhnev gave a name to this conservative idea, 'Mature Socialism', the absurd doctrine that a socialist society had been successfully created and that all that was now needed was to consolidate its gains, which he invoked when he introduced the 1977 'Brezhnev Constitution', the third and last of the Soviet regime. But at sixty years Soviet socialism was older than mature. It was at retirement age.

Along with the ending of political reform there was a reversal of initiatives to loosen state controls on the economy. The Kosygin reforms, drawn up under Khrushchev and introduced in 1965, aimed to stimulate production by giving enterprises greater independence and relying more on market mechanisms within the planned economy. But they were regarded as politically dangerous, particularly after similar reforms in Czechoslovakia resulted in demands for political liberalization and the Prague Spring in 1968. They were killed off by the Brezhnev government.

No amount of tinkering (which is what the Kosygin reforms were) could have turned around the failing Soviet economy. It was not enough to introduce reforms into the planned economy. The problem *was* the planned economy. But without reform the economy was doomed— along with the Soviet system—to terminal decline.

Economic stagnation would not have been so damaging politically if consumer expectations had not been raised so high in the Khrushchev period. A new Party Programme in 1961 had forecast that the Soviet Union would overtake the United States' economy by 1970. It pledged that Communism would be built by 1980, ensuring 'an abundance of material and cultural benefits' so that 'everyone will live in easy circumstances'.[2] Previously the revolution had been based on the idea of personal sacrifice for the collective good. But now that situation was reversed: the Party was acknowledging an economic obligation to the individual. It was issuing IOUs.

The gains for the consumer were considerable during the 1960s. Tens of millions of Soviet families moved into new apartments—an improvement of political significance since it gave them space for a private way of life and conversations free from the scrutiny of neighbours and informers in the communal apartments of the Stalin period. Fridges and TVs were introduced in many homes.

But growth rates lagged behind the West and slowed to less than 2 per cent in the 1970s. There were shortages, especially of meat and dairy products, and long queues for anything that was worth buying in the drab and almost empty shops. People became disenchanted, cynical about the propaganda claims of the regime. No longer fearful of repression, they told jokes to let off steam:

Why isn't there any flour in the shops?

Because they've started adding it to bread.

What would happen if they introduced a Five Year Plan in the Sahara Desert?

Nothing at first, but in a few years there would be a shortage of sand.

Despite massive state investment, the collective farms worked inefficiently. Machines were always breaking down, sometimes going years without repair. There was not enough incentive for the kolkhoz labourers, who were very poorly paid, in those sectors where the state took all the crops (cereals, sugar beet, cotton, flax and cattle production). They worked harder on their garden plots where they grew fruit and vegetables, and kept rabbits, pigs and poultry, which they sold on roadsides or in peasant markets in the towns. By the end of the 1970s, these small garden plots, which took up 4 per cent of the country's agricultural land, were producing 40 per cent of its pork and poultry, 42 per cent of its fruit and over half its potatoes.

Brezhnev responded to the agricultural crisis by allowing larger garden plots to stimulate production. He might have improved the Soviet system's chances of survival by doing what the Chinese were doing at this time: de-collectivizing agriculture and returning to an NEP-like system of cooperatives and household farms on contracts, with the state allowing them to sell what they produced beyond their quotas on the free market. Soviet reformers were not unsympathetic to these policy ideas, even if they stopped short of recommending them. Gorbachev, who at this time was in the Agricultural Department of the Secretariat, proposed giving more autonomy to enterprises and associations in deciding various production and financial questions in a memorandum to the Central Committee in May 1978 (an idea repeated by Andropov on becoming General Secretary in 1982). But the Brezhnev leadership would not accept these proposals—even as trial policies. The old guard was too committed to the Stalinist collective farm system which they had implemented as young men. The Party's power was heavily invested in the direct management of the collective farms by thousands of officials in the localities. Perhaps, in any case, fifty years of collectivization (twice as long as in China) had destroyed any hope of bringing the Soviet peasantry back to life.

Relying on their tiny garden plots to feed themselves, the kolkhoz workers lived in squalid poverty. Many inhabited houses without running water or electricity. The ablest and most enterprising, mostly men of conscript age, ran away from the countryside, which became a ghetto of the old, the infirm and the alcoholic, who worked badly. Entire villages were abandoned or left to rot with only a few elderly inhabitants where once perhaps a hundred families had lived.

Alcohol consumption more than doubled in the Brezhnev years. People drank out of despair. By the early 1980s, the average kolkhoz family was spending one third of its household income on vodka—an official figure which does not include the moonshine made by kolkhoz workers in their homes (for every bottle bought from shops, they drank a bucket of moonshine). Alcoholism was the national disease. It had a major impact on crime rates (around 10 million people every year were detained by the police for drunkenness) and a bad effect on male life expectancy, which declined from 66 in 1964 to just 62 in 1980. The regime was unconcerned by the problem. It increased its vodka sales to extract money from the population which had little else to buy. Better to have people drunk than protesting against shortages.

Oil revenues rescued the regime from probable food riots and possible collapse. They gave a lease on life to the Soviet economy, which would have been in severe trouble without a five-fold increase in crude oil prices as a result of the 1973 crisis. The Soviet Union doubled oil production in the 1970s, mainly by developing new fields in Siberia. With its dollar earnings from the sale of oil and gas, the government was able to buy consumer goods and foodstuffs from the West. Before the revolution, Russia had been a major agricultural exporter. But within sixty years it had turned into the biggest food importer in the world. One third of all baked goods in the country were made from foreign cereals. Cattle production was totally dependent on imported grain.

High oil prices also allowed the Soviet Union to be more assertive in its foreign policy. They financed an eight-fold increase in military spending under Brezhnev's rule. By 1982, the military budget consumed approximately 15 per cent of the country's GNP. The rise showed the growing power of hardliners in the Brezhnev government, particularly in the KGB, the armed forces, and the defence and foreign ministries, who were committed at all costs to maintaining military superiority over NATO as the foundation of Soviet security.

Their confidence was boosted by the failure of NATO to respond to the Soviet invasion of Czechoslovakia to crush the reformist government of Alexander Dubcek in August 1968—an invasion that the Soviet Defence Minister, Andrei Grechko, had pledged to carry out 'even if it leads to a third world war'. The Kremlin emerged from the crisis with renewed boldness. 'The new correlation of forces is such that [the West] no longer dares to move against us,' claimed Andrei Gromyko, the Foreign Minister.[3]

Moscow justified its invasion and reinforced its grip on Eastern Europe by issuing the Brezhnev Doctrine, outlined in a speech by the Soviet leader to the Polish Communists in November 1968. When 'forces hostile to socialism try to turn the development of a socialist country towards capitalism,' Brezhnev warned the Poles, 'it becomes not only a problem of the country concerned, but a common problem and concern of all socialist countries.'[4] In practice what this meant was that the Soviet Union reserved for itself the right to intervene in the internal affairs of any Warsaw Pact country if it deemed it necessary for its own security.

Revolutionary ambitions also fuelled the Kremlin's military spending. While Brezhnev talked détente with the Americans, the hardliners in his government were increasingly directing Soviet arms in support of Third World socialist revolutions and anti-colonial movements. The Americans approached détente in the belief that the Soviet leadership was becoming more pragmatic and less ideological or revolutionary in its foreign policy—a rational approach allowing them to 'manage' and contain it through deterrents and rewards. A CIA report of 1969 maintained that the 'USSR tends to behave more as a world power than as the center of the world revolution'.[5] But this assumption soon proved wrong.

The Soviets were involved in Vietnam, where the northern Communists shifted their allegiances from Beijing to Moscow in the early 1970s, largely on account of China's rapprochement with the United States and Soviet aid for their war against the south. After the Communist victory in Vietnam, Cambodia and Laos in 1975, the Soviet leaders succumbed to hubris, imagining that they were on the brink of the world revolution they had been waiting for since 1917.

As Brezhnev's health deteriorated following a major stroke in 1975, real power passed into the hands of Yuri Andropov, Gromyko and Dmitry Ustinov, the new hawkish Defence Minister, who pushed for an even bolder policy abroad. The Bolshevik commitment to exporting revolution remained as strong as ever to the end. Military aid flowed to Marxist revolutionaries in North Africa, the Middle East and South Asia. Soviet forces were involved in the Angolan Civil War, the Somalian–Ethiopian conflict and the revolution in Nicaragua, which Moscow saw as a 'second Cuba'.

The last foreign adventure was in Afghanistan, from December 1979, where Soviet forces were sent to support a Communist regime against the Afghan Mujahideen, armed and supported by the USA. The nine-year invasion was a catastrophe—the Soviet Union's 'Vietnam'—militarily and politically. The Mujahideen were impossible to beat in their mountainous strongholds, however many Soviet forces were sent there. The Muslim resistance gave rise to the jihadism of Afghanistan and neighbouring lands. The invasion also ended America's commitment to détente. President Reagan pledged to paralyse the Soviet nuclear threat by developing space-based weapons (the Strategic Defense Initiative or SDI) which Moscow could not afford. The Soviet empire was seriously overstretched.

In the summer of 1980, Moscow hosted the Olympic Games. It was a chance for it to demonstrate the superiority of Soviet athletes and the achievements of the USSR to the entire world. The United States organized a boycott to protest against the invasion of Afghanistan. Sixty-five countries did not send teams to the games. The Soviet Union led the medal table, followed by East Germany, the two nations winning more than half the medals between them. But it was a hollow victory.

In Moscow the Olympics were overshadowed by the death of Vladimir Vysotsky, the singer, songwriter, poet, movie star and stage actor, much loved by the Soviet intelligentsia and non-conformist youth, whose funeral attracted massive crowds. Attendance at the games was noticeably lower on that day. For his mourners, Vysotsky was a symbol of dissent, the disillusioned voice of a generation that had grown up with the hopes of the Khrushchev thaw. A heavy drinker and smoker, Vysotsky sang his songs in the gravelly voice of a prisoner, which led many of his fans to think mistakenly that he had been in prison too. But his songs were full of street jargon and bitter allusions to politics, they were at once sad and angry, and this gave them an emotional appeal to people who had suffered, or disliked the regime, even if they did not want to make their opposition known.

How many people could be counted in this category? Disenchantment with the Soviet regime had probably affected everyone to some degree by 1980. No one really believed any longer in the propaganda that surrounded them. They barely noticed the banners in the streets, or inside public buildings, with slogans such as 'Forward to the Victory of Communism!' or 'Bring the decisions of the XXVIth Congress of the CPSU to life!' But they lived in ways that took for granted many of the regime's values and ideas, which became embedded in their attitudes and habits, in the questions they allowed themselves to ask, in the moral judgements they allowed themselves to make, and this prevented them from stepping out of line. They might tell jokes to ridicule the regime's propaganda claims, jokes about the surreal nature of daily life in the Soviet Union:

THE SEVEN WONDERS OF SOVIET POWER:

1. There is no unemployment, but no one works.

2. No one works, but the plan is fulfilled.

3. The plan is fulfilled, but there is nothing in the shops.

4. There's nothing to buy, but there are queues everywhere.

5. There are queues everywhere, but we are on the threshold of plenty.

6. We are on the threshold of plenty, but everyone is dissatisfied.

7. Everyone is dissatisfied, but everyone votes yes.

They might express their disillusionment, even cynicism, to their friends. Or reject the system's public culture and look instead to rock music, films and fashions from the West for their values and ideas. The Beatles were illegal in the Soviet Union but their music—recorded from Western radio stations and passed around on tapes—was listened to by millions of kids who despised the authorities for trying to ban it.

Yet, for all these signs of non-conformity, very few would cross into the opposition circles of the dissidents. United less by politics than by moral principles and the fight for human rights, the dissident movement had begun in response to the political trials of the poet Joseph Brodsky in 1964 and of the writers Andrei Sinyavsky and Yulii Daniel in 1965–6. By the end of the 1970s, it included human rights campaigners like the Moscow Helsinki Group (founded in 1976 to monitor Soviet compliance with the Helsinki Accords on individual freedoms), activist *refuseniks* (mostly Jews denied permission to emigrate abroad), dissenting priests and public intellectuals like Andrei Sakharov, the Nobel physicist exiled to Gorky in 1980. KGB harassment and surveillance kept the dissidents from drawing more supporters from the intelligentsia who sympathized with them. By the end of the 1960s, the KGB had 166,000 agents involved in phone tapping, bugging apartments, opening mail and following suspected dissidents—fewer than the number needed for an omnipresent police state (the East German Stasi had ten times as many agents per capita of population) but enough to act as a deterrent to those who might be drawn into oppositional activities. The key to the power of the KGB was the popular belief that they were 'everywhere'. Fear of the police—passed down through the generations by the collective memory of the Stalin years—produced an in-built compliance that goes a long way to explain why the Soviet regime lasted for so long after it had spent its revolutionary energies.

The dissident historian Roy Medvedev—frequently harassed by the KGB—wrote in his book *On Socialist Democracy* (published in the West in 1972):

> There is now a very widespread feeling that the way we live and work has become untenable, and this applies not just to the intelligentsia but also to much of the working class, white collar workers, and perhaps some of the peasantry. But there is still no mass movement demanding change or democratic reform, and without this it is difficult to count on any rapid transformation of our political system or on a change of attitude at the top.[6]

There comes a moment in every old regime when people start to say: 'We cannot go on living like this any more.' That feeling started in the 1970s. But there was no social force to bring about a change. The people were too cowed, too passive and conformist, to do anything about their woes. They were more inclined to take to the bottle than the streets. The dissidents had little influence, either on the people or on the leadership. But some of their ideas were taken up by reformers in the Party, including Gorbachev, who would cite Medvedev's words in justification of his policies of perestroika and glasnost after 1985.

In the end it was not the dissidents or a mass movement but 'a change of attitude at the top' that brought about the Gorbachev reforms. Gorbachev was one of many Bolsheviks—all of them the children of the Twentieth Party Congress—who believed sincerely in the Leninist renewal of the Soviet project. They spent the Brezhnev era in the political wings, many of them working in the research institutes connected to the Central Committee and its Secretariat (a huge apparatus with more than twenty departments, each responsible for a particular area of Soviet life). A large number of the most important figures in the Gorbachev reforms were acquainted with each other from these years: Alexander Yakovlev, the main intellectual force behind perestroika, was head of the Central Committee's Department of Ideology and Propaganda from 1969 to 1973, when he was dismissed and sent to Canada as the Soviet ambassador as a punishment for criticizing Russian nationalism in an article; Anatoly Chernyaev, Gorbachev's main foreign policy adviser after 1985, was the deputy head of the Central Committee's International Department in the 1970s; Abel Aganbegyan, the man behind Gorbachev's economic reforms, was the Director of the Institute of Economics at Akademgorodok ('Academic City') in Siberia, a scientific refuge where reformist ideas were allowed free rein.

None of the ideas of perestroika were particularly new. Even the term had been used by reformist bureaucrats going back as far as the Khrushchev period. Glasnost too was a concept that went back to the early 1960s, when it was used in reform proposals to suggest that the work of government should be transparent and open to the media. The concept was even mentioned in the 1977 Constitution.

Essentially, then, Gorbachev's ideas were shaped by the Khrushchev Thaw, the defining intellectual influence on the revolution's third and final generational phase. Born in 1931, Gorbachev came from a younger generation than the Party leaders who preceded him—Khrushchev (born in 1894), Brezhnev (1906), Andropov (1914) and Chernenko (1911) all having been born before 1917. Unlike them, he had not made his career in Stalin's time. He was the first leader to have played no part in Stalin's crimes. In fact his family—peasants from the Stavropol region in southern Russia—had been victims of Stalin's war against the peasantry during the 1930s. His paternal grandfather was sent into exile in Siberia for failing to fulfil the sowing plan for 1933—a year of famine when three of his six sons and half the population of his village died of starvation. His maternal grandfather, who was the kolkhoz chairman, was arrested as a 'Trotskyist' in 1937. Gorbachev concealed this 'spoilt biography' until 1990. He made his way through life and rose through the Party despite the stigma of his background as the grandson of an 'enemy of the people'. That experience was no doubt at the root of his commitment to overcome the legacies of Stalinism.

With a good school record and Komsomol report and an Order of the Red Banner of Labour from his kolkhoz, Gorbachev won a place at Moscow University to study law (he was the first leader since Lenin with a university degree). Joining the Party in 1952, he was fairly orthodox in his Stalinist opinions at this time. He did not yet connect his family's suffering to Stalin's policies. But his world-view was transformed by Khrushchev's Secret Speech. Gorbachev was a 'man of the sixties' (*shestidesiatnik*) defined by the ideas of Leninist reform advanced by Khrushchev and the thaw. One of his close friends at university, Zdeněk Mlynár, was later to become an important figure in the Prague Spring. His wife, Raisa, whom he also met at university, became a rural sociologist in Stavropol, where the couple lived from 1955. Her research highlighted the social failures of collectivization.

In Stavropol Gorbachev began his political career in the Komsomol before switching to the Party's city organization. In 1970, at the age of thirty-nine, he became the Party Secretary of the Stavropol region, the youngest regional First Secretary in the Soviet Union. It was a useful position on the ladder to the top. Known for its spas, Stavropol was a place where Kremlin bosses came for holidays. Gorbachev took full advantage of the opportunity to impress them with his efficiency, intelligence and charm. Two frequent visitors were Mikhail Suslov, the Politburo's main ideologist, and Andropov, who brought Gorbachev to the attention of Brezhnev. In 1978, Gorbachev was called to Moscow, where he supervised the ministries involved in agriculture, and he was promoted to the Politburo the next year.

On Brezhnev's death, in November 1982, Andropov became the Party's new leader, the first to come from the KGB. He signalled his intention to tighten discipline in the workplace, to fight corruption in all areas of the administration, and to decentralize the Soviet economy to improve productivity. It was a typically KGB approach to the challenges confronting the country—to beat it into shape. Andropov was a modernizer who believed the system could be made to work if only it was run more rationally, like a police state. He was in favour of moderate reform, he widened the parameters of possible debate within the Party, and he rewarded young talent. In his fifteen months in office he promoted Gorbachev and other reformers like Nikolai Ryzhkov, who was put in charge of industry, to counteract the influence of Chernenko, who represented the old guard of Brezhnevites in the Party leadership.

Who knows what would have happened if Andropov had lived longer. Perhaps the Soviet Union might have undergone a more gradual transition from the old command system, modernizing the economy without relinquishing political controls, as done by the Chinese, though one wonders if this could have been achieved given the extent of the Party's opposition to de-collectivization, the key to China's revival. As fortune would have it, Andropov became terminally ill with kidney failure only nine months after coming into power and died, at the age of sixty-nine, in February 1984. From his death-bed in hospital, he wrote a speech to be read out at the Plenum of the Central Committee recommending Gorbachev to succeed him. But the crucial paragraph was cut by the old guard in the Politburo, opposed to reform, who on his death voted to replace him with Chernenko. Within weeks of his appointment the 73-year-old Chernenko became terminally ill. The Bolsheviks were dying of old age.

Gorbachev bided his time—careful not to alarm the old guard by giving the impression that he might go on with Andropov's reforms yet building his support in the Central Committee and increasing his prestige by trips abroad, where he impressed the British leader, Margaret Thatcher, in particular, on a visit to London in December 1984. Such impressions were important to the Soviet government, which needed Western credits and disarmament. They no doubt helped him make the deal with Gromyko, the Foreign Minister, by which Gorbachev agreed to promote him to head of state (Chairman of the Presidium of the Supreme Soviet) if he supported him to succeed Chernenko as the Party's General Secretary. It was the backing of Gromyko, a veteran Brezhnevite, that tipped the scales in Gorbachev's favour in the Politburo vote on Chernenko's death the following March. There was no battle for the leadership: the old guard simply stepped aside to let in a younger man.

The selection of Gorbachev was arguably the most revolutionary act in the history of the Party since 1917. Had the Politburo known where he would lead the Party in the next few years, it would never have allowed him to become its General Secretary. But at this stage Gorbachev's intentions were still far from clear.

19

THE LAST BOLSHEVIK

Nobody expected the Soviet regime to come to an end so suddenly. Most revolutions die with a whimper rather than a bang. Some people say that the events of 1985–91 constitute a revolution in themselves. This is not quite right. But the speed with which the system fell apart took everybody by surprise, and this seemed to earn the name.

In 1985 the Soviet Union seemed as permanent as any state. None of the problems Gorbachev intended to address through reform threatened the existence of the Soviet system. The economy was stagnant, with annual growth rates at less than 1 per cent, living standards were falling far behind those of the West, and the sharp decline in oil prices (to one third of their 1980 prices) dealt a heavy blow to the regime's finances. But things had been much worse at more politically unstable periods of Soviet history. The people had grown used to shortages, and there were no signs of mass protest. The regime could have soldiered on for years without reform. There are plenty of examples of dictatorships that have managed to survive with poor living standards in permanent decline. Most of them have done so in far worse economic circumstances than those experienced in the Soviet Union during the 1980s.

The military budget was a heavy burden, and set to become even more so with the start of Reagan's SDI. The cost of supporting Communist regimes in Eastern Europe with cheap oil and food was equally a serious strain. The Kremlin had to spend $4bn just to deal with the 1980 crisis in Poland, when mass strikes led to the emergence of the Solidarity opposition movement and the imposition of martial law by the Jaruzelski government. But by 1985 Solidarity appeared to be running out of steam, and the Soviet empire seemed secure.

To explain the speed with which it all collapsed, we need to look, not at the structural problems of the Soviet Union, but at the way the regime unravelled from the top. There was no pressing need for the radical restructuring of the system. If there was a 'crisis', it was in the minds of Gorbachev and other reformers who sensed it in the growing divergence between Soviet realities and their socialist ideals. It was Gorbachev's reforms that brought about the real crisis: the disintegration of the Party's power and authority. The conceptual revolution begun by glasnost allowed people to question the regime and demand an alternative. As de Tocqueville wrote of the old regime in eighteenth-century France, 'the most dangerous moment for a bad government is when it begins to reform . . . Patiently endured so long as it seemed beyond redress, a grievance comes to appear intolerable once the possibility of removing it crosses men's minds.'[1]

Gorbachev began from Leninist ideals. Like Khrushchev, whose programme of de-Stalinization had shaped his political development, he believed in the possibility of 'returning to Lenin'. Where other leaders paid lip-service to the founder of the Soviet state, Gorbachev took Lenin seriously in the belief that his ideas were still relevant to the revolutionary challenges he confronted. He identified with the Lenin of the Testament—Lenin's final writings, which had grappled with the issue of concessions to the market in the NEP and the need for more democracy to reform the revolution which had gone so wrong in the Civil War— seeing parallels with what he thought he had to do over sixty years later. At a time of growing cynicism in the Soviet population and political élites, he remained optimistic, a genuine believer in the reformability of the system. He sincerely thought that Lenin's revolution could be made to work through moral and political renewal. In this sense, at least, Gorbachev was the last Bolshevik.

There is no better example of his idealistic belief in reform than his first initiative: the anti-alcohol crusade announced by the decree of 4 April 1985, which tripled vodka prices and reduced wine and beer production by three quarters. 'We can't build Communism on vodka,' Gorbachev announced. As he later acknowledged, some of his ideas at this early stage were 'naive and utopian'.[2] Not to be deterred, the country's alcoholics purchased cheap and dangerous brands of moonshine from the black market (sugar disappeared from shops overnight) or drank colognes and lotions. The state lost precious revenues from vodka sales, 17 per cent of all its revenues in 1985, reducing its capacity to import consumer goods and food, and with less to buy or drink people became more dissatisfied.

Without a pro-reform majority in the Party leadership, Gorbachev was conscious of the need to proceed carefully if he was to avoid Khrushchev's fate. In 1985–6 he talked only of a 'quickening' of the economy (*uskorenie*), an echo of the Andropov approach to tightening discipline and raising productivity which fitted with the ban on alcohol. It was not until the January 1987 Plenum of the Central Committee that Gorbachev announced the launching of his perestroika programme, describing it as a 'revolution' in its radical restructuring of the command economy and the political system. Gorbachev invoked the Bolshevik tradition to legitimize his bold initiative, closing his speech with the lofty words: 'We want to force even the skeptics to say: Yes, the Bolsheviks can do anything. Yes, the truth is on their side. Yes, socialism is a system that serves man, his social and economic interests and his spiritual elevation.'[3] This was the voluntarist spirit of another October 1917.

Economically, perestroika had a lot in common with the NEP. It rested on the hopeful assumption that market mechanisms could be added to the structures of the planned economy to stimulate production and satisfy consumer needs. State controls on wages and prices were loosened by a 1987 Law on State Enterprises. Cooperatives were legalized in 1988, resulting in an NEP-like sprouting up of cafés, restaurants and small shops or kiosks, selling mostly vodka (now re-legalized), cigarettes and pornographic videos imported from abroad. But these measures failed to ease the shortages of food and more important household goods. Inflation grew, exacerbated by the lifting of controls on wages and prices. Only the dismantling of the planned economy could have solved the crisis. But ideologically that was impossible until 1989, when Gorbachev began to break free from the Soviet mould of thinking, and even then it was too radical for him to legislate until August 1990, when the 500-Day Plan for the transition to a market-based economy was at last introduced by the Supreme Soviet. But by then it was too late to halt the economic crash.

Gorbachev presented perestroika as a 'revolution' in socialist thinking, justifying it in terms of Lenin's writings—in his own idealized reading—at every turn. He called for more 'democracy' in government, with genuine elections of officials, talked about the need for 'pluralism', previously a taboo word, and urged the Party to return to the 'socialist humanism' of its founders. 'The aim of perestroika is fully to restore Lenin's conception of socialism in its theoretical and practical respects,' Gorbachev declared on the seventieth anniversary of the October Revolution.[4] Little of this 'humanism' or 'democracy' was to be found in Lenin's theory or practice. But Gorbachev was forced to invoke Lenin's name if he wanted the support of the Party leadership for his reforms.

In foreign policy this 'new thinking' meant renouncing the Party's Cold War paradigm of class struggle in favour of the promotion of 'universal human values'. This entailed a more practical and 'common sense' approach towards disarmament in the interests of the Soviet economy. It also involved the renunciation of the Brezhnev Doctrine. Gorbachev made it crystal clear to the Communist leaders of Eastern Europe that they were now on their own. Moscow would not intervene to help them if they failed to win the support of their people, which he wanted them to do through perestroikas of their own.

Glasnost was the really revolutionary element of the Gorbachev reforms, the means by which the system unravelled ideologically. The Soviet leader intended it to bring transparency to government and break the power-hold of the Brezhnevite conservatives opposed to his reforms. Early calls for glasnost were reinforced by the shameful cover-up of the Chernobyl nuclear accident—the worst in history and affecting much of Europe—in April 1986. But the consequences of glasnost quickly spiralled beyond Gorbachev's control.

By relaxing censorship, glasnost meant that the Party lost its grip on the mass media, which exposed social problems previously concealed by the government (poor housing, criminality, ecological catastrophes, etc.), thereby undermining public confidence in the Soviet system.

Revelations about Soviet history had a similar effect. One by one the legitimizing myths of the system—its material and moral superiority over capitalist societies, its vindication by the defeat of Nazism, its modernization of the country through collectivization and the Five Year Plans, and its founding in a mass-based revolution in October 1917—came under assault as the dark facts emerged from the newly opened archives and books published in translation from abroad. Every day the media came out with disclosures filling in the 'blank spots' of the country's violent history—details about mass terror, collectivization and the famine, the Katyn Massacre, the full extent of the horrors of the Gulag, the reckless waste of Soviet lives in the Great Patriotic War— which undermined the regime's credibility and authority by exposing its official record of these events as a tissue of lies and half-truths.

Popular belief drained away from the government—much of it transferring to the media outlets which revealed these truths. The most daring newspapers and magazines had fantastic circulations. The weekly subscription to *Argumenty i fakty* (Arguments and Facts)—which ceased to be a propaganda organ and became a source of once-secret facts and critical opinions on Soviet life—grew from 2 million to 33 million copies between 1986 and 1990. Every Friday night tens of millions of younger viewers watched the programme *Vzglyad* (View), which pushed subversively on the boundaries of taste, let alone of Soviet censorship, in its

TV mix of current affairs, interviews and investigations into history (it was eventually banned in January 1991).

Glasnost politicized society. Independent public bodies formed. By March 1989, there were 60,000 'informal' groups and clubs in the Soviet Union. They held meetings and joined demonstrations in the streets, many of them calling for political reforms, civil rights, national independence for Soviet republics and regions, or an end to the Communist monopoly of power. The major cities were returning to the revolutionary atmosphere of 1917.

What made this a revolutionary situation was the possibility of the ruling élites changing their allegiances and joining the people's side. Challenged by the democratic forces of society, the one-party state began to crumble as reformers in the system lost the will to defend the status quo or made their sympathies for the opposition known. Yakovlev, the intellectual architect of Gorbachev's reforms, began to think and sound less like a Bolshevik than a European social democrat. Boris Yeltsin, the populist Moscow Party boss, openly attacked the hardliners in the Communist establishment. On the seventieth anniversary of the October Revolution, he even called for the Party to renounce its Leninist inheritance, effectively suggesting that it should revert to the democratic socialist mainstream and compete for power in multi-party elections (as Kamenev and Zinoviev had argued it should do in 1917). Attacked by the hardliners, Yeltsin resigned from the Politburo and began to rally popular support against the Party leadership.

Gorbachev as well was slowly evolving from a Leninist position towards something resembling a social democrat. His views developed in office as he came to understand the failures of the system and saw the limitations of its possible reform. From 1988 he began to talk about the need, not just to restructure the 'command-administrative system', but to dismantle it. He spoke about the need for checks and balances, for a separation of powers, within the state. He supported the idea of contested elections, and even came round gradually to favour the demands of the democrats to end the Communist monopoly of power enshrined in Article 6 of the 1977 Constitution. The one-party state established by Lenin was falling apart from the top.

Communist hardliners were alarmed by the speed with which the system seemed to be unravelling. Political reform was threatening to become a revolution undermining everything the Party had achieved since 1917. Their opposition to Gorbachev's reforms was articulated by Nina Andreeva, a chemistry lecturer in Leningrad, in an article entitled 'I Cannot Give Up Principles', published in the newspaper *Sovetskaya Rossiia* in March 1988. Approved by several Politburo members, the article attacked the blackening of Soviet history, defended Stalin's achievements 'in building and defending socialism', and called on the country's Communists to defend their Leninist principles, 'as we have fought for them at crucial turning points in the history of our fatherland'.[5]

Gorbachev decided to fight back, pushing ahead with a series of more radical reforms. At the Nineteenth Party Conference in June 1988, he forced the introduction of contested elections for two thirds of the seats in a new legislative body, the Congress of People's Deputies, which would then elect a Supreme Soviet. This was not yet a multi-party democracy (87 per cent of the elected deputies were Communists) but voters could force out Party leaders if they were united against them: thirty-nine Party First Secretaries, along with the then Prime Ministers of Latvia and Lithuania, suffered the humiliation of defeat in the Congress elections in early 1989.

The Congress became a democratic platform against the one-party state. The opening sessions at the end of May were watched by an estimated 100 million people on TV. An Inter-Regional Group was formed within the Congress by reformists in the Party and non-Party democrats, whose main demand was the scrapping of Article 6. Gorbachev agreed with the proposal and steered it through the Politburo in February 1990. Having started his reforms to save the one-party state, he was now dismantling it. 'In place of the Stalinist model of socialism,' he said in a televised address on 2 July, 'we are coming to a citizens' society of free people. The political system is being transformed radically, genuine democracy with free elections, the existence of many parties and human rights is becoming established and real people's power is being revived.'[6] Russia was returning to the February Revolution of 1917.

Within the Party there were many different factions by this stage, although only two that really mattered: the hardliners who wanted to defend their Leninist inheritance and social democrats like Gorbachev and Yeltsin who had evolved politically since 1985 and who now wanted to 'be finished with the old Bolshevik tradition', as Gorbachev recalled in later years.[7] With the Party so divided, one may ask why Gorbachev did not attempt to split it into two, or at least to lift the ban on factions imposed by Lenin in 1921, and create a social democratic movement in support of his reforms. Many of his closest advisers had long been urging him to do precisely that—Yakovlev from as far back as 1985. Such a move would have established a multi-party system in the Soviet Union. The two wings of the CPSU would have each inherited millions of members, newspapers and other media channels, thereby creating a more plural system than the one established following the downfall of the Party in 1991. But Gorbachev refused to force this split. Hesitant and conciliatory by political temperament, he feared a bitter struggle, possibly a civil war, over the control of the armed forces, the KGB and the Party's national apparatus, which he naively thought he could still control.

By maintaining the Party's unity Gorbachev ensured that it fell as one with the collapse of the Soviet system in 1991. That collapse began in the outer reaches of the Soviet empire with the revolutions in Eastern Europe during 1989. Without the military support of Moscow the Communist regimes were unable to resist the democratic movements that forced them out of power and elected new leaders.

In Poland the Communists were forced into round-table talks with Solidarity by mass strikes and protests, leading to a parliamentary vote of no-confidence in the government and semi-free elections in June 1989, when Solidarity won a sweeping victory in every seat where they were permitted to compete. Communist authority was undermined. Jaruzelski resigned as President and Tadeusz Mazowiecki, the Solidarity activist, became Prime Minister, the first non-Communist to lead a government in Eastern Europe for forty years, in September 1989.

In Hungary the Communists negotiated their own abdication of power with the opposition activists of the Democratic Forum, which won the largest vote in the multi-party elections to the new parliament. The Hungarian revolution led to the collapse of the Berlin Wall and the downfall of the Communist regime in the GDR. The crisis began when the Hungarians opened their border to Austria, allowing thousands of East Germans to travel to the West. Attempts to stem the exodus led to mass protests, especially in Leipzig, putting pressure on the government. Speaking on US television, a Politburo spokesman gave the impression that citizens were free to leave—a story picked up by West German stations which were watched in the East. Thinking that the Wall was open, tens of thousands of East Germans arrived at the border from 9 November. Without clear instructions from the government, the guards let them pass through to the West. The Wall came down.

In Czechoslovakia its fall inspired a broad protest movement headed by the Civic Forum organized by Václav Havel and other veteran dissidents. By 25 November, there were 800,000 protestors on the streets of Prague. Two days later a general strike was joined by three quarters of the population. The Communist regime conceded free elections and resigned from power, allowing Havel to become President by a unanimous vote of the Federal Assembly on 29 December.

The East European revolutions added fuel to nationalist movements in the inner empire of the Soviet Union. The Baltic nations were the first to call for independence, followed by the Georgians and Armenians and substantial segments of the population in Ukraine and Moldavia. Slower to react were the Central Asian republics, where the élites depended on the Soviet system and the popular alternative was likely to be Islamic.

Gorbachev's reforms created the conditions for the rise of nationalist movements in two ways. First, his appointment to the newly created post of Soviet President, in March 1990, established a precedent for the republican leaders to form their own power base. Yeltsin's election as Russia's President in June 1991 gave him more authority than the unelected Soviet President within the Russian republic. Second, the introduction of contested elections for the Supreme Soviet in each republic allowed nationalists to win control of these sovereign parliaments and use them to declare their independence from Moscow. In the Baltic states nationalists swept to victory in the 1990 elections. The Communist Party divided under pressure, as factions favouring sovereignty left the CPSU and competed for the nationalist vote.

Police repressions also fuelled the independence movements in Georgia and the Baltic states. In Tbilisi nineteen demonstrators were killed and several hundred wounded by the Soviet police in April 1989. In Lithuania and Latvia seventeen were killed and hundreds wounded in the crackdown of January 1991. These repressions were largely the initiative of Communist hardliners in the KGB and military who were hoping to provoke a violent response by the nationalists which they could use to argue for the imposition of a state of emergency to prevent the break-up of the Soviet Union. Rather than resist them and run the risk of splitting the Party, Gorbachev conceded to the hardliners, appointing Boris Pugo as Minister of the Interior and Gennady Yanaev as his Soviet Vice-President.

Gorbachev needed their support for his plans to reconstitute the Soviet Union. The Soviet President proposed to negotiate a new union treaty with the republics, if they approved this in a referendum vote. He wanted to agree on a federal structure that would keep the Soviet Union together but thought that it was wrong to maintain it by force. Like Lenin, he believed it could survive as a voluntary union.

Six republics were determined to break free completely from the Soviet Union and refused to vote (Georgia, Armenia, Moldavia and the three Baltic states). In the nine other republics, 76 per cent of the population voted for maintaining the federal system of the Soviet Union in a referendum on 17 March 1991. A draft treaty was negotiated between the Soviet government and the nine republican leaders (the '9+1' agreement) and signed on 23 April at Novo-Ogarevo near Moscow. In these negotiations Yeltsin (in a strong position after his election as the Russian President) and Leonid Kravchuk (angling to become the Ukrainian President by reinventing himself as a nationalist) managed to extract from the Soviet President a large number of powers for the republics which had previously belonged to the Kremlin.

By August, eight of the nine republics had approved the draft treaty— the one exception being the Ukrainians, who had voted for the union on the basis of the 1990 Declaration of State Sovereignty. The draft treaty would have converted the USSR into a federation of independent states, not unlike the European Union, with a single president, foreign policy and military force. The treaty would have renamed it the Union of Soviet Sovereign Republics (with 'sovereign' replacing 'socialist'). On 4 August, Gorbachev left Moscow for a holiday in Foros in the Crimea, intending to return to the capital to sign the new union treaty on 20 August.

Although the treaty was meant to save the union, the hardliners feared it would encourage its breakup. They decided it was time to act. On 18 August, a delegation of conspirators flew to Foros to demand the declaration of a state of emergency and, when Gorbachev refused their ultimatum, placed him under house arrest. In Moscow a self-appointed State Committee of the State of Emergency (which included Yanaev and Pugo in addition to Valentin Pavlov, the Soviet Prime Minister, Vladimir Kruchkov, the head of the KGB, and Dmitry Yazov, the Defence Minister) declared itself in power. A tired-looking Yanaev, his hands all-an-alcoholic-trembling, announced uncertainly to the world's press that he was taking over as the President.

The putschists were too hesitant to have any real chance of success. Perhaps even they had lost the will to take the necessary measures to defend the system at its very end. They failed to arrest Yeltsin, who made his way to the White House, the seat of the Russian parliament (the Supreme Soviet), where he organized the defence of democracy against the coup. They failed to give decisive orders to the tank divisions they had brought into Moscow to put down resistance to the coup. The senior army commanders were divided in their loyalties in any case. The Tamanskaya Division, stationed outside the White House, declared its allegiance to Yeltsin, who climbed on top of one of the tanks to address the crowd. Without a bloody struggle there was no way from this point that the putschists could succeed in an attack on the White House. But they did not have the stomach for a fight.

The coup soon collapsed. Its leaders were arrested on 22 August. Gorbachev returned to the capital. But like Kerensky after the Kornilov plot of August 1917, he found his own position had been undermined. The coup had discredited the Communist Party and handed the initiative to Yeltsin as the President of Russia and 'defender of democracy'. On 23 August, he issued a decree suspending the CPSU in Russia pending an investigation into its role in the coup. Late that night, crowds in Moscow toppled the statue of the Cheka's founder, Dzerzhinsky, outside the KGB headquarters at the Lubianka. The next day, Gorbachev resigned as the Party's General Secretary. On 25 August, its property, including all its archives and bank accounts, were seized by the Russian government.

On 6 November, Yeltsin banned the Communist Party in Russia. His decree was technically illegal in that it exceeded the constitutional powers of the Russian President. But Yeltsin justified it on historical grounds, declaring that the Party was responsible 'for the historical cul-de-sac into which the peoples of the Soviet Union have been driven and for the state of disintegration we have reached'.[8]

Gorbachev still wanted to revive the union treaty talks. But Yeltsin turned against them, seeing the disbanding of the Soviet Union as a victory for Russia, while the other republics, especially Ukraine, were now wary of any sort of union with Moscow, whose repressive potential had been exposed by the coup. When the Novo-Ogarevo talks restarted in November, Yeltsin and Kravchuk demanded more concessions from the Soviet government. It looked as if the USSR would be converted into a Union of Sovereign States. But on 1 December a Ukrainian vote for independence blew a massive hole in the Soviet ship of state. A week later, Yeltsin, Kravchuk and the Belorussian leader, Stanislav Shushkevich, met in Belarus to announce the dissolution of the Soviet Union. A Commonwealth of Independent States would take its place.

In effect it was a coup by the three republican leaders (Yeltsin, Kravchuk and Shushkevich) to break away from the USSR and establish their own national governments. In a televised farewell address broadcast from the Kremlin on Christmas Day, Gorbachev declared that he could not support the abolition of the Soviet Union because it had not been ratified by constitutional procedures or by a democratic vote. Popular opinion had been in favour of a union. It was leaders and élites who had ended it.

The collapse of the Soviet Union was not a complete revolution. Although society had been activated and politicized by Gorbachev's reforms, it was not through its efforts that the Soviet regime was brought down; and if history since has demonstrated anything, it is the chronic weakness of democracy in Russia—the inability of the people to effect real change.

Gorbachev was the key player in the events that led to his downfall. Judged by his initial plan, to save the Soviet Union through reform, he must be deemed a failure. But his intentions changed as his own views evolved and in these terms he should be credited with many achievements, not least laying the foundations for democracy in Russia, liberating nations from Soviet domination, and ending the Cold War. Perhaps his main achievement was to engineer a peaceful abdication by the Bolsheviks, whose power had depended on terror and coercion for almost three quarters of a century. He managed to dismantle their dictatorship without civil war or major violence, which had been a serious possibility, and for this he deserves his status in the West (if not in Russia) as one of the great figures in contemporary history. It had not been his aim to end the revolution when he started out. As a Leninist he had been convinced that it was possible to build socialism by reforming the Soviet system. In later years he would argue otherwise, that it had always been his plan to steer a course from Communism to democracy. But in truth he was a political Columbus, setting out to find the promised land, only to discover something else.

The real test of a successful revolution is whether it replaces the political élites. By and large this is what the revolutions in Eastern Europe did achieve. But in Russia there was not much change as a result of the events of 1991. The Yeltsin government had no lustration laws compared to those in most of Eastern Europe to expose officials who had taken part in the abuses of the Communist regime and keep them out of high office. The majority of politicians and successful businessmen in Yeltsin's Russia had been part of the Soviet nomenklatura (Party leaders, parliamentary deputies, regional leaders, factory bosses and so on). Three quarters of the posts in Yeltsin's presidential administration and almost three quarters of those in the Russian government were occupied by former nomenklatura members in 1999. In regional government the proportion was over 80 per cent, with more than half the leaders having been a part of the nomenklatura under Brezhnev.

The business élite of the 1990s was also made up of former Soviet and Party officials. The legal chaos of the Gorbachev era enabled them to convert state assets into private property. From 1986 Komsomols were legally allowed to set up commercial businesses (import–export companies, shops and even banks) and convert their paper earnings into liquid cash. This was Mikhail Khodorkovsky's route from being a Komsomol official at the Mendeleev Institute of Chemistry and Technology to becoming the head of Menatap, one of the first private banks. Officials became rich by setting up joint ventures with Western companies and using foreign credits to profit personally from currency dealings on the black market in Russia. From 1987, Soviet officials began buying state assets, long before the rest of the population received any shares in them. Ministries were commercialized and partly run as businesses by their senior officials, who sold the assets they administered at knockdown prices to themselves. Factories and banks were sold off in the same way.

The collapse of the Soviet system did not democratize the distribution of wealth or power in Russia. After 1991, the Russians could have been forgiven for thinking nothing much had changed, at least not for the better. No doubt many of them had thought much the same after 1917.

20

JUDGEMENT

Yeltsin's ban on the CPSU was challenged by the Communists. The case was heard in the newly founded Russian Constitutional Court in a five-month televised trial from July 1992. Billed as a 'Russian Nuremberg', it amounted to a political trial of the Communist Party, although, unlike the trial of the Nazis in 1945, there were no defendants charged with criminal actions, not even the leaders of the August putsch, who were soon released from prison and granted an amnesty.

Gorbachev refused to appear as a witness, fearing that he would be made the scapegoat in a show trial. He dismissed the comparison with Nuremberg, where 'specific people' had been 'judged for committing specific atrocities', he later wrote in his *Memoirs*. 'But the CPSU leaders who were really guilty of crimes had passed away, and they can be judged only by history.'[1] So what sort of trial was this?

Yeltsin's legal team produced thirty-six volumes of archival documents spanning the entire history of the October Revolution—backed up by the testimony of over sixty expert witnesses—to argue that the CPSU was not a proper party but a criminal regime. Lev Razgon, a victim of Stalin's terror, pleaded for a proper reckoning of the number who had died in the Gulag. Others testified to the persecution of dissidents and priests during the post-Stalin years. The Communists presented their own version of the Party's history, emphasizing the achievements of Soviet industrialization, the victory in 1945 and the Sputnik space programme.

The court announced itself incompetent to judge on Soviet history, and reached a compromise in its legal verdict, approving Yeltsin's ban of the CPSU, whilst allowing the Communists to reconstitute themselves as a party in Russia. The Communist Party of the Russian Federation was legally established shortly after the court's ruling on 30 November 1992. By February 1993, it had more than half a million registered members, making it by far the biggest party in Russia's new 'democracy'.

What kind of judgement could be passed on the Party's history? Who had the legal or the moral right to reach a verdict on its 'criminal' record? At Nuremberg there were obvious war crimes to be punished and military victors to impose the jurisdiction of the court under international law. But there were no liberating powers to establish justice for the former Soviet Union. The Constitutional Court was in no position to assume such high authority. Twelve of its thirteen judges were former Communists. So who were they to judge? A new Russian constitution was not passed until December 1993, meaning they would have to reach their legal decision according to the Brezhnev Constitution, which gave the Party almost unchecked powers to implement its policies.

Who was to be judged? Gorbachev? The Party leadership? The KGB? Or the millions of rank-and-file officials, policemen, guards, who made the Soviet system operate? Yeltsin made it clear in his presidential edicts that individual Communists should not be held responsible for the crimes of the Party (he no doubt had much to answer for in his own record as the Sverdlovsk Party boss between 1976 and 1985). In a TV interview during the trial he underlined the meaning of this moderate approach: 'Probably, for the first time since 1917, we have not embarked on the course of revenge, so to speak. You understand, it is important that Russia has restrained itself from doing this.'[2]

The court was also thinking of the need for national unity and reconciliation when it reached its compromise. As its chairman stated at the start of the hearings, 'on whatever side of the courtroom the parties sit, they must live together afterwards rather than destroy each other in the manner of the Whites and the Reds.'[3]

The result of this conciliatory approach was a failure to bring anybody to justice for the human rights abuses of the Soviet regime. There were no prosecutions of former KGB or Communist officials in Russia, as there were in other countries of the former Soviet Union, notably Estonia and Latvia, where there were a number of high-profile trials of retired NKVD men, who had carried out the mass arrests and deportations of Baltic nationals to the Soviet Gulag during the 1940s. Nor were there lustration laws or policies, like those in Eastern Europe and the Baltic states to expose those who had taken part in crimes and keep them out of high office.

This was certainly a useful outcome for the Russian government, which was staffed by former Communists. But without a legal framework to deal with the abuses of the Soviet regime, there was nothing to prevent the Communist élites from returning to the top. Spared real scrutiny of its activities in the Soviet period, the KGB was allowed by Yeltsin to reform itself as the Federal Counter-Intelligence Service in 1991, and, four years later, as the Federal Security Service (FSB), without substantial changes in its personnel. A lustration bill proposed by the democratic politician and human rights campaigner Galina Starovoytova in December 1992—to impose only a temporary restriction on First Party Secretaries and KGB officials from holding governmental posts—was rejected by the Russian parliament (which then ruled out any further efforts to introduce lustration by making the identity of KGB agents a state secret). Starovoytova was assassinated, allegedly by the FSB, in 1998.

Perhaps the failure of her lustration bill was a chance missed by the Yeltsin government—the best chance it would have—to make a clean break from the Soviet past and promote a culture of democracy. In new democracies emerging from dictatorships, justice tends to come quickly or not come at all. As it happened, the old Communist élites quickly recovered from the shock of 1991 and, with new political identities, restored their domination of politics, the media and the economy, enough to prevent further attempts at making them accountable for anything they might have done in the Soviet period—or afterwards.

But how would any Russian court or prosecutor go about deciding whom to prosecute or ban from office? Perhaps the situation in Russia was too complicated for any judgement to be made. In Eastern Europe and the Baltic states, the Communist dictatorship had been imposed by foreigners. It was easy and convenient for the nationalist leaders there to blame Russia (and the *Russian* Revolution) for the abuses of the Soviet period. They could build new states and national identities by distinguishing themselves from the Russians (in Estonia and Latvia the large Russian minorities were excluded from public life by stringent laws of citizenship). But the Russians did not have a foreign force to blame. The revolution grew from Russian soil. Millions of Russians were members of the Party, and virtually everybody had collaborated in some way with the Soviet regime. There was no simple way to draw a line between perpetrators and victims. The members of Memorial, the largest public organization representing 'victims of repression', included children of the Bolshevik élite, Gulag bosses, Soviet officials—functionaries of the Stalinist regime who were themselves repressed by it. In this sense what needed to be judged in the Party trial was not just the people who had carried out the revolution's crimes but the whole nation that had gone along with them. As Alexander Yakovlev put it at the time, 'We are trying not the Party but ourselves.'[4]

Rather than a trial, perhaps what Russia needed was a commission on truth and reconciliation, something on the lines of the one established in South Africa to give a public hearing to the victims of apartheid and listen to appeals for amnesty from the perpetrators of its violence. If it was inappropriate to prosecute or ban a selected group of former Party officials, it was arguably right and therapeutic for the Russians to confront the truth about their past and recognize the traumas suffered by the victims of the Soviet regime through public hearings and state apologies for crimes committed in the past ('restorative justice').

In a limited way this process had begun with glasnost under Gorbachev. Victims of repression were rehabilitated and allowed to clear their names. After the collapse of the Soviet system, Yeltsin had an opportunity to develop this system as part of the institution-building needed for a new democracy and civil society. He did not take that chance. Part of the explanation for this was political: the KGB was too powerful and could not be forced to open up its archives to public scrutiny; the Constitutional Court was too new to play an effective democratic role; public bodies like Memorial remained too weak; and there was no pressure from the West, which was interested only in economic liberalization. But history was an explanation too. The country was divided by its Soviet past. There was no consensus about the revolution's history, no agreed historical narrative on which the nation could unite in its search for truth and reconciliation. In South Africa there was a decisive moral victory against apartheid that allowed a unifying narrative to be imposed on the history of the deposed regime. But in Russia there was no such victory in 1991. Many Russians saw the collapse of the Soviet Union as a terrible defeat.

Truth and reconciliation mean historical judgement. But what sort of verdict could the Russian people pass on their own country's history? They had lived their lives in the belief (or at least with some acceptance) that the Soviet system was 'normal', if not the best system in the world.

Comparisons are sometimes drawn with Nazi Germany. After 1945, the West Germans underwent a long and painful process of self-examination in the light of their own recent history. The Nazi regime lasted just twelve years. But the Soviet system went on for three quarters of a century. By 1991, the entire Russian population had been educated under it, made their careers under it, brought up their own children under it, and given all their lives to building its achievements, with which they naturally identified.

People were confused by the loss of Communism as a system of beliefs and practices. They felt a moral vacuum. For some, religion filled the gap. Orthodoxy was a ready-made alternative to Marxism–Leninism. It offered reconnection with a Russian way of life that had been lost since

1917, repentance for the repression of ancestors, and self-purification from the moral compromises involved in living with the Soviet regime. For others, monarchism was a substitute. The early 1990s witnessed a resurgence of Russian interest in the Romanovs. There was talk of the family's descendants returning from exile, and of Russia becoming a constitutional monarchy. The monarchist revival culminated in the reburial of Nicholas II and his family in the Peter and Paul Cathedral in St Petersburg on 17 July 1998, exactly eighty years after they were executed by the Bolsheviks. Two years later, the Imperial family were canonized by the Moscow Patriarch.

Divided by their history, the Russians were unable to unite around the symbols of the nation or the state. The Imperial tricolour (white-blue-red) was readopted as the Russian national flag; but nationalists and monarchists preferred the Imperial coat of arms (black-yellow-white), while Communists adhered to the Red Flag. The Soviet wartime anthem was replaced with the 'Patriotic Song' by the nineteenth-century composer Mikhail Glinka. But the latter proved unpopular. It did not inspire Russian athletes or footballers, whose performances on the international stage became a source of national shame. Shortly after his election as President in 2000, Putin brought back the old Soviet anthem with new words by the 87-year-old writer Sergei Mikhalkov, who had written its original lyrics in 1942. Putin justified its restoration by talking of the need for historical respect and continuity. To deny the country's Soviet past, he said, would be to deprive the older generation of a meaning in their lives. Democrats opposed the restoration of the Stalin-era anthem, but Communists supported it, and most Russians welcomed its return.

The commemoration of the October Revolution was similarly divisive. Yeltsin replaced Revolution Day with a Day of Accord and Reconciliation 'in order to diminish confrontations and effect conciliation between different segments of society'. But Communists continued to commemorate the Revolution's anniversary in the traditional Soviet manner with a demonstration in massed ranks with red banners. Putin tried to resolve the conflict by establishing a Day of National Unity on

4 November (the date of the end of the Polish occupation of Russia in 1612). It took the place of the 7 November holiday in the official calendar from 2005. But the Day of National Unity did not catch on. According to a 2007 poll, only 4 per cent of the population could say what it was for. Six out of ten people were opposed to the dropping of Revolution Day.

No more consensus could be achieved on what to do with the founder of the Soviet state. Yeltsin and the Russian Church supported calls to close the Lenin Mausoleum and bury Lenin's body next to his mother at the Volkov Cemetery in St Petersburg, as he had wanted for himself. But the Communists were organized and vocal in resisting this, so the issue remained unresolved. Putin said he was opposed to removing Lenin from the Mausoleum, on grounds similar to his argument about the Soviet anthem, that it would offend the older generation by implying they had cherished false ideals during seventy years of Soviet rule.

From the start of his regime, Putin aimed to restore pride in Soviet history. It was an important part of his agenda to rebuild Russia as a great power. His initiative was popular, particularly when it played to nostalgia for the Soviet Union. The collapse of the USSR was a humiliation for most Russians. In a few months they had lost everything: an economic system that had given them security and social guarantees; an empire with a superpower status; an ideology; and a national identity shaped by the version of Soviet history they had learned in school. Russians resented the besmirching of their country's history in the glasnost period. They felt uncomfortable about the questions they were forced to ask about their relatives in the Stalin period. They did not want to listen to lectures about how 'bad' their history was. By reasserting Russia as a 'great power' with achievements to be proud of since 1917, Putin helped the Russians to feel good as Russians once again.

His initiative began in schools, where textbooks deemed too negative about the Soviet period were denied approval by the Ministry of Education, effectively removing them from the classroom. In 2007, he told a conference of history teachers:

As to some problematic pages in our history, yes, we have had them. But what state hasn't? And we've had fewer of such pages than some other [states]. And ours were not as horrible as those of some others. Yes, we have had some terrible pages: let us remember the events beginning in 1937, let us not forget about them. But other countries have had no less, and even more. In any case, we did not pour chemicals over thousands of kilometers or drop on a small country seven times more bombs than during the entire World War II, as the Americans did in Vietnam. Nor did we have other black pages, such as Nazism, for instance. All sorts of things happen in the history of every state. And we cannot allow ourselves to be saddled with guilt . . .[5]

Putin did not deny Stalin's crimes. But he argued for the need not to dwell on them, to balance them against his achievements as the builder of the country's 'glorious Soviet past'. In a manual for history teachers commissioned by the President and heavily promoted in Russian schools, Stalin was portrayed as an 'effective manager' who 'acted rationally in conducting a campaign of terror to ensure the country's modernization'.[6]

Polls suggest that the Russians share this troubling attitude to the revolution's violence. According to a survey conducted in 2007 in three cities (St Petersburg, Kazan and Ulyanovsk), 71 per cent of the population believed that Dzerzhinsky, the founder of the Cheka, had 'protected public order and civic life'. Only 7 per cent considered him a 'criminal and executioner'. More disturbing still was the survey's finding that while nearly everyone was well informed about the mass repressions under Stalin—with most acknowledging that 'between 10 and 30 million victims' had suffered—two thirds of these respondents still believed that Stalin had been positive for the country. Many even thought that under Stalin people had been 'kinder and more compassionate'.[7] Even with a knowledge of the millions who were killed, the Russians, it appears, continue to accept the Bolshevik idea that mass state violence can be justified to meet the revolution's goals. According to another survey, 42 per cent of the Russian population would like the return of a 'leader like Stalin'.[8]

In the autumn of 2011, millions of Russians watched the TV show *The Court of Time* (*Sud vremeni*), in which various figures and episodes from Russian history were judged in a mock trial with advocates, witnesses and a jury of the viewers who reached their verdict by voting on the telephone. The judgements which they reached do not hold out much hope for a change in Russian attitudes. Presented with the evidence of Stalin's war against the peasantry and the catastrophic effects of collectivization, 78 per cent of the viewers still believed that collectivization had been justified (a 'terrible necessity') for Soviet industrialization, and only 22 per cent considered it a 'crime'. On the Hitler–Stalin Pact, 91 per cent thought that it was necessary; only 9 per cent considered it a factor contributing to the outbreak of the Second World War. The same voting figures were recorded on the Brezhnev period, with 91 per cent believing it to have been a 'time of possibilities', and on the break-up of the Soviet Union, with 91 per cent agreeing with the verdict that it was a 'national catastrophe'.

It will take many decades for the Russians to be cured of the social traumas and pathologies of the Communist regime. Politically the revolution may be dead, but it has an afterlife in the mentalities of the people swept up in its violent cycle of one hundred years.

NOTES

INTRODUCTION

1. S. Fitzpatrick, 'Ending the Russian Revolution: Reflections on Soviet History and Its Interpreters', Elie Kedourie Memorial Lecture, *Proceedings of the British Academy*, vol. 162 (Oxford, 2009), pp. 36–7.

1. THE START

1. R. G. Robbins, *Famine in Russia, 1891–92* (New York, 1975), p. 6.
2. L. Tolstoi, *Pis'ma grafa L. N. Tolstogo k zhene, 1862–1910 gg.* (Moscow, 1913), p. 208.
3. L. Haimson (ed.), *The Making of Three Russian Revolutionaries: Voices from the Menshevik Past* (Cambridge, 1987), p. 68.
4. A. M. Romanov, *Once a Grand Duke* (London, 1932), pp. 168–9.
5. R. Zelnik (ed.), *A Radical Worker in Tsarist Russia: The Autobiography of Semën Ivanovich Kanatchikov* (Stanford, Calif. 1986), pp. 151–52.
6. J. Słomka, *From Serfdom to Self-Government: Memoirs of a Polish Village Mayor, 1842–1927* (London, 1941), p. 171.
7. R. Suny, 'Nationality and Class in the Revolutions of 1917: A Re-examination of Categories', in N. Lampert and G. Rittersporn (eds.), *Stalinism: Its Nature and Aftermath* (London, 1932), p. 232.
8. J. Brooks, *When Russia Learned to Read: Literacy and Popular Literature, 1861–1917* (Princeton, 1985), pp. 55–6.
9. T. von Laue, 'A Secret Memorandum of Sergei Witte on the Industrialization of Imperial Russia', *Journal of Modern History*, 26, 1954, p. 71.

10. L. Trotsky, *1905* (New York, 1972), p. 291.

11. J. Simms, 'The Famine and the Radicals', in E. Judge and J. Simms (eds.), *Modernization and Revolution: Dilemmas of Progress in Late Imperial Russia. Essays in Honor of Arthur P. Mendel* (New York, 1992), p. 16.

12. A. Resis, '*Das Kapital* Comes to Russia', *Slavic Review*, 24, 1970, pp. 221–2.

13. N. Valentinov, *Encounters With Lenin* (London, 1968), p. 23.

14. D. Volkogonov, *Lenin: Life and Legacy* (London, 1991), pp. 8–9.

15. M. Gorky, *Untimely Thoughts: Essays on Revolution, Culture and the Bolsheviks, 1917–1918* (New Haven, 1995), p. 88.

16. Valentinov, *Encounters*, p. 148.

17. L. Fischer, *The Life of Lenin* (London, 1965), p. 329.

18. Haimson (ed.), *The Making of Three Russian Revolutionaries*, p. 126.

2. THE 'DRESS REHEARSAL'

1. W. Sablinsky, *The Road to Bloody Sunday: Father Gapon and the St Petersburg Massacre of 1905* (Princeton, 1976), p. 344.

2. Ibid., pp. 241–3.

3. Ibid., pp. 251–2.

4. V. Gurko, *Features and Figures of the Past: Government and Opinion in the Reign of Nicholas II* (Stanford, 1939), p. 304.

5. A. Ascher, *The Revolution of 1905: Russia in Disarray* (Stanford, 1988), p. 112.

6. B. Pasternak, *Stikhotvoreniia i poemy* (Moscow–Leningrad, 1965), p. 204.

7. J. Neuberger, *Hooliganism: Crime, Culture and Power in St Petersburg, 1900–1914* (Berkeley, Calif., 1993), p. 118.

8. V. Lenin, *Collected Works*, 45 vols. (Moscow, 1960–80), vol. 29, p. 310.

3. LAST HOPES

1. V. Obolenskii, *Moia zhizn', moi sovremenniki* (Paris, 1988), pp. 338–9.

2. B. Pares, *My Russian Memoirs* (London, 1931), p. 139.

3. A. Ascher, *P. A. Stolypin: The Search for Stability in Late Imperial Russia* (Berkeley, Calif., 2002), p. 209.

4. Ibid., p. 374.

5. F. Golder, *Documents on Russian History, 1914–1917* (New York, 1927), p. 21–2.

4. WAR AND REVOLUTION

1. A. Brussilov, *A Soldier's Notebook 1914–1918* (London, 1930), p. 37.
2. A. Pireiko, *V tylu i na fronte imperialisticheskoi voiny* (Leningrad, 1926), pp. 35–6.
3. Brussilov, *Soldier's Notebook*, pp. 170–71.
4. B. Pares (ed.), *Letters of the Tsaritsa to the Tsar* (London 1923), p. 157.
5. O. Figes and B. Kolonitskii, *Interpreting the Russian Revolution: The Language and Symbols of 1917* (New Haven, 1999), p. 25.
6. R. Pearson, *The Russian Moderates and the Crisis of Tsarism, 1914–1917* (London, 1977), pp. 117-18.
7. V. Gurko, *Tsar' i tsaritsa* (Paris, 1927), pp. 70–71.
8. Lenin, *Collected Works*, vol. 23, p. 253.

5. THE FEBRUARY REVOLUTION

1. T. Hasegawa, *The February Revolution: Petrograd 1917* (Seattle, 1981), p. 258.
2. *Padenie tsarskogo rezhima*, vol. 1 (7 vols.; Petrograd, 1924–7), p. 190.
3. A. Mordvinov, 'Otryvki iz vospominanil', *Russkaia letopis'*, 5, 1923, p. 113.
4. RGIA (Russian State Historical Archive, St Petersburg), f. 1278, op. 10, d. 4, ll. 241–2.
5. L. Trotsky, *The History of the Russian Revolution* (London, 1977), p. 193.
6. R. H. B. Lockhart, *Memoirs of a British Agent* (London, 1933), p. 304.
7. S. Mstislavskii, *Five Days Which Transformed Russia* (London, 1988), p. 65.
8. N. Sukhanov, *The Russian Revolution: A Personal Record* (Princeton, 1984), pp. 444–7.
9. Ibid., p. 450.
10. Lenin, *Collected Works*, vol. 25, pp. 176, 179.

6. LENIN'S REVOLUTION

1. House of Lords Records Office, Historical Collection, London, 206, Stow Hill Papers, DS 2/2, Box 8, O. Kerenskaia, 'Otryvki vospominaniia', p. 8.
2. L. Trotsky, *My Life* (London, 1975), p. 331.
3. Lenin, *Collected Works*, vol. 26, pp. 19, 21.
4. Ibid., p. 84.
5. A. Bone (ed.), *The Bolsheviks and the October Revolution: Minutes of the Central Committee of the RSDLP(b), August 1917–February 1918* (London, 1974), p. 98.

6. A. Rabinowitch, *The Bolsheviks Come to Power: The Revolution of 1917 in Petrograd* (New York, 1978), p. 272.
7. Ibid., p. 294.
8. *Vtoroi vserossiiski s'ezd sovetov rabochikh i soldatskikh deputatov* (Moscow, 1957), pp. 43–4; I. Getzler, *Martov: A Political Biography of a Russian Social Democrat* (London, 1967), p. 162.
9. 'Pis'ma moi k tebe, konechno istoricheskie', *Voprosy istorii KPSS*, 2, 1991, p. 43.
10. G. Leggett, *The Cheka: Lenin's Political Police* (Oxford, 1981), p. 17.
11. Lenin, *Collected Works*, vol. 26, p. 382.
12. B. Sokolov, 'Zashchita vserossiiskogo uchreditel'nogo sobraniia', *Arkhiv russkoi revoliutsii*, 13, 1924, p. 16.
13. L. Trotskii, *Sochineniia* (Moscow, 1925–7), vol. 17, part 1, pp. 290–91.
14. Lenin, *Collected Works*, vol. 26, p. 414.
15. J. Reed, *Ten Days That Shook the World* (London, 1977), p. 133.
16. Bone (ed.), *The Bolsheviks and the October Revolution*, p. 174.
17. Ibid., p. 220.

7. CIVIL WAR AND THE MAKING OF THE SOVIET SYSTEM

1. L. Trotsky, 'How the Revolution Armed', in *The Military Writings and Speeches of Trotsky*, trans. B. Pearce, vol. 1 (5 vols.; London, 1979), p. 85.
2. *Odinnadtsatyi s'ezd RKP(b). Steongraficheskii otchet* (Moscow, 1922), pp. 103–4.
3. Lenin, *Polnoe sobranie sochinenii* (Moscow 1958–65), vol. 37, p. 41.
4. Trotsky, *Sochineniia*, vol. 12, pp. 136–7.
5. M. McAuley, 'Bread without the Bourgeoisie', in D. Koenker, W. Rosenberg and R. Suny (eds.), *Party, State and Society in the Russian Civil War: Explorations in Social History* (Bloomington, Ind., 1989), p. 163.
6. N. Krupskaia, *Vospominaniia o Lenine* (Moscow, 1968), p. 54.
7. L. Trotskii, *O Lenine* (Moscow, 1924), p. 101.
8. L. Trotsky, *Terrorism and Communism: A Reply to Kautsky* (London, 2007), p. 63.
9. *Kronshtadstkii miatezh: sbornik statei, vospominanii i dokumentov* (Leningrad, 1931), p. 26.
10. Lenin, *Polnoe sobranie sochinenii*, vol. 43, p. 82.

8. LENIN, TROTSKY AND STALIN

1. Leon Trotsky, *My Life: An Attempt at an Autobiography* (London, 1988), pp. 527–8.

2. Lenin, *Collected Works*, vol. 36, pp. 605–11.

3. Ibid., p. 596.

4. *Istoriia TsK*, 12, 1989, pp. 193, 198.

9. THE REVOLUTION'S GOLDEN AGE?

1. E. Goldman, *My Further Disillusionment in Russia* (Garden City, N.Y., 1924), p. 79.

2. A. Barmine, *One Who Survived: The Life Story of a Russian under the Soviets* (New York, 1945), pp. 124–5.

3. Goldman, *My Further Disillusionment*, pp. 79.

4. Lenin, *Polnoe sobranie sochinenii*, vol. 43, pp. 27, 329.

5. V. Zenzinov, *Deserted: The Story of the Children Abandoned in Soviet Russia* (London, 1931), p. 27.

6. W. Benjamin, 'Moscow', in *Selected Writings*, 4 vols. (Cambridge, Mass., 1996–2003), vol. 2, p. 30.

7. See, e.g., J. Hellbeck, *Revolution on My Mind: Writing a Diary under Stalin* (Cambridge, Mass., 2006); I. Halfin, *Terror in My Soul: Communist Autobiographies on Trial* (Cambridge, Mass., 2003).

8. H. Kuromiya, *Stalin's Industrial Revolution: Politics and Workers, 1928–1932* (Cambridge, 1988), p. 110.

10. THE GREAT BREAK

1. *Pravda*, 7 November 1929; I. Stalin, *Sochineniia*, vol. 12 (13 vols.; Moscow, 1946–55), p. 174.

2. N. Patolichev, *Ispytaniia na zrelost'* (Moscow, 1977), p. 170.

3. V. Kravchenko, *I Chose Freedom* (New York, 1946), p. 91.

4. R. Davies, *The Socialist Offensive: The Collectivization of Soviet Agriculture, 1929–1930* (London, 1980), p. 198.

5. R. Conquest, *The Harvest of Sorrow: Soviet Collectivization and the Terror-Famine* (London, 1986), p. 137.

6. Vittenburg Family Archive, 'Vospominaniia', ms., p. 8.

7. A. Zverev, *Zapiski ministra* (Moscow, 1973), p. 54.

8. L. Kopelev, *The Education of a True Believer* (London, 1981), p. 235.

9. H. Kuromiya, 'The Soviet Famine of 1932–1933 Reconsidered', *Europe-Asia Studies*, vol. 60, no. 4 (June 2008), p. 665.

10. *Pravda*, 5 February 1931.

11. S. and B. Webb, *Soviet Communism: A New Civilization?*, vol. 2 (2 vols.; London, 1935), p. 591.

11. STALIN'S CRISIS

1. S. Allilueva, *Twenty Letters to a Friend* (London, 1967), p. 102.
2. S. Montefiore, *Stalin: The Court of the Red Tsar* (London, 2003), p. 96.
3. J. Haslam, 'Political Opposition to Stalin and the Origins of the Terror in Russia, 1932–1936', *The Historical Journal*, vol. 29, no. 2 (1986), p. 396.
4. All jokes in these pages can be found in B. Adams, *Tiny Revolutions in Russia: Twentieth Century Soviet and Russian History in Anecdotes and Jokes* (London, 2005).
5. R. Tucker, *Stalin in Power: The Revolution from Above, 1928–1941* (New York, 1990), p. 210.
6. J. Getty and O. Naumov, *The Road to Terror: Stalin and the Self-Destruction of the Bolsheviks, 1932–1939* (New Haven, Conn., 1999), pp. 54–7.
7. *Pravda*, 11 Oct. 1932.
8. Getty and Naumov, *The Road to Terror*, p. 127.
9. E. Bonner, *Mothers and Daughters* (London, 1992), p. 148.
10. L. Siegelbaum and A. Sokolov (eds.), *Stalinism as a Way of Life: A Narrative in Documents* (New Haven, Conn., 2000), pp. 124–5 (translation slightly altered for clarity).
11. L. Trotsky, *The Revolution Betrayed* (New York, 1972), pp. 136, 138.
12. J. Stalin, *Works*, 13 vols. (Moscow, 1952–5), vol. 13, p. 250.
13. Tucker, *Stalin in Power*, pp. 244–6.
14. Getty and Naumov, *The Road to Terror*, p. 248.

12. COMMUNISM IN RETREAT?

1. RGASPI [Russian State Archive of Social and Political History, Moscow], f. 17, op. 120, d. 138, 11. 78–9.
2. *Pravda*, 20 May 1935, p. 3.
3. Trotsky, *The Revolution Betrayed*, p. 156.
4. N. Timasheff, *The Great Retreat: The Growth and Decline of Communism in Russia* (New York, 1946), pp. 199–200, 202.

13. THE GREAT TERROR

1. MM [Archive of Memorial Society, Moscow], f. 1, op. 1, d. 169 (V. A. Antonov-Ovseenko to S. I. Antonov-Ovseenko, 11 October 1937).
2. R. Conquest, *The Great Terror: A Reassessment* (London, 1992), pp. 424–5.
3. O. Khlevniuk, *Master of the House: Stalin and His Inner Circle* (New Haven, Conn., 2009), p. 174.

4. Ibid., p. 175.

5. *Istochnik*, 1994, no. 3, p. 80; N. S. Khrushchev, *Khrushchev Remembers: The Last Testament*, trans. and ed. S. Talbott (London, 1971; Boston, 1974), p. 283; M. Jansen and N. Petrov, *Stalin's Loyal Executioner: People's Commissar Nikolai Ezhov, 1895–1940* (Stanford, Calif., 2002), pp. 89, 201.

6. Getty and Naumov, *The Road to Terror*, p. 557. For the text of Bukharin's statement at his trial, see http://www.marxists.org/archive/bukharin/works/1938/trial/1.htm.

7. Kravchenko, *I Chose Freedom*, p. 213–14.

8. MM, f. 1, op. 1, d. 169 (S. I. Antonov-Ovseenko to V. A. Antonov-Ovseenko, 16 October 1937).

14. REVOLUTION FOR EXPORT

1. Figes and Kolonitskii, *Interpreting the Russian Revolution*, pp. 151–2.

2. K. McDermott and J. Agnew, *The Comintern: A History of International Communism from Lenin to Stalin* (London, 1996), p. 28.

3. Tucker, *Stalin in Power*, p. 230.

4. *Pravda*, 30 Jan. 1925.

5. T. Snyder, *Bloodlands: Europe between Hitler and Stalin* (London, 2010), p. 74.

6. R. Gellately, *Stalin's Curse: Battling for Communism in War and Cold War* (Oxford, 2013), p. 46.

7. Alexander Dallin and F. I. Firsov, eds., *Dimitrov and Stalin: 1934–43: Letters from the Soviet Archives* (New Haven, Conn., 2000), p. 151.

15. WAR AND REVOLUTION

1. Montefiore, *Stalin*, p. 330.

2. *Pravda*, 3 July 1941.

3. *Moskva voennaia 1941–1945: memuary i arkhivnye dokumenty* (Moscow, 1995), p. 478.

4. *Vecherniaia Moskva*, 8 November 1941.

5. D. Samoilov, *Podennye zapisi*, vol. 1 (2 vols.; Moscow, 2002), p. 140.

6. Interviews with Rita Kogan, St Petersburg, June and November 2003.

7. P. Kapitsa, *V More Pogasli Ogni. Blokadnye Dnevniki* (Leningrad, 1974), p. 281.

8. *Pravda*, 24 June 1944, p. 2.

9. H. Smith, *The Russians* (London, 1976), p. 370.

10. *Pravda*, 27 June 1945.

16. REVOLUTION AND COLD WAR

1. Gellately, *Stalin's Curse*, p. 48.
2. S. Berthon and J. Potts, *Warlords: An Extraordinary Re-creation of World War II through the Eyes and Minds of Hitler, Churchill, Roosevelt, and Stalin* (New York, 2007), p. 289.
3. M. Djilas, *Conversations with Stalin* (London, 1962), p. 90.
4. A. Gromyko, *Memoirs* (New York, 1983), p. 117.
5. See the original: www.trumanlibrary.org/whistlestop/study_collections /coldwar/documents/pdf/6-6.pdf.
6. *Pravda*, 7 Nov. 1946.
7. J. Brent and V. Naukov, *Stalin's Last Crime: The Doctors' Plot* (London, 2003), pp. 9, 129, 176, 184.

17. THE BEGINNING OF THE END

1. MM, f. 12, op. 30, d. 2, l. 22.
2. L. Chukovskaia, *Zapiski ob Anne Akhmatovoi*, vol. 2 (3 vols.; Paris, 1980), p. 137.
3. A. Solzhenitsyn, *The Gulag Archipelago*, vol. 3 (3 vols.; New York, 1973), p. 451.
4. http://www.guardian.co.uk/theguardian/2007/apr/26/greatspeeches1.
5. Khrushchev, *Khrushchev Remembers*, p. 79; A. Hochschild, *The Unquiet Ghost: Russians Remember Stalin* (London, 1994), p. 223.
6. R. Medvedev, *Let History Judge: The Origins and Consequences of Stalinism* (New York, 1989), epigraph.
7. W. Taubman, *Khrushchev: The Man and His Era* (New York, 2004), p. 272.
8. L. Alexeyeva and P. Goldberg, *The Thaw Generation: Coming of Age in the Post-Stalin Era* (Boston, 1990), p. 4.
9. F. Burlatsky, *Khrushchev and the First Russian Spring* (New York, 1988), p. 93.
10. J. Brodsky, 'Spoils of War', in *On Grief and Reason: Essays* (London, 1996), p. 8.
11. S. Farber, *The Origins of the Cuban Revolution Reconsidered* (Chapel Hill, NC, 2006), p. 147.

18. MATURE SOCIALISM

1. R. Medvedev, *Khrushchev* (New York, 1983), p. 245.
2. *Programme of the Communist Party of the Soviet Union. Adopted by the 22nd Congress of the CPSU, October 31, 1961* (Moscow, 1961), pp. 9, 62.
3. Haslam, *Russia's Cold War*, p. 248.

4. *Our Course: Peace and Socialism: A Collection of Speeches by L. I. Brezhnev* (Moscow, 1973), p. 226.

5. A. Konchalovsky, *The Inner Circle: An Inside View of Soviet Life Under Stalin* (New York, 2007), p. 85.

6. R. Medvedev, *On Socialist Democracy* (London, 1975), p. 314.

19. THE LAST BOLSHEVIK

1. A. de Tocqueville, *The Old Regime and the Revolution* (London, 2012), p. 214.

2. V. Zubok, *A Failed Empire: The Soviet Union in the Cold War from Stalin to Gorbachev* (Chapel Hill, N.C., 2007), p. 314.

3. R. Daniels (ed.), *A Documentary History of Communism in Russia: From Lenin to Gorbachev* (Hanover, N.H., 1993), p. 347.

4. M. Gorbachev, *Oktiabr' i perestroika: revoliutsiia prodolzhaetsia* (Moscow, 1987), p. 32.

5. I. Tarasulo (ed.), *Gorbachev and Glasnost: Viewpoints from the Soviet Press* (Wilmington, Del., 1989), pp. 277–90.

6. A. Brown, 'Gorbachev, Lenin and the Break with Leninism', *Demokratizatsiya*, vol. 15, no. 2, April 2007, pp. 235–6.

7. Ibid., p. 237.

8. S. Toymentsev, 'Legal but Criminal: The Failure of the "Russian Nuremberg" and the Paradoxes of Post-Soviet Memory', *Comparative Literature Studies*, vol. 48, no. 3, 2011, p. 298.

20. JUDGEMENT

1. M. Gorbachev, *Memoirs* (London, 1995), p. 680.

2. J. Henderson, 'The Russian Constitutional Court and the Communist Party Case: Watershed or Whitewash?', *Communist and Post-Communist Studies* 40, 2007, p. 14.

3. Ibid., p. 12 (translation slightly altered for clarity).

4. *Pravda*, 22 October 1992.

5. Leon Aron, 'The Problematic Pages', *The New Republic*, 24 Sept. 2008.

6. A. Filippov, *Noveishaia istoriia Rossii, 1945–2006: Kniga dlia uchitelia* (Moscow, 2007), p. 74.

7. D. Khapaeva and N. Koposov, *Pozhaleite, lyudi, palachei: Massovoe istoricheskoe soznanie v postsovetskoi Rossii i Stalinizm* (Moscow, 2007).

8. *Moscow News*, 4 March 2005.

A SHORT GUIDE TO FURTHER READING

The following are books in the English language I would recommend. Not every subject has been covered. This is a personal and selective list. I do not mention my own books (listed in the front matter) on which I have drawn in these pages.

On Imperial Russia: Duncan Mackenzie Wallace, *Russia* (1905); Wayne Dowler, *Russia in 1913* (DeKalb, Ill., 2010). On the Romanovs: Richard Wortman, *Scenarios of Power* (vol. 2; Princeton, N.J., 1995). On the revolutionary movement: Tibor Szamuely, *The Russian Tradition* (London, 1974). On Lenin and Trotsky: Louis Fischer, *Life of Lenin* (London, 1965); Isaac Deutscher, *The Prophet Armed: Trotsky, 1879–1921* (1954).

On 1905: Abraham Ascher, *The Revolution of 1905* (Stanford, Calif., 2004). On Stolypin and the Duma: Geoffrey Hosking, *The Russian Constitutional Experiment* (Cambridge, 1973); Abraham Ascher, *P. A. Stolypin: The Search for Stability in Late Imperial Russia* (Cambridge, 2001). On the peasant problem: Teodor Shanin, *The Awkward Class* (Oxford, 1972).

On Russia in the Great War: D. C. B. Lieven, *Russia and the Origins of the First World War* (London, 1983); Norman Stone, *The Eastern Front, 1914–1917* (London, 1976); Allan Wildman, *The End of the Russian Imperial Army* (2 vols.; Princeton, N.J., 1980, 1987); Bernard Pares, *The Fall of the Russian Monarchy: A Study of the Evidence* (London, 1939).

On the February Revolution: Tsuyoshi Hasegawa, *The February Revolution: Petrograd, 1917* (London, 1981); Diane Koenker, *Moscow Workers and the 1917*

Revolution (Princeton, N.J., 1981); Steve Smith, *Red Petrograd: Revolution in the Factories, 1917–18* (Cambridge, 1983); Ziva Galili, *The Menshevik Leaders in the Russian Revolution: Social Realities and Political Strategies* (Princeton, N.J., 1989); Nikolai Sukhanov, *The Russian Revolution: A Personal Record* (London, 1955). On October: Leon Trotsky, *The History of the Russian Revolution* (London, 1967); John Reed, *Ten Days That Shook the World* (London, 1977); Alexander Rabinowitch, *The Bolsheviks Come to Power: The Revolution of 1917 in Petrograd* (New York, 1976); Maxim Gorky, *Untimely Thoughts: Essays on Revolution, Culture, and the Bolsheviks* (New Haven, Conn., 1995); John Wheeler-Bennett, *Brest-Litovsk: The Forgotten Peace, March 1918* (London, 1938).

On the Civil War period: Victor Serge, *Year One of the Revolution* (London, 1972); Ronald Suny, *The Baku Commune, 1917–1918* (Princeton, N.J., 1972); Peter Kenez, *Civil War in South Russia* (2 vols.; Berkeley, Calif., 1971, 1977); Thomas Rigby, *Lenin's Government: Sovnarkom, 1917–1922* (Cambridge, 1979); Sergei Melgunov, *Red Terror in Russia* (London, 1925); Eric Landis, *Bandits and Partisans: The Antonov Movement in the Russian Civil War* (Pittsburgh, Pa., 2008).

The 1920s and the First Five Year Plan: Viktor Danilov, *Rural Russia under the New Regime* (London, 1988); Richard Stites, *Revolutionary Dreams: Utopian Vision and Experimental Life in the Russian Revolution* (New York, 1989). On collectivization and the First Five Year Plan: Lynne Viola et al. (eds.), *The Tragedy of the Soviet Countryside: The War against the Peasantry, 1927–1930* (4 vols.; London, 2005); Sheila Fitzpatrick, *Education and Social Mobility in the Soviet Union, 1921–1934* (Cambridge, 1979); Hiroaki Kuromiya, *Stalin's Industrial Revolution: Politics and Workers, 1928–1932* (Cambridge, 1988); Robert Conquest, *The Harvest of Sorrow: Soviet Collectivization and the Terror-Famine* (London, 2002).

On Stalin and the 1930s: Robert Tucker, *Stalin in Power: The Revolution from Above, 1929–41* (London, 1992); Sheila Fitzpatrick, *Everyday Stalinism: Ordinary Life in Extraordinary Times: Soviet Russia in the 1930s* (New York, 1999); J. Arch Getty et al. (eds.), *The Road to Terror: Stalin and the Self-Destruction of the Bolsheviks, 1932–1939* (New Haven, Conn., 2010); Oleg Khlevniuk, *Master of the House: Stalin and His Inner Circle* (London, 2009); Robert Conquest, *The Great Terror: A Reassessment* (London, 2008). On the Gulag: Alexander Solzhenitsyn, *The Gulag Archipelago, 1918–1956: An Experiment in Literary Investigation* (3 vols.; London, 1974–8); Anne Applebaum, *Gulag: A History of* *the Soviet Camps* (London, 2003); Lynne Viola, *The Unknown Gulag: The Lost World of Stalin's Special Settlements* (Oxford, 2009). On Soviet foreign policy and the Comintern: Kevin McDermott and Jeremy Agnew, *The Comintern: A History of International Communism from Lenin to Stalin* (Basingstoke, 1996).

On the revolution during the Second World War and the Cold War: Catherine Merridale, *Ivan's War: The Red Army 1939–45* (London, 2005); Amir Weiner, *Making Sense of War: The Second World War and the Fate of the Bolshevik Revolution* (Oxford, 2001); Timothy Snyder, *Bloodlands: Europe between Hitler and Stalin* (London, 2010); Robert Gellately, *Stalin's Curse: Battling for Communism in War and Cold War* (Oxford, 2013); Jonathan Haslam, *Russia's Cold War: From the October Revolution to the Fall of the Wall* (London, 2011).

From Khrushchev to Gorbachev: William Taubman, *Khrushchev: The Man and His Era* (London, 2003); Archie Brown, *The Rise and Fall of Communism* (London, 2009); Polly Jones (ed.), *The Dilemmas of De-Stalinization: Negotiating Cultural and Social Change in the Khrushchev Era* (London, 2006); Vladislav Zubok, *A Failed Empire: The Soviet Union in the Cold War from Stalin to Gorbachev* (Chapel Hill, N.C., 2007); Edwin Bacon, *Brezhnev Reconsidered* (Basingstoke, 2002); Alexei Yurchak, *Everything Was Forever, Until It Was No More: The Last Soviet Generation* (Princeton, N.J., 2005); David Remnick, *Lenin's Tomb: The Last Days of the Soviet Empire* (London, 1993).

The after-life of the revolution: Adam Hochschild, *The Unquiet Ghost: Russians Remember Stalin* (Harmondsworth, 1994); David Satter, *It Was a Long Time Ago, and It Never Happened Anyway: Russia and the Communist Past* (New Haven, Conn., 2012).

ACKNOWLEDGMENTS

Thanks are due to my editors, Simon Winder at Penguin and Sara Bershtel at Metropolitan, to Marina Kemp at Penguin, who also read the second draft, to Bill Bowring and above all to my agent, Deborah Rogers, who has overseen the entire cycle of my books on revolutionary Russia, from which I have drawn in these pages.

INDEX

320 INDEX

Volunteer Army, 90, 109
Volynsky Regiment, 70–71
Voroshilov, Kliment, 172, 233, 245
voting, 41, 47–48, 115
Voznesensky, Nikolai, 239
Vyborg Manifesto (1906), 41
Vyrubova, Anna, 61
Vysotsky, Vladimir, 267
Vzglyad (TV programme), 277–78

Wall Street Crash of 1929, 208
War Communism, 111–14, 123, 137–38
War Industries Committee, 59, 66
Warsaw Pact, 253, 259, 265
Warsaw uprising, 231
war scare of 1927, 146–47
Webb, Beatrice, 162, 212
Webb, Sidney, 162
West, 50–51, 104–5, 162, 181, 192–93,
    210–14, 228–29, 234, 253–56, 267–68,
    272, 286–87, 292
Western Zemstvo Bill (1911), 48
We (Zamiatin), 143
What is to be Done? (Lenin), 23
White armies, 90, 104, 109, 112, 116,
    118–21
White Guards, 104, 109
White Sea Canal, 161–62
Wilhelm II, Kaiser of Germany, 53, 61
Witte, Count Sergei, 15–16, 33, 41
women, 16, 68–69, 80, 184–85
Women's Battalion of Death, 84
Women's Union for Equality, 28
Workers' Opposition, 122–23, 132
working class, 18, 110, 129, 159, 184–85.
    See also labour; trade unions; strikes
    October Manifesto of 1905 and, 33
    pay and privileges and, 170–71, 177–80
World Festival of Youth, 255

World War I, 4, 27, 35, 50–57, 65–67, 74,
    77–78, 82–87, 89, 99, 104–9, 118, 205–6,
    218, 222, 230
World War II (Great Patriotic War), 2, 5, 57,
    140, 156, 158, 192–93, 209–10, 213–32,
    277, 296
Wrangel, Baron Peter, 120
Writers' Union, 180, 242

xenophobia, 242

Yagoda, Genrikh, 160, 174, 194–96
Yakir, Iona E., 195
Yakovlev, Alexander, 269–70, 278, 280, 291
Yalta Conference, 231
Yanaev, Gennady, 282–83
Yazov, Dmitry, 283
'Year of the Great Break, The' (Stalin), 149
Yeltsin, Boris, 278, 280, 282–86, 288–90, 292,
    294
Yenukidze, Abel, 174
Yezhov, Nikolai, 174, 194–96, 203
Yugoslavia, 230, 232, 236
Yusupov, Prince Felix, 64

Zamyatin, Yevgeny, 143, 241
Zemgor, 59
zemstvos, 8–10, 26–28, 44, 47–48
Zemstvo Union, 59
Zhdanov, Andrei, 237, 239–40, 242–43
Zhdanovshchina, 240
Zhukov, Georgi, 57, 219, 232, 238–39
Zinoviev, Grigorii, 20, 94, 106, 109, 114, 127,
    129, 131–33, 146, 167, 174–75, 194, 196,
    278
Zinovievites, 174, 192
Znamenskaya Square massacre, 70
Zoshchenko, Mikhail, 241
Zvezda (journal), 241

ABOUT THE AUTHOR

ORLANDO FIGES is the author of numerous books on Russia, including *A People's Tragedy*, *Natasha's Dance*, *The Whisperers*, and *The Crimean War*. His works have been translated into twenty-seven languages. A professor of history at Birkbeck, University of London, and a frequent contributor to *The New York Review of Books*, Figes is the recipient of the Wolfson History Prize, the W. H. Smith Literary Award, the NCR Book Award, and the Los Angeles Times Book Prize, among others.